THE POLITICAL THEOLOGY OF HANNAH ARENDT

THE POLITICAL THEOLOGY OF HANNAH ARENDT

AUGUSTINE AND THE INVENTION OF MODERNITY

Michael Weinman

EDINBURGH
University Press

Edinburgh University Press is one of the leading university presses in the UK. We publish academic books and journals in our selected subject areas across the humanities and social sciences, combining cutting-edge scholarship with high editorial and production values to produce academic works of lasting importance. For more information visit our website: edinburghuniversitypress.com

Edinburgh University Press Ltd
13 Infirmary Street
Edinburgh EH1 1LT

First published in hardback by Edinburgh University Press 2025

Typeset in 10/12.5 Adobe Sabon by
IDSUK (DataConnection) Ltd, and
printed and bound by CPI Group (UK) Ltd,
Croydon, CR0 4YY

A CIP record for this book is available from the British Library

ISBN 978-1-3995-2554-1 (hardback)
ISBN 978-1-3995-2555-8 (paperback)
ISBN 978-1-3995-2556-5 (webready PDF)
ISBN 978-1-3995-2557-2 (epub)

MIX
Paper | Supporting responsible forestry
FSC® C013604

This book is printed using paper from well-managed forests, recycling and other controlled sources

CONTENTS

ACKNOWLEDGEMENTS

This book is the first major research project I have undertaken as an individual writing effort in more than a decade. This makes me only more aware of the truth, fundamental to the spirit and the letter of Hannah Arendt's work, that no human artifact is the work of a single human being. With only me to hold responsible for the faults of what follows, there are a number of people to whom it is my honor and duty to offer my thanks for their part in bringing this to light.

First, to Dick Bernstein, may his memory be for a blessing, mentor and teacher, later friend and critic, whose critical yet kind eye I was not fortunate enough to consult in drafting this book, but whose last conversation with me inspired me to believe that there was, in fact, more to be said about "Hannah Arendt and the Jewish Question" two decades after his pioneering work on the subject and despite all the contributions others have made in his wake, and that perhaps I might be someone to say it.

To Isaac Ariail Reed, for helping me come to the conviction that a version of the main thesis of this book would make a contribution to both Arendt scholarship and the history of political thought in the first place, for jointly writing pieces closely cognate to the argument of this book together with me, and for calling me to account as I developed and reworked material I originally wrote with an eye on joint publication as parts of this solo-authored book.

To Jeffrey Champlin, for reading virtually every word of this manuscript in very rough first drafts and providing feedback that was both constructive and incisively critical at three distinct stages in the drafting process where it felt like this project was a fool's errand.

To Siobhan Kattago, Katarzyna Eliasz, Maria Robaszkiewicz, Joel Pierce, and Aaron Tugendhaft for their comments on one or more of the chapters. And to Shree Agnihotri for sharing with me her doctoral thesis on "Arendtian Constitutional Theory," which was immensely helpful in helping me round out my discussion of scholarship on Arendt in the field of Constitutional Theory.

To Roger Berkowitz, Jana Schmidt, Jana Mader, and Tina Stanton, as well as the wonderful staff at the Hannah Arendt Center for Politics and the Humanities at Bard College, for intellectual stimulation and incredibly kind hospitality at three different events over the course of 2022 and 2023, at which, during which, and through which, the argument of this book came into focus. The June 2023 Reading Group in particular was absolutely vital for the Arendt text selections that form the basis of three of the chapters and the Epilogue.

To Ben Robinson, Jeffrey Isaac, and Mark Roseman for inviting me to present an early version of Chapter 3 to the departments of Germanic Studies and Political Science and the Borns Jewish Studies Program at Indiana University, and to the audience there for helpful feedback that eventually turned what was then-conceived as a one-off "article" into this book project. And to audiences at Oxford University, the Hannah Arendt Center, the University of Virginia and Boston University for their kind attention to and suggestions for early versions of different parts of this manuscript.

To the Borns Jewish Studies Program and its Faculty Affairs Committee for providing me with a Supplemental Research Grant to make it possible to share parts of the manuscript both in the United States and in Germany over academic year 2023–24.

To Ersev Ersoy, for all her help in bringing the book that preceded this one to press and for making the suggestion to think about publishing this one with Edinburgh University Press and then for making that happen. And to Sarah Foyle, Helena Heald, and Sam Johnson and all else at the Press for their professionalism and dedication in making this book the best it could be and reach the widest audience it could reach.

Finally, to Irit, my life partner, and Ido and Rona, my children: you have heard and discussed many of the arguments in this book with me, sometimes over and over again as I rethought what exactly I wanted to say; you have challenged me to make it clearer and to explain why it matters; and you have been generous in understanding the time it took that making this manuscript come about, even when you and I would have wanted some of that time to be used otherwise. For this, and for all you do to make the private space we share a space of love and growth, I am most grateful.

These Acknowledgements were drafted, in large part, in various rooms at Lennox Hill Hospital in New York City, where my godfather Edward Platt was diagnosed with the lung cancer that—so far as human probabilities can be certainly known—will bring about the end of his time in my life and in this world before this book comes to press. Fitting, then, that it was always my intention to dedicate this work to him, which I humbly do now. Arendt, and he, I believe, would appreciate the irony of this book about the Hebrew and Roman theocratic elements of Arendt's putatively secular liberalism being dedicated to the member of my very Jewish family who has always understood himself as stridently secular.

Bloomington, IN / New York
February 2024

LIST OF ABBREVIATIONS

LOTM1	*The Life of the Mind, Vol. 1: Thinking*
LOTM2	*The Life of the Mind, Vol. 2: Willing*
LSA	*Love and Saint Augustine* (translation of *Der Liebesbegriff bei Augustin*)
OR	*On Revolution*
OT	*Origins of Totalitarianism*
OV	*On Violence*
RP	"Religion and Politics"
RLR	"Reflections on Little Rock"
THC	*The Human Condition*

INTRODUCTION: REFIGURING ARENDT'S *CORPUS* AS INTERVENTIONS IN POLITICAL THEOLOGY

Hannah Arendt has recently come to be seen as a figure central to the growing interest in what is called, generally with reference to the work of Carl Schmitt or Giorgio Agamben, "political theology." Comparatively few of those participating in this scholarly conversation attend to Arendt's engagement with the influential work in politics and religion done by three of her German émigrée contemporaries: Eric Voegelin (on "the political religions"); Ernst Kantorowicz (on "sacred secrets of the state" and, more famously "the King's Two Bodies"); and Leo Strauss (on "Athens and Jerusalem," Spinoza's *Theological–Political Treatise* and Hobbes' *Leviathan*, among numerous other interventions). Arendt shares with these three contemporaries an urgent need to understand the irrational aspects of political life, both the particular perversions that made Fascist and National Socialist totalitarianism possible and the religious-like appeal of Bolshevism. Like these three, Arendt also acknowledges the traces of similar phenomena within liberal democracies. At the same time, her focus on spontaneity and her distrust of institutionalization, and of the bureaucratization and delegation adjacent to such institutionalization, provide her with a unique point of critical entry to political theology. What brings her close to Strauss, Voegelin, and Kantorowicz and what sets her apart merit much attention than is usually given.

Why so? Answering this question will require a careful critical reconstruction of the scholarly analysis of political theology since the 1920s, a task I aim to begin in Chapter 1 through a discussion of what Seyla Benhabib (2018:

190) has called "Weimar syndrome." But, in essence and in brief, we can say that while Arendt is rightly received as a critic of bureaucratic rationality like Habermas and other followers of Weber on the left, she is also, and I will argue more fundamentally, trying to correct Max Weber's error of attempting what cannot be done: the evacuation of normativity from the project of the human sciences. It is this that brings her work closest to that of Strauss, Voegelin, and Kantorowicz, for all their many and important disagreements. Arendt insists, like these critics of Weber, on an extra-rational—or at least non-rational—form of value commitment that binds together those who would act in public.

My attempt to situate Arendt in this conversation requires a critical review of the main ways in which the term "political theology" is deployed in contemporary conversations and how using it as a lens that permits an overview of selections from the entirety of Arendt's corpus adumbrates a distinctively different sense of the term. But before we can unpack these senses of what we mean by political theology, we need first to address what it means to take up Arendt as engaged in theological thought at all. This may, indeed, seem quite surprising, if not outright wrong-headed. After all, one might well ask, isn't Arendt a secular thinker, a non-observant German-Jewish philosopher (or political theorist)? What, then, does Arendt's work have to do with Christian theology and what does that theology have to do with our attempts to come to terms with her work at all, let alone as a necessary contribution to the discourse around political theology? To address these questions, we begin (in the next section) with a discussion of the juncture of Hannah Arendt's thinking and Christian theology, in critical conversation with John Kiess' (2016) *Hannah Arendt and Theology*.

From there, the analysis connects the debates of the 1920s with contemporary arguments about the limits of liberalism—in particular, two positions that will here be dubbed "New Augustinianism" and "Black Protestant Theology" as central, competing articulations of the contemporary importance of Augustine's thinking—before concluding that Arendt is an ideal interlocutor for a renovated liberalism as a political theology today insofar as she: (i) like both the New Augustinians and Black Protestant theologians engages (in *Origins* and elsewhere) substantially with the "dark side" of liberal modernity and its characteristic rationality; (ii) like Kantorowicz, Strauss, and Voegelin has a sophisticated and principled disagreement with a certain mainstream form of political liberalism and the narrative of progress; and yet (iii) unlike all those mentioned does not succumb to either an overly rejectionist or accepting response to what Arendt called "the tradition."

Hannah Arendt and (Liberalism as a Political) Theology

What is, as I am calling it here, New Augustinianism? I have in mind a certain approach to Augustine and the Augustinian tradition that understands itself as developing in the aftermath of the Second World War and as a response to

Hannah Arendt and *Origins* in particular. John Kiess (2016: 3) rightly observes: "There is a need for a fuller, more integrated picture of Hannah Arendt, one that situates her engagement with theology within the broader contours of her thought, and one that can help readers navigate the various responses her work has generated." And while Kiess (2016: 3) often makes good on his intention to take "stock of how Arendt appropriates or criticizes theological perspectives in the course of developing original positions" on core aspects of her thinking such as "evil, worldliness, natality, and the life of the mind," there are key respects in which his account seems nevertheless to occlude recourse to Arendt as a resource for expanding or improving our understanding of political theology. In this section, I first address two insights that Kiess develops out of Benhabib (1996) and Richard J. Bernstein's (1996) approaches to Arendt's work. I then go on to show why, notwithstanding his helpful expansion of the reception on Arendt through these thinkers and further theological resources relevant for understanding what these commentators are taking from her work, there are two key respects in which we still need, even after Kiess' intervention, a more fundamental reconstruction of the place of theological disputes in reading Arendt. And, on that basis, a renovation of our understanding of Arendt as an interlocutor within the discourse on political theology.

The first interpretive point that Kiess (2016: 125) emphasizes entirely correctly in my view—working in the wake of Benhabib's (1996: 90–91) account of how Arendt's basic worldview and life experiences inform her thinking about judgment—is that and why "Arendt's turn to worldliness represented an attempt to reflect more deeply upon the underlying conditions that enable us to exercise our basic human capacities," and her corresponding articulation of "citizenship in terms of the everyday task of forging a common world, a task sustained by the *amor mundi* of each citizen." Here we see the first and most principal debt to Augustine in her political thinking: the notion that, for all the perils involved in introducing emotional or passionate investment into the space of politics—and of bringing love into public, which as we will see troubles Arendt to no end, throughout her writing career—the standard liberal understanding of public life as an arena of deliberation and debate, of consensus and compromise, requires an amendment in which such rational commitments to democratic life are embedded within a prior and extra-rational, if not irrational, commitment to the possibility of sharing *this* world, the only one there is for humankind, with others. Moreover, others with whom we are—by no choice or contract of our own—in community. In this respect, as Kiess (2016: 125) rightly notes, Arendt "remained indebted to key Augustinian insights about the world's fragility and the importance of love in ensuring its ongoing existence."

It may well be that Arendt distances herself from Augustine insofar as the latter's conception of love ultimately leads one to a set of commitments that are other-worldly rather than this-worldly, insofar as she concludes, as

Kiess (2016: 126) puts it, that the church is primarily "a social 'body' bound together through charity [*caritas socialis*—MDW], not the worldly in-between of things"; this is a complex interpretive question to which we will devote ourselves in Chapter 1. All the same, as Kiess (2016: 127–28) argues in conversation with Benhabib's (1996: 14–22) discussion of Arendt's early work on Rahel Varnhagen, Arendt's thought is alive to the ways in which church communities, like the salons of the late eighteenth century "are not merely 'social' and certainly not unworldly; on the contrary, they serve as powerful alternative or experimental 'publics' that offer glimpses of new possibilities for the broader common world." Yet, as members of pluralist democratic societies, we may well not find ourselves at all called to build a world in common with those who "experiment" in such churches understood as latter-day salons; the avowedly extra-rational and non-contractual nature of membership and participation in these spaces entails that there is no way in advance to ensure that the convictions and aims that emerge in themselves contribute to the building of a world in common that is truly in common with other members of the democratic societies in which these churches are embedded.

This is the problem of democratic societies as inherently exclusionary, with which Arendt struggled throughout her career and which will haunt the argument of Chapters 2–4 as we try to uncover a positive and constructionist liberalism as a political theology out of Arendt's engagement with Augustine in her key mature works before setting Augustine directly into view as the object of analysis in Chapter 5. There, we will confront most directly the deepest faultline in Arendt's engagement with Augustine: how can it simultaneously be the case *both* that democratic citizenship, understood as the task of building the common world, is based on the love of the world *and* that love is a private capacity that dies if it is made public and upon which no action can rightly be based. That these views are both Arendt's—as we will see in detail below—is indisputable; that they are in tremendous conflict with one another, if not outright mutually exclusive, is also immediately clear. The main line of argument in this book will proceed in awareness of this deep faultline without trying to resolve it; in Chapter 5, I will argue that accepting the central lesson of Arendt's continual returns to Augustine in search of an antidote to a chronic illness in liberalism might well require that we abandon the second of these two commitments, in part at least, in order to preserve and extend the salutary benefits of the first.

In so arguing, I am surely in concert with the second of Kiess' core insights in trying to better integrate Arendt scholarship and contemporary debates in theology and ethics, namely, that Arendt is a needed voice for contemporary theological discussions of evil and that Arendt scholarship would benefit from listening further to what theologians are saying about evil in response to Arendt—though with an important amendment discussed below. As Kiess

(2016: 53) notes, our examination of this dimension of Arendt's engagement with Augustine begins with another head-scratching seeming paradox: "Arendt consistently and emphatically disavows the relevance of tradition in making sense of the unprecedented nature of totalitarian evil, and yet much of what she has to say about evil inadvertently confirms the continued relevance of the Augustinian tradition." This seeming paradox is best resolved, as Kiess (2016: 63) argues following Bernstein (1996: 139–53), if we understand the purported "changing of her mind" between the discussion of radical evil in *Origins* and the "banality of evil" in *Eichmann in Jerusalem* as not a changing-of-mind at all, but rather a shift of emphasis and a difference of argumentation regarding the reception of the tradition.

We will engage the details of this just below; for the moment, what is crucial is what lesson, on the best interpretation of Arendt on the problem of evil, ought we to draw for thinking about Arendt and the tradition, and in particular Augustine, today. For Kiess (2016: 54) it is that there is "a tendency in Arendt to dismiss traditional resources too prematurely and, in the case of the privation account, on the basis of a mischaracterization of the position in question" because "Arendt's disavowal of tradition is based upon one rather static conception of tradition," which for Kiess is neither the only nor the best "way to conceive tradition." Here, I disagree with Kiess in two ways. First, I do not believe that Arendt engages the tradition as static or one-sided; as we will see in detail in Chapters 1 and 3 especially, she is keenly attuned to the polyvocality within the tradition itself and the various ways in which it can be and has been taken up by both thinkers and actors since, especially, the Atlantic revolutions of the late-eighteenth century. Second, and more importantly, however static her notion of tradition is, it is undeniable that she considers it to be a "lost treasure": yes, we can engage with, and "dive for pearls and coral" among the various jewels that have been "left to us by no testament."[1] But, for Arendt, there is no possibility of retrieving and repurposing the wisdom of the past for the purposes of the present. This holds for Augustine's arguments as much as for anything else that Arendt admires in the tradition that "had its definite beginning in the teachings of Plato and Aristotle" and "came to a no less definite end in the theories of Karl Marx" (Arendt, "Tradition and the Modern Age": 17).

This matters, primarily, not for Arendt interpretation, but for the problem we face in trying to take up the task of building a world in common in a pluralist

[1] Fusing the image that she borrows from Walter Benjamin (1968: 50: "Like a pearl diver who descends to the bottom of the sea, not to excavate the bottom and bring it to light but to pry loose the rich and the strange, the pearls and the coral in the depths, to carry them to the surface, this thinking delves into the depths of the past—but not in order to resuscitate it the way it was and to contribute to the renewal of extinct ages.") with the aphorism of René Char with which Arendt (1993 [1968]: 3) begins the Preface to *Between Past and Future*.

democracy where we do not, in fact, share a tradition with all of our fellow citizens, but rather participate in and critically respond to different clusters of different strands of a tradition—call them "Athens and Jerusalem" or "Rome and Jerusalem" or "Athens and Alexandria/Constantinople" *and* "Rome and Jerusalem" and so on—that is no longer authoritative for us in any clear way. In this light, let us briefly review two key points in Arendt's reception of what she frames as "the tradition" that are essential to her understanding of Augustine and which Kiess reconstructs in less than the best light. Doing so will help us to see why I think he is mistaken about Arendt's rejectionism—not that I disagree that Arendt rejects the salience of tradition as we seek "to think without banisters," but rather that I think he is wrong to think that she is wrong in doing so. More importantly, though, it will help us to see why and how the best developed Arendtian line in response to Augustine—one that never quite entirely surfaced in her written works, but which is there to be uncovered—can help us articulate a better, renovated liberalism as a political theology that can do better than both the putatively secular, or largely secularized, articulations of liberalism and their expressly non-secular alternatives.

The first of the two points, discussed in greater detail below, is the afterlife of the Pelagian controversy. If we take the view of tradition and its contemporary salience that he advocates, then we might well draw the conclusion, as Kiess (2016: 2) does[2] that, in her appeal to "the Greek striving for immortality and the human capacity for spontaneity" Arendt "falls victim to precisely the Pelagian pride and optimism that Augustine and others warned against long ago." When Kiess (2016: 162–67) develops this argument in the fourth chapter of his book, he largely endorses the view of Charles Mathewes (2001), albeit in somewhat softer tones. I respond to Mathewes' argument to this effect in the following section, but for the moment let us note the chief point of conflict, which is that "Arendt relied upon Augustine for his basic insistence upon freedom," while "her own account of action 'effectively Pelagianizes' his thought by unmooring it from any account of grace." We can debate—and will in the following section—the extent to which Arendt, like many liberals, takes sides with the view of Pelagius and Celestius in their fifth-century controversy with Augustine—and in this way the extent to which Arendt "Pelagianizes" action. But the prior point and the one salient for our current concern of "what to do with the tradition" is that is only a problem that she is Augustinian about freedom and anti-Augustinian about action if, in the first place, we think that there is a stable and core "traditional" Augustine that needs to be accepted or rejected in the first place. But Arendt's attitude to Augustine's works is that, like other "pearls," they are there like lost treasure for us dive for and among, but

[2] Or at least cites Charles Mathewes (2001) as concluding (Kiess 2016: 9 n.6).

which we will never retrieve in their wholeness as they were meant for readers in their times—even if we wanted to so recover them.

The same holds for the second main point of difference between Kiess' attempt to bring Arendt scholarship and theology into a fuller engagement with one another, which in fact builds from this problem with Pelagianism and connects back with the problem of radical evil: it is the place of judgment in Kant's thought; in particular, his response to Leibniz and others on the idea of theodicy. With great justice, clarity, and concision, Kiess (2016: 84–86) reconstructs the ultimately Kantian character of Arendt's judgment of the Israeli court's failure to judge Adolf Eichmann in the manner she considered correct; namely, on the basis of his crimes against humanity with the court's competence settled by universal jurisdiction.[3] Kiess (2016: 86) connects this judgment to Arendt's call, in *Origins*, for recognition of the universal right to have rights because "responding to evil required nothing less than a recovery" of these rights for the rightless. As we will see in Chapter 5 and the Epilogue, I believe it is wrong to see Arendt as defending the "right to have rights" in Chapter 9 of *Origins*, but the basic point of agreement with Kiess is that the argument about universal jurisdiction in *Eichmann* must be read together with the "new law of the earth" that Arendt calls for in the first Preface to *Origins*.

More serious than a disagreement with Kiess' attempt to bring Arendt's Augustine more fully into conversation with standard views of her major works is that he neglects what Susan Neiman (2001: 66) has argued in providing a substantiation of Arendt's rather offhand remark that *Eichmann in Jerusalem* is a work of theodicy: the view that, in Jerusalem, "what was on trial was not (only) German war crimes, or Jewish complicity in them, but Creation itself." To come to terms with Arendt on evil, then, is not merely to settle her accounts with Augustine but also to directly address the ways in which Augustine's discussion of freedom (where Arendt largely borrows from him) and his discussion of action (where she disavows him) are accessible to her in response to Kant's own attempts to secularize practical thinking, so as to evade the antinomy of freedom and grace for which Mathewes takes Arendt to task for attempting to avoid in her "partial Augustinianism."

Thus, for all the virtues of Kiess' attempt to provide an overview of the "state of play" as regards Arendt's reception within theological discourses today, and notwithstanding the significant debt that my account owes to his treatment of Arendt as a voice with which contemporary theology must reckon, there is something substantial he misses about the problem of evil and how it structures both Arendt's impact on theological debates in the second half of the twentieth

[3] Rather than for his crimes against the Jewish people; on this see Leora Bilsky (2010) and Robaszkiewicz and Weinman (2022: 104–6).

century and her relevance today. Namely, as both Neiman (2002) and Bernstein (1996) show, it is crucial to note (as Kiess does not) just how *and why* postwar political philosophy, moral thought, and popular discourse generally were so silent about the problem of evil.[4] This, from Arendt's perspective, is not merely the actual proper content of the discourse we call (or to which we refer under the sign of) "political theology," but actually the fundamental question of our time. The fact that this was so poorly heard and so little received, despite all the influence Arendt has had, is central to advancing the "fuller, more integrated picture of Arendt" that Kiess calls for and tries to bring about. For this reason, in the rest of this section, I will reconstruct these arguments from Neiman and Bernstein as a supplement to Kiess' overview.

In the opening moments of her instant classic treatment of the problem of evil, offered not so much as a philosophical investigation of a topic (though it is that) but as "an alternative history of philosophy" itself, Neiman (2002: 2) observes that: "In 1945 Arendt wrote that the problem of evil would be the fundamental problem of postwar intellectual life in Europe, but even there her prediction was not quite right. No major philosophical work but Arendt's own appeared on the subject in English, and German and French texts were remarkably oblique." Neiman (2002: 3) recognizes that most philosophers today will find her claim that you can tell the history of modern philosophy through a conceptual analysis of evil and how its meaning changed from the mid-eighteenth century to the mid-twentieth century "to be less false than incomprehensible"; for, "the problem of evil is thought to be a theological one [and] such questions have been off-limits to philosophy since Immanuel Kant argued that God, along with many other subjects of classical metaphysics, exceeded the limits of human knowledge." It is precisely this Kantian commitment, I want to show in what follows, that had brought Arendt to engage seriously and substantially with Augustine already before the horrors of the mid-twentieth century, in her 1929 dissertation on the concept of love in Augustine (*Der Liebesbegriff bei Augustin*, published in English translation as *Love and Saint Augustine* only in 1996, more than twenty years after her death). It also brought her back to Augustine again and again, in each of her major mature works and in her last, *The Life of the Mind*.

As Neiman (2002: 68) relates, Kant's steadfast and principled rejection of Leibniz's cause of defending this as "the best of all possible worlds" is not meant

[4] For sure, Kiess (2016: 51) notes that "it may have taken other intellectuals longer to come around [to the importance of the question of evil] than she anticipated," but his longer discussion of the issue seems to entail that, in the long run, the engagement with the problem of evil that she imagined would be required after the Second World War occurred. For reasons that the rest of this section will hopefully show, I do not believe that the reckoning Arendt had in mind is the one that Kiess documents and joins.

so much to refuse theodicy as to diffuse it and led Kant "to insist that faith in a world which coordinates happiness and virtue can't be faith in another world to come but in a transformation of the world we live in." In this, we can see at once why Arendt could say that once she read Kant he was "always looking over her shoulder": Kant's persistent this-worldliness is integral to her long-standing quarrel with Marx and emblematic of her antipathy for any other-worldly or messianic visions in politics, be they Marxist–Hegelian, Socialist, or Zionist. But together with this, Kant's attempt to please neither Leibniz nor Hume while doing justice to the empirical and moral arguments they advance carries with it a constant companion that dissatisfies Arendt. For, Neiman (2002: 83) even if "no one worked harder to show that the question of whether the world is made for us cannot even be properly formulated, no one seems more tempted to give it a positive answer." It is precisely in the face of Kant's inability to dispel this philosophical optimism, and theodicy, once and for all that Arendt is drawn to her appropriation (perhaps, less generously, we could say her decontextualization or even her bastardization) of Augustine's claim that rather than the world being created for human beings, human beings are in order to fashion and re-fashion the world, giving rise both to time and to history. The this-worldliness of this conviction, however partial an understanding of Augustine's intent in book XII of *City of God*, is a sign that only with Augustine, as she understands him, can the problem of the world and humankind as created and good point to the embrace of freedom in and as natality, which together with plurality is as close to a foundational principle as we can find in Arendt.

This, as Neiman (2002: 111) notes, brings us face to face with "the power of contingency," which is one of two axes (the impotence of God to prevent disasters and suffering being the other) "on which reason falters": here, too, Kant provides inspiration, for "his vision of metaphysics as unending rests on his view that the gap [between is and ought] is permanent" leads him to imagine the relation of the thinking subject "as that of unsatisfied yet unwavering lover." This is one ground of the love of the world that remains Arendt's basic orientation from the 1920s straight through to the end of her life; it is also, as Neiman (2002: 258–67) argues the basis of Arendt's unique response to the putative novelty of Nazi wrongdoing and the Second World War as ending any modern theodicies. The connection between contingency as the source of human freedom and contingency as the source of the love of the world stands at the very center of Neiman's (2002: 261) reading of Arendt and her account of evil more generally, for what Arendt was rejecting in making her own judgment was the desire to remove "the sting of contingency by showing individual misery to be necessary for human history as a whole" as "a way of reconciling us to a world where such misery occurs."

In a recent analysis of *Evil in the Western Philosophical Tradition*, Gavin Rae (2019: 202) also notices this irreducible element of contingency by which

Arendt critically appropriates "the Augustinian–Kantian tradition" and "challenges its claim that evil is grounded in the individual's autonomous will"; Rae's view, however, is that Arendt's account of evil repeats "the basic Augustinian–Kantian claim that the individual can always choose to alter his or her morality and is therefore ultimately responsible for it." On Rae's (2019: 203) reading, this is a weakness of Arendt's account, which requires a turn to post-structuralist and psychoanalytic thinkers—Jacques Lacan and Cornelius Castoriadis in particular—in order to understand "the linguistic structures and practices that structure individual understanding and actions." I, following Arendt's intuition about the ineluctable return of contingency whenever action (rather than behavior) is concerned, believe that Neiman and Bernstein's account of evil—hewing closer to Arendt—ultimately offers a plausible and workable answer to the ongoing impasses that rest beneath Arendt's turn to Augustine.

Yet, even as we must see Arendt, like Jean Améry and Hans Jonas and Theodor W. Adorno, as opposed to any "modern theodicy" as a classical form of consolation and reconciliation, Neiman (2002: 270) insists that *Eichmann in Jerusalem* nevertheless is (as we have seen above) an attempt at theodicy,[5] insofar as: "Resolving to take responsibility for some piece of the world in the absence of convincing metaphysical grounding is part of what it means to grow up in it." Here, we can see the Augustinian orientation behind the appeal to Kantian responsibility and judgment: as human beings we were not born as isolated individuals, we were born into a world, with an unending end in mind: to begin anew, again. Taking up that mantle, as Neiman (2002: 300) understands Arendt, is the only form of reconciliation that could either make sense of events or resolve the question of "whether human beings fit into the world"; it is a form of reconciling not with the past but with the uncertain future. But even though, as Neiman (2002: 300) argues, Arendt believes that any attempt "to show that we are at home in the world would make us too comfortable," it is also the case, as Neiman (2002: 303, 304) also argues, that "Arendt compared the feeling of understanding to the feeling of being at home" and that, in her exchange with Mary McCarthy, Arendt described her experience in writing *Eichmann in Jerusalem* as a having been "a curious state of euphoria," which suggests that, for Arendt, facing even the extermination camps, their causes and their effects, we "may be at home in the world after all."

This incongruence was also clear to Richard J. Bernstein (1996), who calls our attention to the disparate directions in which Arendt's analysis of evil in the design and operation of National Socialism before and after the Final Solution takes us, when reading her discussion of radical evil in *Origins*

[5] Or, more precisely, as Neiman (2002: 300), a work that could "formulate the task that might replace theodicy."

together with her argument about evil's banality in *Eichmann in Jerusalem*. Bernstein (1996: 137) begins, like Neiman, by noting the centrality of the problem of evil for Arendt and the lack of wider attention to this problem, even as her work in general garnered more and more attention over the 1950s and 1960s: "In 1945, Arendt declared: 'The problem of evil will be the fundamental question of postwar intellectual life in Europe.' She was wrong. Most postwar intellectuals avoided any direct confrontation with the problem of evil. But it did become fundamental for Arendt. She returned to it over and over again, and she was still struggling with it at the time of her death."

Bernstein (1996: 147–48) very helpfully and persuasively points to a famous exchange of letters between Arendt and Karl Jaspers in 1946, surrounding the latter's publication of *Die Schuldfrage* (published in English almost immediately after as: *The Question of German Guilt*) as demonstrative of the ways in which the banality of evil was already on Arendt's mind—because Jaspers uses the phrase himself—before she publishes the first version of the argument about totalitarianism and/as "radical evil" (in the first instance as "absolute" evil, later revised to "radical" (Bernstein (1996: 139–42))). This exchange of letters and the way the same ideas come to be expressed in the introduction to *The Life of the Mind* decades later, Bernstein (1996: 151) concludes, "shows how strikingly Arendt departs from the traditional, entrenched conception of evil understood as a manifestation of 'evil motives.' This departure from the tradition is what is so disturbing in her analysis of the banality of evil. But she had already made the same point about radical evil." By going back to the 1946 correspondence with Jaspers, and in particular Arendt's engagement with Jaspers' discussion of "German guilt," Bernstein persuasively shows that Arendt has not, truly, changed her mind in the twenty years between the end of the catastrophe and the Eichmann trial in Jerusalem.

On this basis, Bernstein (1996: 152) argues that "the question, Did Arendt change her mind?" (that is, between her presentation of the totalitarian experiment as an expression of radical evil and her presentation of the banality of evil) must be answered "emphatically in the negative"; though in saying this, he is no less emphatic that there was a "major shift of focus," from superfluousness (in *Origins*) to thoughtlessness (in *Eichmann*). Bernstein (1996: 153) reconstructs the way in which the central arguments of both works can be read together as a major shift of emphasis rather than as a change of mind thus: "Totalitarianism opens for us the abyss of radical evil, the evil that seeks to make human beings superfluous and even to eradicate the concept of humanity. What is most frightening is that this monstrous deed . . . can result from the thoughtlessness—the inability to think—of ordinary normal people." Here, the first sentence of this abridged summary finding can be read as the central conclusion of *Origins* and the second that of *Eichmann*; framed thus, we can see both why and how there is no "changing of the mind" for Arendt between the two works.

Bernstein thus exposes the same inner tension within Arendt's thought that Neiman exposes when trying to determine whether Arendt, at least as the author of *Eichmann in Jerusalem*, does or does not ultimately believe that the exercise of judgment—hers, not the Israeli court's—vindicates her being at home in the world. As Ronald Beiner (1996: 280) notes, this tension (or in his words, "paradox") in Arendt's understanding of human life in terms of both belonging and estrangement not only manifests in her judgment of Eichmann and his trial, but already in *Der Liebesbegriff*, where she reads Augustine as already setting the terms of a love-of-neighbor that appears at least to lead one to equally love the world and view it as a desert. Beiner (1996: 280–81, 284 n.56) suggests that responding to this dynamic tension between loving the world and feeling alienated from it as a source for making a home in this world is the task of both the *vita activa* and the *vita contemplativa*, as Arendt confronted in both *The Human Condition* and then *The Life of the Mind*. Following this insight, when we "pull back the lens" from both the immediate context of her writings and the controversies surrounding them and the problem of evil as such, we can see that this tension ultimately points to the very question of secularization and Weber's disenchantment thesis that made Augustine's concept of love relevant for her as a dissertation topic. For this reason, we now need to bring the issues raised by Arendt's works of the 1950s and 1960s in this section into conversation with those that motivated her first turn to Augustine as a graduate student in the 1920s.

Liberalism as a Political Theology and its Roots in the Pelagian Controversy

Responding to Kiess' account of Arendt's importance for contemporary theology, and the role of theological arguments in her thinking, expanded and revised through the lessons drawn from Neiman and Bernstein about the reckoning with evil Arendt saw as central and necessary for postwar intellectual life but about which very few other than herself had very much to say for about fifty years, this section aims to demonstrate two points. First, Neiman and Bernstein are both absolutely right to point to the problem of evil as both Arendt's chief and abiding object of interest and her inescapable contribution to moral and political thought. Second, and as Joanna Vecchiarelli Scott and Judith Chelius Stark also stress in their essay on *Liebesbegriff* (LSA: 131), we need to widen the scope beyond the horrors of the Second World War and take Arendt's undeniably theological analyses of evil back into her doctoral dissertation (published in 1929, before the rise of the National Socialists). When we do so, we see that already before, and then during, the emergence of patterns of action and thinking she would later come to identify as totalitarian Arendt had already come to identify the problem of theodicy as the deepest of the unresolved impasses that bubbled up from underneath the cracks in the foundations of the liberal and secular order attempting to entrench itself in the wreckage of a rebuilding Europe in the wake of the First World War.

Particularly telling in this regard is Neiman's (2002: 314) observation that the problem of evil continually reemerges in Rawls' work, "despite his own best efforts (and those of his friends) to avoid metaphysical pitfalls," and her contention that this "reemergence" demonstrates that "this engagement was increasingly unavoidable almost in spite of personal inclinations suggests something about the problem of evil itself." Eric Nelson (2019: 51) has recently advanced a rather strong reading of this persistent reemergence of the problem of evil in Rawls' mature works, arguing that the publication of Rawls' "undergraduate senior thesis, *A Brief Inquiry into the Meaning of Sin and Faith*, has given us an invaluable new perspective" on the development of "his idea of 'moral arbitrariness.'" In particular, Nelson (2019: 51) finds it very significant that Rawls develops this crucial element of political philosophy—which Neiman (2002: 310–14) very deftly and concisely summarizes within the horizon of the analysis of contingency highlighted in her alternative history of philosophy as discussed above—"in the context of a fierce attack on the Pelagian heresy." Even if a reader is not entirely persuaded by the degree of emphasis that Nelson wants to place on Rawls' undergraduate thesis—it was, after all, an undergraduate thesis, even if one written by the most important political philosopher trained in the Anglo-American tradition in the mid-twentieth century—what is undeniable is that, just as much as the original liberals or protoliberals of the seventeenth and eighteenth centuries, Rawls is still operating within an argumentative space opened up by Augustine in his response to Pelagius and Celestius.

For this reason, the persistence of the Pelagian heresy as foundational for the development of the liberal worldview is surely not simply or solely, or even mostly, important for Rawls as a liberal; it is a problem that all liberals, however explicitly Christian or avowedly secularist, must have in mind when debating the wickedness of the world and the possibility of moral improvement through political progress. Nelson (2019: 5) argues that "those we identify in retrospect as 'protoliberals' arrived at their political commitments because they all, to varying degrees, took the Pelagian side of the theodicy debate. Liberalism, in other words, began life as a theodicy."

Nelson's claims about Rawls in particular are and ought to be read as claims about a very surprising development in one line, perhaps the main line, of what could be called orthodox liberalism as a political theology, at least in his sense. Put baldly, Nelson's (2019: 52) idea is that while "all of the early modern theorists who laid the foundations for what we have come to call 'liberalism'—from Milton to Locke to Kant—were committed Pelagians, Rawls' "orientation was stridently anti-Pelagian." How can we account for this? A partial answer might be to note with Neiman, as discussed above, that Kant himself is, quite literally, the crucial figure here; to whatever extent he inherits the Pelagian worldview that motivates the theodicy with which liberal thinkers hope to work through the problem of salvation, grace, and foreknowledge, Kant cannot in fairness simply be grouped with the other "protoliberals." But this does not really solve the question of just how strongly and correctly Rawls is identified with the liberalism of Locke and Kant while also being very much on the other side of this crucial debate about the moral fabric of the world. What can, in fact, explain that?

Nelson's (2019: 51) account of this "striking fact" begins with the recognition that "Pelagianism was always regarded as a 'Judaizing' or 'Hebraizing' doctrine. Its enemies saw in it the sin of 'pride'—the prideful insistence of the 'chosen people' that one can follow God's law and earn election without Christological intercession." It is this putative Pelagian pridefulness that prompted, through the doctrine of original sin, the Augustinian orthodoxy that founded and grounded Christendom precisely as the Roman Empire began to recede as a political force. Nelson (2019: 53) argues that while Rawls "was no longer a Christian and certainly had no interest in vindicating the doctrine of original sin" by the time of the publication of *A Theory of Justice* (1971), his "essential anti-Pelagianism remained intact as a habit of mind. When outlining his principle of moral arbitrariness, he straightforwardly returned to the very same language and arguments he had first employed at Princeton thirty years earlier."

But is this "pattern of thought" in Rawls really so telling? Does it really matter for our reception of his theory of justice and his immensely influential defense of liberalism as a political and moral order? Nelson (2019: 66–67) carefully considers the argument that the alignment of thought forms between his anti-Pelagian convictions as a student and his mature defense of moral arbitrariness in his secular political philosophy is ultimately of only superficial interest and that one need not take the anti-Pelagian legacy seriously in responding to his theory of justice as fairness. Nelson (2019: 67) concludes, however, that this view "is nonetheless mistaken," for "when religious arguments are secularized, they tend to leave behind the set of premises that initially made sense of them"; in this case, while "in Rawls' thesis, the uprightness of the upright man is said to be the consequence of the actions of others," it is (for the Augustinian argument that is presupposed for the argument Rawls is advanced in a secularized vein) "God acting through others that makes us act in ways that seem 'deserving.'" For this reason, Nelson (2019: 69) concludes, extrapolating from this example of the theory of agency operative in his account of distributive justice to the way his thought undergirds liberalism as both a political practice and a political philosophy: "The point is not that the mature Rawls continued to accept the doctrine of original sin, but rather that he continued to write and think *as if he did*. And to the extent that many of his disciples have tended to regard human responsibility as quite robust in the retributive realm and highly attenuated in the distributive realm, they are likewise operating under the shadow of a theological claim."

This last claim concerning how liberals following in the wake of Rawls, of which there are many, operate "under the shadow of a theological claim" cannot help but resonate in our ears with Schmitt's usage of political theology and its influences. I turn to this in the next section, situating Arendt as a central figure in this ongoing debate that begins with Augustine's theology of original sin as a response to the original Pelagians and continuing through the thinkers generally taken to be canonical for political theology: Carl Schmitt, of course, as well as Leo Strauss, Eric Voegelin, and Ernst Kantorowicz, though in different ways. We will find that Arendt's appropriation of Augustine offers us a viable and livable way through the Pelagian debate; without Arendt, we might well be left with an Augustinianism, like Rawls', that however completely secularized, is still fighting against Pelagian pridefulness. Arendt, on the other hand, is trying to recover a sense of love of neighbor in Augustine's thought that can provide a different way through the Pelagian debate that is not grounded in original sin and the pathway out of the theodicy debate it pretends to offer.

Arendt's Engagement with Augustine: An Overview of the Coming Chapters

We will turn to Arendt's potential pathway, as she begins to pave it in *Der Liebesbegriff*, in Chapter 1. But first, before concluding this Introduction, let me provisionally answer a question that may well be posed here: why should we, with or without Arendt, bother with Augustine at all, given all the problems we have just, with Nelson, noted in attempts to take on the theodicy debate in contemporary political philosophy? An answer to this in all its fullness, at least within the horizon of Arendt's thinking, can only come with an account of each of the momentous occasions where Arendt turns to Augustine in her work. But the short answer might well be: look at the alternatives. And the two main alternatives we seem to have at hand are Weber's *Entzauberung* ("disenchantment" in the usual translation but maybe more like "demystification" as will be discussed later in this Introduction and in Chapter 1) or Schmitt's rebellion against Weber and the various explicitly and unreconstructedly theological thinkers of the political right, such as the Catholic integralists, or the political left, such as Giorgio Agamben. With that sort of a rock and a hard place as alternatives, Arendt's Augustine is an ally worth searching for sympathetically if skeptically. We can ultimately only understand why Arendt turns to Augustine in her dissertation, and then returns to him again and again, if we see this move as an attempt to work through liberalism's deepest self-contradictions as a form of political theology that seeks individual liberation universally, by means of communally legitimated and inherently particularist constitutional regimes grounded in majoritarian decision-making processes.

In the coming chapters, we read why Augustine is a continual interlocutor for Arendt as she engages different manifestations and dimensions of that tension. First, in Chapter 1, "Weimar Syndrome: *Der Liebesbegriff* and Weber's Disenchantment Thesis," we situate Arendt's first substantial engagement with Augustine as one of a handful of expressions of the need to move beyond the usual horizon of liberal politics emerging in the late Weimar period. Having placed this short and imperfect work in that light, I argue in conversation with Kampowski's (2008: 230) critical construction of Arendt's main line of argumentation there, for all the flaws of her dissertation, its conclusion (we ought to "see the human condition of plurality as a gift rather than a liability" and her esteem for "the human capacity to begin something new") is not just central to the development of her mature thought but also still relevant for what I am here calling Weimar syndrome and better resolving the impasses of liberalism as a political theology.

In Chapter 2, "Paradoxes of Popular Sovereignty: The People's Two Bodies after Weber's False Prophecy of Disenchantment," I develop a reading of sovereignty and agency as they are described in *The Human Condition*, arguing that we can best understand the impossibility that grounds an articulation of the problem of "the people's two bodies" as both a legacy of the medieval and early modern phenomenon of King's Two Bodies classically analyzed by Ernst Kantorowicz and a central tension that remains unresolved at the heart of liberalism's own, quite modern, political theology.

Chapter 3, "Three Antinomies of Liberalism as a Political Theology: Foundations in *Willing*," attempts to unpack the tension analyzed in Chapter 2 by turning our gaze to the Augustinian themes in *The Life of the Mind*. Examining more precisely both what the three antinomies of liberalism as a political theology have to do with major faultline between liberalism (with its commitments to the rule of law and the protection of minorities) and democracy (as the regime in which sovereignty rests in the people and where decisions are made on the basis of majoritarian rule), I show how Arendt offers new insights into how we might yet heal this fault and the resulting chasms that seem to be opening in many or most liberal democracies today.

Then, in Chapter 4, "Constituting and Constituted Power: The Antinomy of Theocratic Faith and Secular Reason in *On Revolution*," these results are compared with the arguments Arendt makes about these matters in *On Revolution*, read together with relevant passages from *Origins* and the last two chapters of *The Human Condition*. The crucial point here will be to see how Arendt's unique understanding of power in contrast to common depictions of "power-over," in particular as the enhancement of capacity via the act of authoritative delegation, can be best understood by attending to the background of these discussions in Augustine, which is often overlooked.

Finally, in Chapter 5, "The *Eschaton* of Liberalism as a Political Theology: Popular Sovereignty Without Exclusion", we recognize the limits of Arendt's partial Augustinianism, focusing on her rejection of James Baldwin's advocacy of a solidaristic politics of love in "Letter from A Region of My Mind" (1962), and how we might draw on her work with Augustine without endorsing this rejection. In addition to Baldwin, the textual counterpoints will be Howard Thurman (1949) and Bayard Rustin (2003), with whom we will engage two central motifs of great importance for the political theology upon which Black liberationist politics rest, which Arendt misses and which are also absent in the usual picture of political theology, emanating from Schmitt and Kantorowicz and, to a lesser extent, Strauss and Voegelin. The first of these, crucial for Thurman, is the figure of Rome and Israel, both in the Biblical contexts of the Exodus story and of Jesus' life in Palestine and in the analogous, or analogized, context of the dehumanization of Black people and peoples by the "secular" powers of Europe and the United States as "legacies of Rome." The second is the revolutionary character of what we generally call the civil rights movement, but Rustin argues we should rather think of the civil rights revolution.

In the Epilogue, "Arendtian Political Theology and Neighbor-love as Political Principle," I aim to bring the insights from Baldwin, Thurman, and Rustin gleaned in Chapter 5 to bear on the limits of Arendt's partial Augustinianism, arguing that it is possible—and necessary—to push Arendt's turn to Augustine beyond the limits she herself imposes. Liberalism as a political theology of this sort, I will argue, examines how it may be possible to constitute a more just and equitable polity. Inspired by Arendt, and informed by the liberationist Black thought with which she engaged but could not ever quite productively respond to, we will see how irremediably irrational aspects of sharing a common world in a plural, democratic society could still point beyond the quandaries we share with her generation of thinkers.

Arendt's Engagement with Augustine: Is it Plausible?

This development of my reading of Arendt's Augustine aims to show that Stephan Kampowski (2008: xviii) is absolutely correct to insist that, beyond the "sheer fact" that Arendt "begins her academic career with a dissertation on Augustine ends it with [a work] in which Augustine plays again a pivotal role," the "acute reader of Arendt" must also note the "symbolic significance of this fact," which, quoting Remo Bodei in his own translation from Italian, is that Arendt's "span of reflection is thus symbolically brought together under the sign of Augustine." Less poetically, perhaps, we will see that Arendt's early attempt to come to terms with a profoundly practical question: "how for Augustine a Christian believer who loves God and has his mind and heart set on the heavens above is still able to love his neighbor in the world below"

(Kampowski 2008: xviii). More especially, we might underscore, the driving question: how is a Christian believer to love their non-baptized, and putatively therefore unsaved, neighbor? And how can we relate this problem of neighbor-love, in the context of what Scott and Stark aptly describe as Augustine's dual citizenship as a Roman and a Christian, to established central themes in Arendt's mature work such as: the world-destroying effects of bureaucratic rationality; the pernicious "rise of the social" at the expense of political concerns and public life; the lost tradition and its enduring relevance in the face of revolutionary thought and action; and how can we judge while situated within the gap between past and future?

Before trying to show how Arendt's Augustine is central to the best answer for the fundamental questions she raises in *Origins of Totalitarianism*, *The Human Condition*, *Eichmann in Jerusalem*, and *Between Past and Future*, we first need some confidence that Arendt's Augustine offers us something we can use. A good proxy for this would be to understand why Arendt time and again returns to a sentence from *City of God* where Augustine writes: "That there be a beginning man was created." This is the essence of natality, a key term, perhaps the key term for Arendt; for this reason, Arendt has reason to bring it to bear in numerous contexts as we will discuss in each of the next four chapters, with each appeal to this sentence requiring its own account given its unique argumentative purpose.

Here and now, in beginning, however, what we need is an account of why it is Augustine that becomes for Arendt the thinker of beginning *par excellence*. Surely, it is not because Arendt is a Christian or believes that Christology holds the key to solving the inner contradictions of liberalism. Rather, as Arendt (LOTM2: 217) makes clearest in the sentence just before the conclusion of the last chapter of the last work she wrote before her untimely and sudden death, Augustine's chief legacy for her is simply that he understood and best expressed what it means to free: Augustine teaches us, she believes, that "we are *doomed* to be free by virtue of being born, no matter whether we like the freedom or abhor its arbitrariness, are 'pleased' with it or prefer to escape its awesome responsibility by electing some form of fatalism." It is true that this has come to be "Arendt's last word" because, finite being that she is, *Judging*, the intended third volume of *The Life of the Mind*, remained only an intended third volume of *The Life of the Mind*.[6] Nevertheless, we cannot deny that it is fitting that Augustine not only returns in each of Arendt's works, but at the very last moment. For, even if it was Kant's "democratic theory of judgment" that formed the nuts and bolts of the account of judgment as the only possible way through the impasses that rest beneath not just theory but also the practice

[6] Notwithstanding the publication of Lectures on Kant's political philosophy (Beiner 1982).

of legitimate democratic rule, it is Augustine who provides the ultimate rationale and the groundless ground of that iterative and unending practice. If, then, there is an Arendtian solution to the Weimar syndrome, we cannot look to Kant or any other "secular" Kantian; we can only look to Augustine. For, as we see in this second to last sentence of her *corpus*, Arendt identifies with, entirely, Augustine's understanding of freedom—convinced not only that he was the first philosopher of the will but also the only Roman thinker to see both the political and philosophical dimensions of freedom in their antagonism, as will be discussed in Chapter 3.

All the same, and no less importantly for the argument pursued in the coming four chapters, Arendt rejects the doctrine of grace and the related doctrine of original sin that are foundational for Augustine's understanding of action. Charles Mathewes (2001) examined Arendt's partial adoption and partial disavowal of Augustine, ultimately concluding, essentially, that Arendt's Augustine is interesting and sometimes insightful, but not nearly Augustinian enough and chiefly of value to us in pointing to why we need more Augustine in understanding of evil, freedom and action. In build-up to the crescendo of this argument, Mathewes (2001: 184) first unpacks Arendt's debt to Augustine with respect to what he calls her "more sustained and fruitful arguments" in *Eichmann in Jerusalem* in particular: these are, in his mind, primarily two: first, "the political and legal argument about the flawed character of the trial as a trial" and how it proved incapable of dealing with Adolf Eichmann as a "special type of crime and criminal"; and, second, a "larger argument, obliquely advanced, about the character of our response to such evil." It is the second of these arguments that is chiefly interesting to us here.[7] In its regard, Mathewes (2001: 192) concludes that Arendt's response to the trial and its inability to secure justice in the face of the criminal's crimes is her unique form of politics as (what Mathewes deems to be) not so much agonal (Honig 1993: 1995) as participatory; he understands her to be arguing for a form of individual commitment to collective action that "must be *participatory*, involving us in the activity of creating a 'world' which is fit for human habitation."

As Mathewes (2001: 178) acknowledges, he owes a large debt here to Jean Bethke Elshtain's (1995) account "of the relation between Augustine's evil and Arendt's Eichmann," to which Elshtain devotes a chapter in her classic book on *Augustine and the Limits of Philosophy*. It is true that Mathewes draws from Elshtain (1995: 51–67) a critique of "the pridefulness of philosophy" that he attributes to Arendt's rejection of anti-Pelagian commitments without which (to his mind) Augustine's account of love, and therefore Arendt's partial Augustinianism cannot cohere; I would aver, however, that Elshtain herself does not

[7] For my views on the first, that is, Arendt's judgment of Eichmann himself and the uniqueness of his crimes, see Robaszkiewicz and Weinman (2022: ch. 5, esp. pp. 95–102).

see Arendt as guilty of the pridefulness for which Augustine is a necessary corrective. Indeed, after quoting Arendt's conviction that "no more is required, and no more can reasonably be asked, for this planet to remain a fit place for human habitation"—expressed in the closing moments of *Eichmann*, and discussed through Neiman's discussion of Arendt and feeling at home in the world above—Elshtain (1995: 85) concludes that "Arendt's companion in thought, Augustine, would agree with this sober and poignant conclusion" and, more importantly, perhaps, that in order to understand what Arendt says about radical evil in *Origins* and the banality of evil in *Eichmann*, it is necessary to "have some sense of Augustine's grappling with the question of evil." This supposed agreement on Augustine's part, of course, leaves open the question of the extent to which Arendt agreed with or followed Augustine, or even fully understood him; a question to which we turn in earnest just below and then, especially, in Chapter 1.

For the moment, I want to make clear both what seems to me right in the conclusion about Arendt's partial Augustinianism that Mathewes develops from Elshtain, and what seems to mistaken therein. Seeing both, to my mind, is the best way to see in broad terms that it is worth our time to dig deeper into the Augustinian dimensions not only of *Der Liebesbegriff* (1929), *Eichmann in Jerusalem* (1963), and *The Life of the Mind* (1974/1978) but of Arendt's work more generally. Mathewes (2001: 194) rightly concludes that "What is perhaps most surprising about Arendt's attempt [in the Epilogue to *Eichmann in Jerusalem*] to create a new political vocabulary for our new situation is how very Augustinian (albeit, only partially so) her resulting position turns out to be." Yet his account leaves unsaid what perhaps most needs to be said and what my argument here hopes to vindicate: that Arendt's turn to Augustine, already in her doctoral dissertation and very much in her judgment concerning the Eichmann trial, as well as throughout the course of her writing career, is meant as a response to Weber's disenchantment thesis and the hopelessness of his, and other liberals', project of articulating some sort of value-free social science. It is no accident that nothing about this is to be found here; for, on the account Mathewes (2001: 196) offers, Arendt believed that the "interpretation of natality was not essential to the structure of willing" and therefore "sought in her work to 'demystify' it, to strip it of its theological pretenses and show it to be solely a human capacity—properly miraculous, to be sure, but not in need of any supernatural powers"; in this way, for Mathewes, Arendt becomes yet another Pelagian: "this move—a move which effectively Pelagianizes Augustine—ends up rendering the ontology unsustainable, and the anthropology unintelligible."

In other words, Mathewes argues that Arendt's partial Augustinianism is doomed because she ends up trapped within the same secular politics and "demystified" philosophical anthropology as her fellow post-Weberians. I aim to show, on the contrary, that Arendt's Augustinianism—though surely partial—is not only one of a series of attempts in her generation to demystify the theological underpinnings of liberal politics in the wake of the First World War but, actually, was in its time, and remains today, our best hope of finding a way out of liberalism's Pelagianism problem. Mathewes ultimately rejects Arendt as a possible source for a way through the problem of evil and salvation because she is not a sufficiently orthodox Augustinian—because she lacks grace, essentially. I hope to show, on the contrary, that we would do better to reject the orthodox Augustinian view while embracing what Arendt—with whatever justice—identifies as the core Augustinian insight into the cosmic and divine underwriting of human freedom as truly the most viable path still open. This is the central contribution Arendt makes to political theology.

The lesson, then, of our reconstruction of a conversation about Arendt and Augustine through the work of Kiess, as a response to Neiman and Bernstein, and Mathewes is that we are now prepared to understand what it means to speak of Arendt as articulating a unique and potentially salutary political theology. This political theology is not, most properly, about how theological concepts pervade political discourse and its practical forms, although that is the terrain on which this scholarly conversation tends to take place today. Rather, political theology is the attempt to come to terms with the persistence of providence as a way of making sense of the world as one world, at a time when we have no confidence that there is an author or creator of that world. My central contention is that Arendt tries to make this case through Augustine as a response to Kant, albeit only episodically and over five decades.

Before turning to the development of that main line of argument, though, let us acknowledge one key concession that must be made to Mathewes in his rejoinder to Arendt and Arendt's Augustinianism, or her purported or partial Augustinianism. Having concluded that Arendt's hopelessly partial Augustine is fundamentally unsalvageable, Mathewes (2001: 196) concludes his chapter on Arendt and (re)turns to "the theological anthropology she thought she could dismiss." It is my contention, however, that this misrepresents both the exact nature of what is admittedly a partial Augustinianism that is to be found in Arendt's thinking. In order to see why, and to understand Augustine's answer to the problem of evil as Arendt understands and seeks to appropriate it, we need to place *Liebesbegriff* in its earlier Weimar context and own the ways in which and reasons for which her embrace of Augustine must remain only partial, even if as Mathewes (2001: 196) believes this led to "her thought's incoherence and failure." When we do so, we see that far from a Weberian demystification of Augustinian providence, Arendt's engagement with Augustine was about searching for both an ontology and an anthropology that could support both the claim that the world is a fundamentally loveable place and that it is a world because of a *superhuman* power of love.

Conclusion

We saw above, with the help of Nelson's recent critical examination of Rawls' undergraduate thesis on Pelagianism and its ongoing relevance not only for his mature work but also for current defenses of distributive justice that Rawls and his followers have an unresolved problem with secularity and the disavowed political theology that clandestinely undergirds much of liberalism. If we agree with Nelson that Rawls and Rawlsian liberals cannot hope to resolve the problem with Pelagianism that Kant had already tried heroically but unsuccessfully to resolve, why should we have any hope in Arendt offering some way through Kant et al.'s impasse with Augustine? A complete argument to this effect will require the careful reconstruction of what I hope to show is Arendt's partially Augustinian political theology, offered in Chapters 1–4, and the extension and correction of this view in Chapter 5 and the Epilogue. In advance, however, we can make clear what I take to be the grounds of hope that Arendt does in fact do better on this point.

The wager of my argument, as it unfolds in the rest of this work, is this: if, in concert with Mathewes (2001), we insist that one cannot understand Arendt's sense of politics as power as freedom without accounting for her strange Augustinianism, and if, at the same time, we reject his conclusion that Arendt's partial Augustinianism is doomed, then we will see both why and how exactly she offers an alternative to political theology in the sense of Benjamin and Schmitt. For this, we turn in Chapter 1 to a discussion of what Benhabib (2018) calls the "Weimar syndrome" and then Arendt's dissertation as a first response to that condition that does not demystify Augustine, even if she does not yet in that text present a coherent view of the ways in which her partial Augustine might yet ground something we could call a liberalism as a political theology, crucially one that does not fall prey to the impasses that liberalism's unsettled business with Pelagianism prevent it from overcoming, as both Mathewes and Nelson demonstrate.

Before taking that step forward into the details of Arendt's argument in *Der Liebesbegriff*, we must first understand the general problematic in which it is situated, namely, the febrile and inchoate crisis of parliamentary democracy as diagnosed by both Max Weber and Carl Schmitt; in particular, we must attend to and understand the impasses through which Arendt meant her reflection on the concept of love in Augustine to offer some possible ways forward. We begin with the help of Seyla Benhabib's (2018) account of "Weimar syndrome," which is symptomatic of the way in which thinkers as different as Schmitt, Morgenthau, Kantorowicz, Strauss, and Benjamin were investigating and attempting, one way or another, to advance beyond the impasses of the liberal non-solution, principally Weber's, to the problems of "political theology." To see how and why this is so, we must turn to Weber's disenchantment thesis and its perennial discontents, discussed in Chapter 1.

1

WEIMAR SYNDROME: *DER LIEBESBEGRIFF* AND WEBER'S DISENCHANTMENT THESIS

As we have seen, "Weimar syndrome" is the framing device through which it is possible to understand Arendt's corpus as interventions in political theology. But what is this "Weimar syndrome," exactly? I adopt the term from Seyla Benhabib (2018: 190), by which she means the condition in which we, like Kelsen, Schmitt, Strauss, Arendt, and Shklar before us, are "haunted by Weber's questions" concerning "how to defend, intellectually and institutionally, modern constitutional republics and liberal societies in an age of value pluralism as well as class conflict." Arendt offers the best response to this dilemma because of her heterodox liberalism—a better way, I believe, of identifying what Seyla Benhabib (1996) earlier termed Arendt's "reluctant modernism." While my overall understanding of both Arendt's major intellectual projects and her overarching intellectual project both before and after the publication of *Origins* owes much to Benhabib, I believe that we might better understand Arendt as neither a modernist (however reluctant) nor an advocate for the tradition or whatever it is that modernity has supplanted. Instead, we need to understand her as a heterodox liberal; specifically, one attuned to the ways in which liberalism is and always has been a political theology, which can be seen in her recurrent return to Augustine in each of her major works.

As Yotam Hotam (2023: 126) argues while presenting Arendt as one of four twentieth-century Jewish thinkers who make clear the "religious sources of secular thought," we need to come to terms with "how tradition informs [Arendt's] conceptualization of critique and in particular her critique of modernity, making it dependent on theology." Though there are differences between Hotam's sense of the dependence of critique on tradition and my own, as we shall see in Chapters 4 and 5 in particular, I believe it is the unique way in which Arendt acknowledges the dependence of putatively secular modernity on religious sources that characterizes her heterodox liberalism, by which I mean to self-consciously call upon the customary sense of heterodoxy as a deviation from the mainstream view in an organized faith tradition that nevertheless understands itself as belonging to that faith tradition. The implication, of course, being that liberalism is, itself, a faith tradition in the relevant sense; this I take to be a core Arendtian insight. I remain convinced that, as Maria Robaszkiewicz and I (2022: 3) argue, "readers ought to follow her own claim" from a famous 1964 interview[1] (Arendt 2005a: 4) in which she says of "her political awakening in the 1930s: 'I did not belong to a party, nor did I have need to,'" and which "in a more metaphoric way, remained true all her life." All the same, if we feel we need a pithy phrase to characterize her unique positioning in the political theory canon, I would suggest "heterodox liberal" comes closest to hitting the mark—both in the sense that she is heterodox (though not alone, of course) in seeing liberalism as a sort of faith tradition and in the sense that her brand of liberalism itself deviates from that liberalism-as-faith-tradition, in particular as regards the *topos* of "the freedom of a Christian," as we have understood it since Luther's epochal reading of Paul.

This shift of emphasis also helps us to improve on recent work that has received a great deal of specialist and non-specialist attention, in which Samuel Moyn (2023a: 533) has argued that "like Isaiah Berlin, Karl Popper, Judith Shklar, Jacob Talmon, or Lionel Trilling, Arendt is best understood as displacing the intellectual premises of earlier liberalism, while foreclosing a global approach to the universalization of freedom and equality in an era of decolonization and deracialization." While in this article, Moyn (2023a: 534) takes pains to stress that Arendt was not herself a "Cold War liberal" in the sense of his influential book (Moyn 2023b), this is only or mostly because she is not a liberal at all, and that in any case "her very attempt to strike out on her own in developing a new account of freedom proved hostage to many of the intellectual and political premises of Cold War liberalism."

This (mis)representation of Arendt is, in my view, not just wrong but wrong-headed; rather than trying to read Arendt's "reluctance" about the liberal, multilateralist *Pax Americana* of modernity as a sign of her conservatism as Moyn does, we should come to terms with the real appeal for Arendt of the conservative critiques of liberal modernity. This appeal, as I will show in the following, rests in Arendt's perception that Strauss, and even Voegelin, are not

[1] Arendt, "What Remains? Language Remains", interview with Günter Gaus, West German TV.

wrong about the ways in which liberalism fails to understand its debt to what she calls the tradition and projects a false vision of itself as novel and "modern." Yet, while accepting a good deal of these conservative critiques, Arendt thoroughly rejects antiquarianism or anything like a nostalgia for premodern conditions. This is what makes her a liberal after all, but a heterodox one precisely as regards liberalism's reliance on traditional resources that it is eager to disavow. Understanding what makes Arendt a *heterodox* liberal, rather than "reluctant modernist" or a Cold War liberal, we can see why she preserves much of what is most persuasive in conservative and/or anti-modern critiques of liberal modernity, while refusing their cultural pessimism and their rejectionism of the "unfinished project" of modernity.

This chapter proceeds in three parts. In the first, we unpack what Benhabib means by Weimar syndrome and why getting beyond this constellation of concerns requires an engagement with political theology that avoids the antiliberalism inherent in Schmitt's influential version of this line of thought. In the second, we turn directly to Arendt's doctoral dissertation, reading it as her early and explicitly political–theological response to Weimar syndrome, discovering both the promise of her appeal to Augustine and two key unresolved tensions in the "thought train" on which that work is based. In the third, we dive more deeply into the second and more fundamental of those tensions, related to the third of three moments of the concept of love that she derives from Augustine: the *caritas socialis*, or the love of the community (or fellowship) of human beings, and its inescapable entanglement with what we will examine in Chapter 2 as the second body of the People.

Before beginning the first of the three steps outlined above as the central focus of this chapter, it is important to identify two argumentative goals that our work in this chapter might be expected to achieve but will not. First, it might be thought that in framing *Der Liebesbegriff* as a way to call Weber's version of liberalism into question without yielding to Schmitt's understanding of political theology, I mean for the first two sections of this chapter to provide a close analysis of Arendt's response to Schmitt's critiques of liberal democracy. A reader interested in this should consult Ville Suuronen's (2022b: 3–6) recent detailed discussion of how closely Arendt read Schmitt, and when and why. It might similarly be expected that the analysis here will attempt to resolve the debates, actively ongoing among both Arendt and Augustine scholars and between those two largely non-overlapping groups, concerning just how deeply Augustine's views truly shaped Arendt's argument in her early work and the extent to which Arendt, in this book, adequately or faithfully recounts Augustine's view of "the difficult conceptual relation between love for God and love for neighbor" (Gregory 2001: 156). Though, of course, these issues will arise in recounting the main themes of the work, we will not have the time to seek to resolve them. Rather, our focus will be on introducing Weimar syndrome as the most helpful intellectual frame for engaging *Der Liebesbegriff* and then showing what we can learn about Arendt's Augustine as presented there through this analytic lens. Deeper questions related to political Augustinianism as an alternative to the illiberal, and anti-liberal, thought of Carl Schmitt will have to be suspended until our closer examination of the status of modern political institutions as both revolutionary and rhetorically ensconced in tradition in Chapter 4.

Weimar Syndrome and Political Theology: Avoiding Schmitt's Anti-Liberalism

Focusing on the deeper intent behind Arendt's private reflection in a November 1952 letter to Gertud Jaspers that Eric Voegelin "is off the track but the first to ask the fundamental (*prinzipielle*) questions since Weber,"[2] I hope in this section to present Arendt, with Voegelin and Strauss, as thinkers engaging the same political–theological constellation within which Weimar syndrome expresses its symptoms in response to the liberal and secular modernism celebrated, or perhaps tragically accepted, by Max Weber. We aim to understand why, for Arendt, Voegelin is so important, even though he was wrong-headed about so many things, suggesting that it is because he, more than anyone since Weber, is thinking about the problem of political theology. In this way, we will come to see how and why the central problem Weber tries but fails to address in the vocation lectures—how to maintain the fact/value distinction in the domains of both the human (or social) sciences and practical politics—very much remains our problem today as we continue to try, and fail, to overcome the Weimar syndrome.

Is there, though, space to critique Weber's understanding about the inescapable and ineluctable evacuation of value judgments from the realm of knowledge and understanding without simply echoing Schmitt's central argument in *Political Theology*? Yes, because Schmitt deploys the term "political theology" in a way that forecloses the debate between Augustine and Thomas and in so doing frames the problem of the afterlife of Christian values and practices in secular modernity along the lines of the early modern schism between the Catholic Church and Protestant reformers. Facundo Vega (2017: 698) has recently advanced an argument along these lines that brings together Schmitt, Strauss, and Arendt as similarly attempting to "fully apprehend their diagnoses of the modern disenchantment

[2] H. Arendt–K. Jaspers, *Briefwechsel 1926–1969*, hrsg. v. Lotte Köhler und Hans Saner, Piper, München, 1995, 240. A 1992 English translation has it as: "I think the book is on the wrong track, but important nevertheless. The first fundamental debate with the real problems since Max Weber" (*Hannah Arendt and Karl Jaspers: Correspondence*, trans. Robert and Rita Kimber, New York, Harcourt Brace Jovanovich, 1992: 203).

of the world"; while indebted to this insight, I dissent from his conclusion that "their competing responses to the theologico-political problem constitute a singular treatment of tradition and the place of 'the absolute' in the political realm." As I hope to show in what follows, I believe that already in *Der Liebesbegriff*, Arendt is attempting to find, or forge, a different path through her reading of Augustine's concept of love as both plural and pluralist and in this way constitutive of something like a pure imminence that points outside the binary of absolute (and unconditioned) and contingent (and conditioned).

Arendt's Augustine points toward a path beyond the claims and counterclaims she shared with Schmitt, on the one hand, and Strauss and Kantotowicz and Voegelin, on the other, chiefly because her engagement with Augustine points beyond the horizon of theses of secularization that are themselves parasitic on the notion that what precedes secularism is a form of medieval *Catholic* political theology. Montserrat Herrero (2023: 17), in advancing on understanding of Schimitt as a political theologian of revolution and not merely of absolutism or anti-liberalism, has recently suggested that Schmmit's sense of political theology as a practical program is "Christian and monotheistic" and has "one of its representatives in Augustine, whose ideas Schmitt describes in *Political Theology II*"; in her view, Schmitt understands himself as following in Augustine's wake, particularly the latter's theory of the Trinity, insofar as he, like Augustine, "sees in the divine pluripersonality the condition of possibility for plurality and fighting in a political world." Arendt—in demonstrating that Augustine is not, or is not simply, a Catholic thinker in that sense, precisely because of how he tried to bring together the contradictory worldviews of neo-Platonism, Pauline Christianity, and Roman civil religion—points in a different direction.

It is true, as Scott and Stark (LSA: xvii) note in the Preface to their translation of *Der Liebesbegriff*, that her interpretation of *caritas* as neighborly love as "Augustine's intended point of intersection for the neo-Platonic, Pauline, and Roman traditions he inherited" might well be "far more revelatory about Arendt herself" than it is "as a piece of scholarship on Augustine." Be that as it may, my contention would be that this point of departure is nevertheless more fruitful for ongoing attempts to get beyond Weimar syndrome than what can be found elsewhere; including in Herrero's very creative and original reading of Schmitt on revolutionary dictatorship and its theological–political character. To see why, let us first recount the three main ways in which the term "political theology" is deployed today, each with its own historical contextualization.

First, there is the sense (associated principally with Ernst Kantorowicz) of political theology as a paradigmatically medieval phenomenon by which stability in politics and law, specifically the sovereignty of the monarch over his land and his people, was secured through theological resources, specifically the analogy between the incorporation of the body politic into the monarch and the incorporation of body of the church into the godhead through the holy spirit. As Facundo Vega (2017: 701) notes, Kantorowicz and others, principally Leo Strauss, are concerned with the "insoluble tension between Athens and Jerusalem," that is, between reason and revelation, which Weber's account of secularization and the rationalism of the modern political state misses and "Arendt's approach to political tradition proves helpful in clarifying." This is so, Vega (2017: 701) continues, because even though Arendt "never refers to the theologico-political problem as such, it is implicit in her discussions of secularization and the broken thread of tradition" and "her view of the abyssal character of modern politics," which defines "the scope and limits of the theologico-political problem." This is precisely what the rest of this chapter, and then its ramifications in Chapters 2, 3, and 4 following, hopes to make clear.

Second, associated primarily with Carl Schmitt, there is the sense of political theology as the study of political forms within the horizon of modern politics, sovereignty above all, as "secularized theological concepts." Together with this comes the strict anti-modernism of Schmitt and his left-wing interpreters; in this meaning of the term political theology refers directly to the unavoidable irrationality or mystical depth of any true "politics." For Schmitt and leftist thinkers openly inspired by him, such as Chantal Mouffe (2005), the dictates of religion as giving meaning to death continues to exist in modern, liberal capitalist democracies and their politics, though many in those societies are quite determined, in Schmitt's view, to deny this. Catholic political philosopher Peter Simpson (2018) provides a bracingly clear view of political theology from the right in this sense.

Finally, there is the sense of political theology as theological politics today: this kind of study might involve descriptions or conceptualizations of religious political parties or movements in liberal democratic states. A central example of this sort of political theological formation would be Christian Nationalists in the United States, as examined in an influential and widely covered PRRI/Brookings Institution report "A Christian Nation?" (Deckman, Dionne et al. 2023). Another would be the rise of (Jewish) national-religious parties in Israel that, at the time of writing, make up nearly half of the most illiberal and exclusionary government in that country's seventy-five-year history; in the face of which Yotam Hotam (2023: 166; in part quoting Gordon 2020: 147) has recently spoken of the need to "propose a position that differs from the contemporary faultline" that is "situated between 'those who adhere to the principle of secular reason and those who are ready to embrace the temptations of theocracy.'"

Laying these out we can observe two shortcomings in this state of affairs. First, there is a disciplinary differentiation where one or both of the first two usages "dominate" the discussion in theory-world, while the usage in comparative politics and in political sociology gravitates toward the third–with little or no mediation between those two discourses. Second, they display a chronological differentiation where political theology can either be what happened before secularization (following in Kantorowicz's wake), after secularization (following in Schmitt's), or in the non-secularized present (in the sense of theological politics). My aim in re-signifying and re-deploying the term as a way of understanding Arendt's "reluctant modernism" and in particular her continual return to Augustine is to show that each of the three current usage traditions points to something true and important but also that none of them can be understood in their full importance without seeing its interpenetration with the other two. Contemporary theological politics cannot be restricted to the sense one has of this phenomenon if we focus only on "religious parties" and "religious governments" for the same reason that it is wrong to think of the afterlife of medieval political theology in liberal democratic ("modern") societies as one of secularization.

Arendt's unique approach to political theology, in the sense articulated here,[3] is the study of ways in which political actors of very different kinds, with quite different ideological lodestones, contend for legitimation in liberal democratic societies within a system of speech acts and interpretations that is very far from "disenchanted" in Weber's sense. Contrary to Weber's model where the fact-value distinction is strictly upheld in social life, for Arendt the common world and the organizations and institutions through which actors create and participate in that world involve a certain *leap of faith*—that the organization will continue, that the rules will somehow apply in an expected way two weeks or two years from now, that their contributions will continue to be valued, even after they "sign away" their authorship toward the collective author of the larger project to which their work contributes. To engage in political theology as Arendt attempts in *Der Liebesbegriff* is to study of that leap of faith, and its various meanings in the world, as it applies to governance of multiple kinds, between the state and citizens but also in everyday social interactions.

Der Liebesbegriff: Arendt's Political–Theological Response to Weimar Syndrome

One good reason to be skeptical of my suggestion that we read Arendt's dissertation on Augustine as a political–theological response to Weber's analysis of modernity as disenchantment and the Weimar syndrome is that many doubt that Arendt's Augustine book is about theology at all. As Scott and Stark (LSA: 128)

[3] The closest parallel to my usage to my knowledge is that at work in Adam Kotsko's (2018: 129) observation that "one of most curious aspects of political theology as presently understood is that Weber's *Protestant Ethic and the Spirit of Capitalism* is not considered a foundational document alongside Schmitt's and Kantorowicz's work." Both my debt to Kotsko and where I depart from his line of thought are clear in the extended discussion of the term "political theology" in the third section of Chapter 3, below.

note, Elisabeth Young-Bruehl's (1982: 369) claim that "Arendt was no theologian, not even an Augustinian one" set the terms of debate and the tone of most academic treatments of the place of Augustine in Arendt's thinking until at least the publication of the English translation of Arendt's dissertation in 1996. I agree with Scott and Stark about the depth of Arendt's abiding interest in Augustine and share in their refusal to accept Young-Bruehl's (1982: 369) claim (made in her analysis of Arendt's thinking about radical evil in the years between writing *Origins* and *Eichmann*) that Arendt "explained the privative nature of evil in secular terms." Yet I think they somewhat misrepresent the picture of Arendt's doctoral dissertation that Young-Bruehl provides. It is worth pausing to see how and why this is so, as it illustrates the stakes not just of our re-reading of Arendt's Augustine in this text but of thinking of Arendt as a secular thinker, as Young-Bruehl does, rather than as a political theologian.

We can see the distance between Young-Bruehl's characterization of *Der Liebesbegriff* in her philosophical biography of Arendt and the way it has been received both by readers who want to take the dissertation seriously and those ready to dismiss it if we broaden the lens of analysis to encompass the place of the dissertation in Young-Bruehl's (1982: 3) picture of Arendt's life as an evolving series of versions of the "no longer" and the "not yet" as Arendt herself put it when first trying to give an account of herself in 1924–1925. Seen this way, rather than through the lens of what Young-Bruehl (1982: 62–76, *passim*; esp. 74–76) writes about *Liebesbegriff* in the chronological chapter where it belongs, the understanding of the role of the doctoral dissertation in her life's work shifts away from the question of Heidegger's influence on the young Arendt toward the approach that I, following Kampowski (2008), suggest. Two quotes from Young-Bruehl's biography will show this, one where Young-Bruehl references the dissertation in the context of the contrast between her relationships with the two teachers who were most influential for her (Karl Jaspers and Martin Heidegger), and one which offers a synopsis of the text of the dissertation—which would be unavailable for English-language readers for another fifteen years after the publication of Young-Bruehl's book.

Speaking of the ways in which the young Arendt was drawn at least as much by Romantic poetry as by philosophy, Young-Bruehl (1982: 4) notes that while her "gift for philosophy is certainly apparent in the doctoral dissertation she wrote at Heidelberg with Karl Jaspers," the most striking thing about the text is "her longing, her vision of that community-sense which Saint Augustine called 'neighborly love.'" One can debate the extent to which this is an accurate account of "what is most striking" in *Der Liebesbegriff*; all the same, this makes clear that for Young-Bruehl as for our discussion here, it is a mistake to take her view to be that the dissertation belongs to an early and immature Arendt whose thinking is shaped more or less definitively by Heideggerian themes and interests, even if this is the way her discussion of the dissertation shaped Arendt scholarship for two decades or more. This needs to be understood together with the stance that Arendt insists she will maintain in the dissertation, even when discussing issues such as the relation of Creator and creature which seem manifestly theological; for Young-Bruehl (1982: 499) the "apolitical and atheological" nature of the text is Arendt's way to keep "the promise she made in her introduction that her inquiry would be 'analytical throughout'" and "'purely philosophical,' by which she meant that she was not going to consider Augustine's 'dogmatic subservience' to Scriptural and ecclesiastical authority." This underscores the point about Arendt being wholly secular for Young-Bruehl; it is also, as Scott and Stark argue, overly determinative of Augustine's place in Arendt's thinking through at least *Eichmann*.

If, however, we look at the whole of this claim, taken together with the early claim about the worldly and personal bases of Arendt's passionate interest in neighbor-love, and the wider claim here in the appendix about Arendt's own belief in the weakness of the abstraction of the dissertation and its refusal to take a position about the very politically and personally invested man who authored the arguments she engages only abstractly in *Der Liebesbegriff*, I would submit that Young-Bruehl's depiction of Arendt's Augustine is ultimately compatible with that in the 1996 English edition of *Love and Saint Augustine*. In particular, Young-Bruehl's view supports Scott and Stark's (LSA: 129) argument that *Der Liebesbegriff* is both very much about Augustine's unique take on Christian theology and "present throughout *The Human Condition* as a subtext for Arendt's phenomenology of public, private, and social life." I hope in this section to vindicate, with friendly amendments, this account of Arendt's dissertation as integral to and a source for her mature work, through a close reading of Arendt's critical reconstruction of Augustine's *caritas socialis*.

Before turning to that reconstruction, let us note one further infelicity of Young-Bruehl's approach, which Scott and Stark rightly characterize both as dismissive of the importance of the Augustine book for Arendt's later thinking and very well-received in Arendt scholarship; namely, the ways in which it marginalizes the Augustinian background to Arendt's decades-long consideration of evil, from the discussion of radical evil in *Origins* and in texts written while preparing that manuscript to the discussion of the banality of evil in *Eichmann*. In the Introduction, we discussed Bernstein's argument that this shift of emphasis does not involve "changing her mind" about the depth or shallowness of evil, an argument I consider to be persuasive. What remains to be said about this issue in the present context is that, as Scott and Stark (LSA: 130) emphasize, this shift in Arendt's argumentation mirrors "a similar movement in [Augustine's] thought as he evolved from a belief in the material reality of evil during his Manichean period toward his 'mature' position in which evil is described as a bondage to habitual sin, worldliness that free will is powerless to break." While Scott and Stark probably overstate the degree to which

Arendt's position in either *Origins* or *Eichmann* maps with Augustine's in *De Libero Arbitrio* or *De Natura et Gratia*, as we will discuss later in this section, they are right to say that for Arendt theoretical and practical debates about political concerns, such as sovereignty and freedom, need to be returned to their theological context.

Writing precisely when Scott and Stark introduced Arendt's dissertation on Augustine to the English-speaking world, Ronald Beiner (1996: 270) argued that "what the Augustine book may indicate is that Arendt was a political philosopher before she knew that she was one." This approach to reading *Der Liebesbegriff* is definitely superior to one that sidelines, minimizes, or outright ignores Arendt's first finished working out of a "thought train" from the tradition; chiefly because, as Beiner (1996: 280) notes, it "allows us to trace some important continuities that run from Hannah Arendt's first book to her last," and in particular, to what extent "Arendt's philosophical reflection" is "governed by the problems that constitute her reading of Augustine." I believe, however, that Beiner's way of presenting the lessons of (re-)reading the Augustine book puts the matter backwards: it is not that there are certain political philosophical problems that motivate Arendt, continually (if episodically) throughout the nearly five decades of her writing career. Instead, I would argue, there are certain problems of a *theological–political* character that Augustine is the first to grapple with seriously, and to which Arendt is continually and repeatedly drawn. To see what difference this difference makes, and why the latter is the more correct characterization, let me first make the case why Stephan Kampowski (2008) offers us the best way into and through *Liebesbegriff* in connection with Arendt's mature work, especially "Willing," and then offer my distillation of the place of Arendt's view of Augustine's *caritas socialis*.

Doing so entails attending the manner in which Arendt foregrounded, throughout her career, the ways in which Augustine introduced Paul's understanding of the freedom of the will, with all its perplexities and contradictions, into the history of philosophy. As Scott and Stark (LSA: 138) put it, engaging with Arendt's engagement with Augustine's engagement with Paul in "What is Freedom?": in "the essay on freedom Arendt imports the Augustine of her dissertation and adapts him to a discussion of the exemplary power of natality and foundation in the world." In their telling, Augustine's unique insight here rests in his awareness of himself as both Roman and Christian. This dual citizenship is what helps him to help her object to the liberal line that modern republicanism undoes sovereignty altogether. It is this feature of Augustine's worldview, eminently political–theological but *not* to do with his canonical place in the medieval and early modern Church, that indicates for her a vision that could allow us to forge a path beyond what Benhabib has named Weimar syndrome. To see the development of this light of thought, let us now reconstruct her reconstruction of Augustine's *caritas socialis* in her dissertation.

The first point to stress, in mobilizing here the definitive account of the *Liebesbegriff* as a lens on Arendt's mature thought and the basic starting points of her non- (or anti-) foundationalist form of political thinking that Kampowski (2008: 20–21) provides, is that whatever exactly "the merits and demerits of the 1996 English translation/edition of Arendt's dissertation," two points should be clear: first, "the English edition is only of limited value in helping us come to know the original text"; and, second, that "even if we are speaking of the German text . . . there are a number of *prima facie* objections on simple historical and linguistic grounds against assigning a straight-out quintessential role to it." Among these grounds are its brevity, its extreme compactness in terms of quotation, citation, and argumentation, the haste of its composition, and—perhaps needless to say—the fact that Arendt was twenty-two years old at the time of writing and had not yet fully developed her perspective on the issues she means for her close reading to raise.

More serious than these "first blush" reasons not to assign the text too great a value in trying to come to terms with her mature thought and/or her appreciation of Augustine as such are a further set of what Kampowski (2008: 21) calls "questions of its conceptual content," by which he means that in the doctoral dissertation, Arendt's focus on, and exegetical analysis of, certain key phrases and concepts in Augustine is not always either entirely clear or internally consistent. As Kampowski (2008: 21) also stresses, this does not, in any way, make the text "irrelevant"; indeed, his whole project is meant "to show that it *is* significant in that it fits within a broader, life-long intellectual project." And that project, for Kampowski, as for Scott and Stark, is indeed "to think what we are doing." We can understand what Arendt means by this without reading the dissertation, but our understanding is richer and in particular our notion of what she is doing with Augustine is clearer, when we read the later works *not* through the interpretive lens of the doctoral dissertation—as "Rediscovering Hannah Arendt," the interpretive essay Scott and Stark wrote for the 1996 English edition argues—but rather with the text of *Der Liebesbegriff* as a sounding board off which to read key passages of Arendt's later works where its themes are relevant.

The second point to stress, as we turn to the actual text of Arendt's dissertation, is also put eloquently by Kampowski (2008: 25): "While we have to grant that *Der Liebesbegriff* may not serve as a quintessential key to Arendt's later thought, we now want to argue that it is nonetheless an important text, fitting in with the whole of her works and larger projects on action theory and ethics." Kampowski has just taken great pains in the second half of his introduction to document as closely and carefully as possible all the reasons why we ought not, as Scott and Stark (LSA: 118) do, argue that "without the historical and conceptual context of the dissertation, Arendt's thought cannot be completely or authentically appropriated." Yet, turning to his discussion of what he describes as Arendt's theory of action, Kampowski (2008: 25–26) now stresses the importance of Arendt's lifelong engagement with Augustine, which his method is to uncover directly from close readings of *The Human Condition* for her "action theory" and *The Life of the Mind*, in conjunction with *Eichmann* and "Thinking and Moral Considerations," for her view of ethics. We will not follow each of his moves in this respect, focusing rather on the way in which he then relates his key findings from readings of what he calls her "larger projects," written in the 1950s, 1960s, and 1970s to his readings of *Der Liebesbegriff*, which he is working with in the German original rather than the 1996 edition.

The first and foremost example of tracing the presence of Augustine in Arendt's mature works, for Kampowski and for anyone who would wish to understand Arendt's Augustine in any of her individual works or in her *corpus* overall, is undeniably the sentence from *City of God* (Bk XII: 20) that, in her translation in the master passage for understanding the significance of this Augustinian claim, Arendt (THC: 177) parses as holding "that there be a beginning, man was created." According to Kampowski (2008: 46–47, 257 n.95), even though "from 1953 onwards, this citation from *City of God* appears as a constant refrain in Arendt's writings," it is *not* quoted in the doctoral dissertation in the original German, though Arendt did write it into the English translation that she was working on in the 1960s but abandoned the process of seeing through to publication in her lifetime.[4] For Kampowski, this is further evidence of his general approach in (re-)reading the dissertation in the light of *The Human Condition* and *The Life of the Mind*: even Arendt herself reworked her treatment of the second of the three big themes in Augustine—the relation of Creator and creature—with which she is grappling in the dissertation in light of her understanding of Augustine as she came to express it (over and over again) after 1952–1953. Be that as it may, it surely shows that even though the dissertation is the place where *City of God* in particular among Augustine's works received the longest sustained attention from Arendt, it cannot be said that the dissertation provides something like "the key" to unlock the otherwise opaque references to Augustine in her mature works. What, then, can it provide? To answer this question, we must turn to the first and third of the three major themes of the dissertation: love-as-desire (*cupiditas*) and love-as-care [for the earthly community of human beings] (*caritas socialis*).

Earthly love, as seen through Augustine's eyes (at least those eyes seen through Arendt's mediation), manifests in two main forms: a desiring love (a love-as-wish-to-possess) that is fully irredeemable and is indeed the main

[4] The sentence from Augustine appears in the 1996 translation (LSA: 55), B033191; the editors also offer an account—slightly different—of its many manifestations in her work after 1953 (LSA: 147–48).

obstacle to living as a Christian; and a caring love (a love-for-neighbor-and-all-neighbors) that, despite every reason to eschew in favor of a purely transcendent love-of-God as the sole means of salvation, Augustine nevertheless accords a high esteem—even while articulating a theological vision of an earthly city that is of no value, or even of a negative value, when compared with heavenly city that is the true polity of and for a Christian. Given Arendt's resolute and consistent appeal to the world as the ultimate defining feature of the human condition, that is, as the ungrounded ground of the space of appearance in which action and thus a truly and fully human life is possible, it can be hard to imagine why Augustine's concept of love could be the object of deep interest for her, unless as a position *against which* to articulate a view of action as a world-building human activity. But this is not what one finds in examining Arendt's attempt to differentiate *cupiditas* and *caritas* from one another in *Der Liebesbegriff*. As Arendt writes (LSA: 23): "For it is only by its pursuing what is outside that craving turns the neutral 'outside' into a 'world' strictly speaking, that is into a home for man. Only the world constituted by the 'lovers of the world' (*dilectores mundi*) is an evil, and only desire (*appetitus*) for this 'evil' turns into *cupiditas*." Arendt (LSA: 22) working with and within Augustine's terminology, while also claiming that "Augustine's uncritical use not only of Stoic but also of neo-Platonic categories could not help but lead him into inconsistencies," wants to show at the same time that Augustine is committed to a picture where desiring-love and neighborly-love both derive from the same craving[5] for something this-worldly. At the same time, as she turns to the relation of Creator and creature in part II and then to social life in part III, Arendt (LSA: 22) will stress how Augustine "knows of an entirely different kind of *caritas*" that "stands in no relation whatsoever to either *appetitus* or *cupiditas*, and therefore is truly of divine and not human origin."

Here already we see the intensity of the tension in Arendt's relation to Augustine: her "thought-train" in his regard begins from what she deems to be an already existing inconsistency in his thought, where *caritas* is at the same time (and in one sense) wrapped up with *cupiditas* as sharing an origin in craving (*appetitus*) but at the same time (but in another sense) is of divine origin. This inconsistency is not something to solve through exegesis, but rather the sign

[5] While I follow him in just about every particular when it comes to his views about the relative infelicities in working from the "A" and "B" manuscripts of the English translation from which Arendt was working before abandoning the project of bringing out an English version of *Der Liebesbegriff*, and why it is better for the most part to go back to the original German if we want to learn from and about this text today, I dissent when Kampowski (2008: 317 n.7) objects to the translation of *appetere* and its cognates as "craving," rather than "desiring." Wherever he translates Arendt's German translations of Augustine's *appetere* "to desire," I prefer LSA's "to crave"; for, to say "desire" when reading this term obliterates Arendt's attempt to distinguish craving and caring as two forms of desire/love, it seems to me.

of a deep fault in the entirely ontology and eschatology of Christendom and such is of abiding interest to Arendt, in the middle of her writing career (*The Human Condition*) and at its conclusion (*The Life of the Mind, Vol. 2*) no less than at its outset. Why so? Because Augustine finds a way to cast the true *caritas* otherwise than in the fundamental unworldliness that she associates with the tradition of Christian political theology more generally. So great is Arendt's commitment to the world that by the time she is writing *The Human Condition*, a reader could be forgiven for thinking that Augustine's (fully Orthodox) Christian unworldliness makes him just about the last place you might imagine Arendt would find inspiration.

But, as Kampowski (2008: 68–75) shows in a section titled "Love and Hannah Arendt," it would be a grave mistake to imagine that the attack on the unworldliness and antipolitical character of love in *The Human Condition* is somehow a rejection of her early appropriation of Augustine in the doctoral dissertation. Instead, Kampowski (2008: 174) argues, we must see that when Arendt argues in the section of *Der Liebesbegriff* quoted just above that "when Augustine speaks of love as desire, he thinks more or less within a Stoic framework," this is entirely of a piece with her presentation of love as unworldly and apolitical in *The Human Condition*. The critical hinge between the analysis of love as unworldly in the latter work and the analysis of love as world-constituting in the former, is way that human beings constitute the world through desire; in contrast to the divine creation of the universe. As Kampowski (2008: 174) puts the point more succinctly than it is found in either the dissertation or the English edition,[6] Arendt holds that not only human worldliness but also the human constitution of a world in the first place are owed to the fact that that "the *saeculum*, the sum total of temporal goods, [are] objects of human desire." Yes, according to the persuasive gloss Kampowski (2008: 70) provides, even though Arendt (THC: 51–54) yokes together love and charity—here the English terms clearly working as translations of *cupiditas* and *caritas*, respectively, as discussed in the doctoral dissertation—as each "antipolitical" and "unworldly"; there is, however, an important difference in the case of charity, in which "the love of God enters as a *tertium* into the relationship, fulfilling the function that, according to Arendt,[7] the world takes on in other relationships not based on love: 'Charity [is] something which, like the world, is between men.'"

Arendt's Aporetic Augustine: Caritas Socialis and the Second Body of the People

Let us summarize the findings to this point. With Kampowski, we have sought to dispel two plausible accounts of the relationship between the discussions of

[6] Compare: LSA: 54–55 and *Liebesbegriff*, 45.

[7] Here Kamposwki quotes THC: 53.

love and of Augustine that can be found in *Der Liebesbegriff* and *The Human Condition*. The first, which he attributes to Scott and Stark (LSA), suggests that the dissertation is, essentially, required reading for anyone who wants to understand Arendt's mature works, as it contains essential aspects of the issues that motivate her analyses and her keywords there. The second, which both he and Scott and Stark have attributed to Elisabeth Young-Bruehl (1982) among others, would exclude the dissertation from serious consideration as it reflects, more than anything else, the haste of its composition, the influence of her teachers, and, in any case, a set of problems that concerned Arendt in the 1920s but which seemed to her beside the point in the face of changing world events and as she became more and more a political theorist rather than a philosopher.

Rejecting both of these views, we have tried to establish both the divergences as well as the directly overlapping arguments in order to show that the world-constituting character of love-as-craving articulated in *Der Liebesbegriff* accords with the anti-political and unworldly character of love described in *The Human Condition*, and specifically for the reason that despite the seemingly antinomian character of those two claims, they are both grounded in the same condition named by Augustine: that the world-as-world, rather than as a gathering of so many creatures who live and die in a universe that God created, is a pure contingency and the site of human freedom.[8] Having established this, I now show how Arendt's argument that natality and plurality, and not principally mortality, orient the way human beings act in the world is an expression of themes that become salient for her in trying to think through the "inconsistencies" she sees in Augustine's concept of love as expressed in part III of *Der Liebesbegriff* in particular.

Let us begin with how Kampowski (2008: 191) notes Margaret Canovan's (1992: 8) suggestion that the fact that a paragraph concerning "the new beginning" needed to be added to the draft English translation of *Der Liebesbegriff* shows that this argument is "somewhat extraneous to the context and that Arendt's notion of man as a new beginning is an altogether later insight." It is here that I believe we come upon the most significant contribution to understanding Arendt's thinking as a whole made by the 1996 publication of the English translation initially prepared in the 1960s and then abandoned by Arendt for various reasons. For, while it is true that Arendt did not quote Augustine's "that there be a beginning" line (from *City of God*, Bk XII) in the original text of the doctoral dissertation, if we attend to the precise place where Arendt chose to insert in chapter 2, we can see that Arendt herself understands her original argument to be focused on the fact that human beings are, for Augustine as well as

[8] This pure contingency and Augustine's importance for understanding it, will be the subject matter of Chapter 3 below.

for her, *temporal* beings more fundamentally than we are *created* beings. This may not be the point that *Der Liebesbegriff/Love and Saint Augustine* makes as it is written—given that the argumentative focus of her text remains the troubled attempt to resolve the tension she sees in Augustine's account of the love of God and the love of neighbor.

All the same, as Kampowski (2008: 192) concludes: "Once we allow that an origin is a beginning, the insertion of Augustine's "*initium-ut-eset* paragraph" at this point will seem to be well-justified and confirm [that] human temporality is a recurring motif of Arendt's thought that . . . both plays an important role in *Der Liebesbegriff* and stands at the basis of the action theory of her later works." This insertion of Arendt's favorite quotation from Augustine in the process best demonstrates that the essential point for Arendt, in the doctoral dissertation as much as in *Origins* and *Eichmann* and the essays written between the two, is to understand the conditions of possibility for the exercise of our contingent freedom as human beings sharing this world in our plurality and, crucially, *in gratitude* precisely for our limitations—and how those conditions might be satisfied. It seems, however, that the Arendt of the doctoral dissertation does not yet have an account for this—not even one that would satisfy herself: Arendt's insertion of the paragraph on Augustine's "that there be a beginning" into the translation, as well as her abandonment of the translation project, offer ample proof of this, as much as any critical commentary. As such, Kampowski (2008: 227) concludes, in a partial echo of Mathewes' judgment concerning Arendt's incoherence as a reader of Augustine, that "a serious problem still remains as even this *caritas socialis* is far from the evangelical love that never ends. It is a necessity only in this life, and its only purpose is to spur one's neighbor on to the love of God. In a situation where God is 'all in all,' there will be neither room for love of neighbor nor any need of it anymore." While Kampowski shares with Mathewes the understanding that Arendt's Augustine can only ever be a partial one, and that in particular Arendt is unable either to work with or find sufficient reasons to dismiss Augustine's theological anthropology, he does not on this basis condemn her partial Augustinianism to incoherence and impotence.

The beating heart of Augustine's insight and his limitations, as far as Arendt can see, is how *caritas*, as a world-affirming orientation toward other human beings with whom we share the earth, arises from God's grace and the human being's acceptance of their status as God's creature and thus as most fully what they are when they are *not* of this world. The focal point for this discussion is the first chapter of part II of *Der Liebesbegriff*, and the basic orienting claim, as Kampowski (2008: 179) paraphrases the German, is that the "choice of God the Creator" as the ground of the life that matters for a human being, means "recognizing and accepting oneself as a created being, which in turn entails the explicit recognition of one's dependency on one's Creator for one's very being."[9] In a gesture that anticipates Arendt's famous claim that we learn from Pindar the need to carry "a basic gratitude for everything that is how it is *physei*" in a 1964 letter to Gershom Scholem about which we will speak further in the next section, Arendt (LSA: 178) extends this argument to conclude: "By the explicit acceptance of divine grace we accept ourselves as creatures and realize our pre-existing dependence on the Being that has made our own existence what it is." Letting change what changes given the basic world-orientations of the Christian bishop Augustine and the Classical poet Pindar, this does indeed sound very much like the basic gratitude for the existence of oneself and the things of the world as they are. In the Epilogue, I will return to the overlap between, on the one hand, Augustine's position on praise and love—and *not* grace—as that which heals both the mutilated world and the human will which is, of course, for Augustine a feature both constitutive of, and constituted by, that mutilated ("perverted, drunken, earth-bound" as we learn in *Confessions*) world, and on the other hand, her reverence for what she takes to be Pindar's argument about a basic gratitude for everything that is as it is.

But there is a real problem here. For, as Kampowski (2008: 179) argues, however compelling this Augustinian insight about our recognition of our contingency and finitude may be, Arendt finds it "difficult to account for the possibility and meaningfulness of the love of neighbor" on the basis of this *caritas* that "refers to man's return to his origin in the Being of his Creator." Here we directly confront the central inconsistency, if not contradiction, that Arendt sees in Augustine's concept of love: how can *caritas*, which for a Christian is about the turn away from the things of this world possibly come to express itself in the *caritas socialis*, which is explicitly a care for our fellow travelers in this world? As Kampowski (2008: 180, paraphrasing LSA: 94[10]) compellingly dramatizes the disconnect between the love of God as Creator and the love of neighbor for the believing Christian as Augustine depicts that person: "The neighbor is once more added merely as an afterthought, since the world, in its temporality, is essentially a desert for the believer, and it is difficult to explain how someone living alone in a desert can have a neighbor at all." In short, one can see fairly clearly how the ascetic ideal of the hermit can arise as a form of prioritizing *caritas* over *cupiditas* in the recognition of oneself as first and

[9] *Liebesbegriff*, 53 (for the German, see also Kampowski (2008: 322 n.54). In LSA, 77, this is translated: "His existence wholly depends on the Creator who antedates man's choice. In other words, man's choice still depends on the priority of what he chooses, but this choice can only be made on the preceding choice by the Creator himself. . . . Even the choice of *caritas*, in which the referring back becomes reality, requires something prior."

[10] "This view of neighborly love as the commandment of self-denial fails to explain how the absolutely isolated person can have a neighbor at all."

foremost a limited being who owes everything and thus must orient oneself in a "basic gratitude for everything that is as it is." What remains a puzzle is how and why this gratitude is meant to manifest itself in one's care for the neighbor; indeed, where this neighbor is or can be for the person who has chosen eternity and God over temporality and this world.

For Arendt (LSA: 105), in what is undeniably a forced reading, historicity is Augustine's solution to this in *City of God*, book XV: specifically, the world-historical character of humanity's basic sinfulness, that is, each human being's participation in original sin: "[T]he sinful past is common to all, and nothing else could stabilize social life in a community." Once this metaphysical condition of wretchedness was introduced not into the soul of the sinner but into the fabric of the created world as a matter of historical fact, Augustine argues in Arendt's (LSA: 105) view, the neighbor becomes relevant in themselves; for, now, the "neighbor is a constant reminder of one's own sin, which does not cease to be a sin because divine grace has made it a thing of the past." That is to say, Augustine is here trying to resolve what seems like an unsolvable problem posed by trying to fuse a Pauline conception of the gratuitous grace of God in the face of the fundamental and irredeemable wretchedness (evil, baseness) of both the world and human beings with his continuing conviction in the basic goodness of everything that is insofar as it is. In the Epilogue, we will see Arendt return to this problem in *Willing*, her last completed work. Here (at the very beginning of her writing career) and there (at its very end), her solution—or her attempt at a solution—is the same. And it is to be found in the what she figures as the *weight* of love.

Thus, Arendt (LSA: 106)[11] concludes: "the reason you should love your neighbor is that the neighbor is fundamentally just like you, having the same sinful past." As Kampowski (2008: 186) argues, Arendt is right to see this account of the love of neighbor in Augustine as bearing a "fundamental indirectness," insofar as for Augustine, "we love our neighbor as a being capable of beatitude, a being that is *capax Dei*"; he denies, however, that this makes the neighbor "an afterthought" for Augustine. For Arendt, the grounding of the love of neighbor in original sin is both inescapable for Augustine and a basic weakness; Kampowski (2008: 187) counters that in so arguing, Arendt has missed a different Augustinian resource for the grounding of the love of neighbor and the *caritas socialis*: namely, "the idea of God as the supreme *common* good of the whole universe," which "Arendt did not consider in her dissertation." To see both why Arendt excludes this resource and what this implies about the limits both of *Liebesbegriff* and of Augustine's thinking from

[11] As Kampowski (2008, 183) modifies the Ashton translation. The German reads: "Weil der Andere im Grunde dir gleich ist, d.h. die gleiche sündige Vergangenheit hat wie du, deshalb sollst du ihn lieben."

the perspective of Arendt's mature works, let us now trace the trajectory of her interest in the *caritas socialis* from the dissertation to her later works.

Having traversed this course through Arendt's lifelong engagement with Augustine, from the mature works back to the dissertation and back again, we follow Kampowski (2008: 226) back to his main *conceptual* concern with foregrounding *Der Liebesbegriff*, which is first articulated in his introduction; namely, that "most of the solutions Arendt presents in *Der Liebesbegriff*, however, dodge the issue of human contingency. . . . She thus turns to a third context in which she understands Augustine to discuss the human person's existence, and which can be summed up by the expression *caritas socialis*." The problem, in other words, is that Arendt's Augustine cannot but be at odds with himself when it comes to the freedom of will that is required for the choice to love the neighbor as oneself, no matter how much Arendt tries to exclude personal and theological commitments from the version of Augustine she engages in the doctoral dissertation.

For Kampowski (2008: 156–72), the best way to address this self-imposed limitation on the Augustine to which we can turn for an account of neighborly love as the basis of a worldly ethic, whether for a Christian or *tout court*, is to supplement the Augustine to which Arendt limits us with an account of Augustine's thinking about freedom that exceeds what Arendt is willing to allow. Indeed, Kampowski finds Arendt's presentation of his *Freedom of the Will* contracted and unsatisfying not only in the version found in *Der Liebesbegriff* but also in the more patient exposition in *The Life of the Mind*[12]—about which we will have more to say in Chapter 3 and the Epilogue. As we are more interested here in Arendt's main findings in the doctoral dissertation than we are in her as a reader of Augustine, however, let us leave the question of the free will and God's grace to the side and focus on the issue of neighborly love that is truly of God in and through the neighbor that Arendt discusses in part III and which fulfills her promise to find in Augustine that divine love, which perhaps inconsistently, escapes the critique of both cupidity and charity in part I.

The crucial point here, as Kampowski (2008: 187) puts it compellingly, is that "the merit of Arendt's doctorate does not necessarily consist in offering a convincing account of the problem of the relation between the two commandments of the love of God and love of neighbor in Augustine," for—as we have amply seen, Arendt simply does not offer such a convincing account nor even seems to believe that one can be offered. Rather, as Kampowski (2008: 188) rightly insists, what continues to make *Der Liebesbegriff* relevant for understanding Arendt's

[12] In vol. 2, ch. 7, discussed in Chapter 3, below.

thought more generally is its "presentation of the human being as a temporal and conditioned being" who has the freedom to respond to this being-conditioned "in a number of possible ways," from grateful acceptance to self-deceit to active resentment. What is especially striking about Arendt's discussion of this freedom-in-contingency at the center of the thought train that truly and most deeply motivates Arendt's discussion of Augustine in the dissertation is that she is grappling (LSA: 14–15; *Liebesbegriff*: 28–29) with the same passages from *Confessions* book XI from which she draws when discussing these problems in *Willing*; a discussion we will follow closely in the Epilogue. For both texts, the unique human faculty of remembrance is crucial. In the doctoral dissertation Arendt (LSA: 15) stresses that: "For Augustine [it] is in our memory where things are being stored up" so that memory "is the presence of the 'no more'" and thus "I do not measure what is no more, but something in my memory that remains fixed in it."

In the context of Augustine's concept of love, this insight about memory and temporality—and about the reality of time—is quickly brought into the context of cupidity and charity. If, however, we follow Kampowski and take on board the suggestion that what is really motivating her in turning to Augustine on this point is the ontology and ethics that follow from human being not as *created* being but as *temporal* being, then we can see the direct line from Arendt's earliest published work to her last one. For, in *Willing*, Arendt (LOTM2, 117) asserts that in the transition from Augustine to the Scholastics what was lost was not time, in contrast to eternity, but precisely the faculty of memory, which Arendt holds to be "the most specifically Roman" of Augustine's faculties in its attention to what has come before rather than expectation of what is to come; along with the loss of memory, she asserts, comes a loss of a "sense of the thoroughly temporal character of human nature and human existence, manifest in Augustine's *homo temporalis*." We might at first fail to see the connection between this claim from *Willing*, written about a decade after the time Arendt was revising the doctoral dissertation, and Arendt's discussion of Augustine's account of memory and time in the doctoral dissertation; the latter seems typical of her mature analysis—offered in *The Human Condition* and then many texts written later—of human beings as a "new beginning" that grows from our capacity *both* to remember things from the past *and* to expect things in the future are integral to our capacity to act.

As a new beginning, Kampowski (2008: 230) choses to endorse the "only alternative as Arendt sees it," namely, "the grateful acceptance of what is given: to see the human condition of plurality as a gift rather than a liability and to marvel at and esteem man's great capacity to begin something new." It is with precisely this grateful acceptance that Richard Bernstein (1996: 1) opens the introduction to his reflection on *Hannah Arendt and the Jewish Question*, going so far as to quote her 1964 letter to Gershom Scholem on the occasion of their increasingly bitter exchange about *Eichmann in Jerusalem* as an epigraph for his work: "There is such a thing as a basic gratitude for everything that is as it is; for what has been *given* and was not, could not be *made*." (An alternative translation, or rather a translation from Arendt's German in addressing Scholem that leaves the key italicized terms in the Greek that Arendt herself did not translate is at the center of Judith Butler's response to this sense of gratitude at being "a daughter of the Jewish people." Butler (2012: 134), following Arendt in stipulating that "being Jewish" is "an indisputable fact of my life," focuses on Arendt's poetic turn of phrase which itself is an echo of the archaic Greek poet Pindar: "there is such a thing as a basic gratitude for everything that is as it is; for what has been given and is not made; for what is *physei* and not *nomos*." Being a Jew, for Arendt, like being a woman is such a thing that is *physei* and for which one is to express a basic gratitude.

While Butler is ultimately at odds with Arendt's conviction that her being a woman and a Jew is *physei* (is "given," is "by nature"), holding that Arendt illegitimately "naturalized" and de-politicized both her gendered and religious identity in her response to Scholem, she shares with Arendt the conviction that what is political is something that has been made, something that exists by convention (*nomos*), and thus can and must be contested and revised in the public domain. Such agonistic politics, though, must leave some things alone for Arendt: political life emanates from a certain "basic gratitude" for the unpredictable and unique feature of human life, not as God's creation, but as a temporal and conditioned manner of being. This lies at the heart of Arendt's turn to Augustine, which I aim to explore and endorse in response to critiques of her reception of Augustine advanced by Mathewes, discussed earlier in the Introduction.

Inconclusive Conclusion: Augustine and Modernity

In light of this reading of the central conclusion of *Der Liebesbegriff*, let us now turn to the problem of political theology as it posed itself to Arendt and others in the late 1920s in order to see why the former seemed to Arendt a response to the latter. To see this most clearly, let us draw out with greater precision Scott and Stark's claim that the understanding of Augustine's *caritas socialis* advanced by Arendt in the dissertation is motivating the whole account of private, public, and social life in *The Human Condition*. To make this case, I focus on her famous complaint (in the "action" chapter of *The Human Condition*: 189) that action, in distinction from work and labor as she wishes to understand them, is severed from human natality, creativity, and interdependence, when it is separated into two distinct moments of, first, ruling, and then acting. To understand how and why this central feature of her approach to politics as appearance in public rests so critically on this "Homeric" moment in the history of political thought, we must view this chapter in light of "political theology" and in contrast to each of these three key interlocutors. Arendt argues, this separation is best expressed in the Greek verbs *archein* and *prattein*, which she renders respectively as "'to begin,' 'to lead,' and finally 'to rule'" (*archein*), and "'to pass through,' 'to achieve,' 'to finish'" (*prattein*). What this shift in language represents, Arendt (THC: 189) argues, is the difference between what was "the original interdependence of action, the dependence of the beginner and leader upon others for help and the dependence of his followers upon him for an occasion to act themselves," and the (unfortunate) emergence of a functional differentiation of some into "command givers" and others into "command followers." The ruler is isolated as the one who exercises command through force; in contrast, in Arendt's more ideal form of politics, what separates "he who begins" is simply the risk being taken by someone who calls persons to join him in a project.

Significantly, Arendt is highly suspicious, from a political perspective, of something that is sociologically commonplace—the way in which rulers take credit for actions not of their doing, and the eventual results of those actions. This bifurcation of *archein* as ruling ("being in charge") and as originating ("being the source") of action and projects turns out to be the source of Arendt's suspicion about breaking *archein* off from *prattein*. In other words, while Arendt is often taken to be arguing against the division between those who rule and those who act, her deeper worry is the same political theological problem that haunts the work of Voegelin, Kantorowicz, and Strauss in different ways.

Habermas (1996: 147–51), among others, understands Arendt here to be expressing what we might call a Habermasian commitment to the rationality of shared life in public and the necessity for informed participation on the basis of reason-giving. This grossly mis-states Arendt's position. We need rather to understand her, yes, as a critic of bureaucratic rationality like Habermas and other followers of Weber on the left, but one who, in ways similar to but interestingly different from Strauss, Kantorowicz, and Voegelin, is trying to correct Max Weber's error of attempting what cannot be done: the evacuation of normativity from the project of the human sciences.[13] She insists, that is, on an extra-rational—or at least non-rational—form of value commitment that binds together those who would act in public. As Seyla Benhabib (2018: 6–8) argues, whatever Arendt's substantial and important differences with Strauss (and others), there is this crucial point of agreement with her conservative fellow German exile-émigrés.

Benhabib was fundamentally and importantly right about how Arendt, with much trial and tribulation, resolved for herself "the quarrel of ancients and moderns" that is the bedrock—or maybe the quicksand—of all attempts

[13] It goes beyond the scope of this chapter, but Michael Staudigl (2017) has edited a special issue of *Human Studies* that explores the same response to Weber in Alfred Schutz's phenomenological sociology of religion.

to grapple with the limitations of Weber's theory of modernity as a story of secularization and *Entzauberung* ("disenchantment'). Yet if we bear in mind the central lessons from Susan Neiman (2001; 2002) and Richard J. Bernstein (1996) regarding Arendt's characterization of "my Eichmann book" as a work of theodicy and the continuation and refinement, rather than the rejection, of her discussion of radical evil discussed earlier in the Introduction, a surprising depiction of Augustine emerges. Namely, Arendt's lifelong engagement with evil, notwithstanding the limits of her approach from the perspective of a committed Augustinian as we saw Mathewes (2001) argue in the Introduction, comes to light as evidence of Arendt's sense that Augustine inaugurates the crisis of "our" tradition, even as he seems to sit almost at its conception. For Arendt, it is with Augustine that modernity, with its characteristic gap between past and future, is invented.

This is why, as Mathewes (2010: 46) notes, Augustine's framework is inherently transgressive from within the analytic of contemporary, putatively secular, political thought; for, Augustine continually "confuses the crisp lines we often want to draw between 'secular' or 'worldly' matters and 'spiritual' or 'religious' ones"; in particular, even as hope—the basis of the *caritas socialis*—"energizes and orients worldly action" it also has "its origins and its ultimate end in a theological reality." Arendt, of course, cannot be said to wish for the sort of theological politics that Mathewes seeks and defends through this reading of neighbor-love. Yet if our engagement with *Liebesbegriff* in this chapter has been successful, then we can see why and how Arendt's Augustine is a commonplace to which she returns time and again when trying to understand the ungrounded ground of the love of the world in and through which politics becomes not just possible but actual. Surely, this is at least in part because her modernism is reluctant: she mourns the loss of what she often enough refers not as *the* tradition but as *our* tradition.[14] But it is also because, more than any other philosopher whose works remain a touchstone for her with the possible exception of Kant, Augustine's thought not only grows out of the breach opened by the gap between past and future but also lives inside and even celebrates that gap. The political ramifications of this feature of what Arendt (LOTM2: 212–17) figures as Augustine's "Virgilian politics" manifest in what we can call "the second body of the People" as a robustly modern problem of how a political community can persist in "founded freedom" (*constitution liberalis*) through "a new order of the ages" (*novus ordo saeclorum*). Coming to terms with this ramification is focus of the following three chapters.

[14] For instance, at the opening of "Tradition and the Modern Age" and "Introduction *Into* Politics," as well as in chapter 6 of *On Revolution*.

2

PARADOXES OF POPULAR SOVEREIGNTY: THE PEOPLE'S TWO BODIES AFTER MAX WEBER'S DISENCHANTMENT THESIS

In the previous chapter, we saw how "Weimar syndrome" plagues contemporary political thought as it continues, often explicitly and self-consciously in the wake of Max Weber, to describe and defend the principles of liberal constitutionalism as a, or the, proper mode of modern politics. This chapter, taken together with its sequel on what will be called the three antinomies of liberalism as a political theology, argues that Arendt's Augustine offers the best alternative approach to the paradoxes inherent in popular sovereignty as a constituting power within the liberal constitutional order. This is so, we shall see, because, in the chapters on "Action" and "The *Vita Activa* and the Modern Age" of *The Human Condition*, read together with *On Revolution* and the analysis of political and philosophical freedom in *The Life of the Mind*, Arendt examines the continuing afterlife of the "early modern" problem of political theology. In the fourth chapter we will analyze how this constituting power of "the People" as a sacred second body manifests in the constituted power of liberal political institutions, offering an account of the paradoxes of popular sovereignty as distributed sovereignty that demonstrates why the attempt to overcome sovereignty with governance in constitutional orders displays the impossibility of "disenchanting" the mysteries of state.

Introduction

This chapter exposes the paradoxes of popular sovereignty as distributed sovereignty, building on the view that the concept of "power" admits of an understanding in terms of control and even domination, on the one hand, and the enhancement of capacity via the act of authoritative delegation, on the other. Of particular interest is the complex intertwining of the representation of delegation with the execution of power that obtains in societies in which the legitimation of power is, in part, bound up with the representation of power as delegated from a sovereign "people."

A recent burst of work in sociology has examined "agency relations" and "chains of power and their representation," focusing, in particular, on how long chains of relations between individuals and groups—effectively, hierarchical "ties" between nodes in widely dispersed networks of power—come to structure the world (Adams 2005, 2011; Reed 2017, 2020). The impetus of this work has been to combine cultural understandings of dominated consciousness with attention to the formation and reformation of power relations in organizations, thus combining an older, more formal discourse of the human sciences familiar from the locution "A has power over B when . . ." (Lukes 2005 [1974]), with an appreciation of the particular ways in which certain persons, categories of person, or collectivities are made to appear, via cultural representation, as the "natural" source of authority and the "likely" occupants of positions of power. In other words, this work combines cultural sociology with the sociology of the (hierarchical) network.

These sociological accounts show how domination can grow out of delegation, on the one hand, but also recognize that delegation appears in many situations and instances which we would not, *prima facie*, judge as instances of "domination," on the other. That is to say, a theory of power must grasp phenomena as different as the process of delegation to experts whose knowledge is valuable to a community at large, on the one hand, and the expansion of technocratic state control of persons over and against their needs and desires, on the other. That these possibilities increasingly run together in the networked world of late modernity is the central thesis of Julia Adams' (2011) theory of agency. The core of these arguments, in terms of theoretical vocabulary, is derived from a deliberately heterodox reading of a classic formulation of rational choice theory, game theory, and mainstream economic theories of the corporation—the theory of "principal" and "agent" (Adams 2010; Coleman 1998 [1990]). In such theories, principals delegate to agents certain tasks that principals then attempt, through punishment, monitoring, and incentives, to have agents complete. Such theoretical accounts, Adams shows, both grasp and distort (given the late modern capitalist relations of domination they fetishized) the social relations that obtain when humans engage in projects via the recruitment of other humans as allies and complicit spectators, and via the exclusion of other humans as inimical to a given project.

Isaac Ariail Reed (2017) extends this account of agency relations by theorizing "chains of power and their representation" through which a person or group seeks to become *rector* (formerly *principal*), who in turn sends and binds *actors* (formerly *agent*) into the world on behalf of a project, and in so doing excludes. This is accomplished with varying degrees of discrimination and violence, *others* (undertheorized in rational choice theory) whose relationship to the project is conceived (from various perspectives) as antagonistic. The upshot of the Reed–Adams theory of agency relations is that the sociological abstraction has three "types" or "positions"—rector, actor, and other—and that the act of power has two fundamental features: (1) turning someone else into your agent (which may or may not amount to domination); and (2) excluding someone else from the rector–actor game, thus making them other (which may be variably destructive or debilitating).

Rector and actor, as positions of power occupied by individuals or collectivities, are engaged in a struggle for recognition and redistribution, and agency accrues to certain persons and groups that are able to send and bind allies. This hierarchical production of agency means that what Judith Butler (1990: 9–12, 146–49, 153 n.21; 2015: 29–34) calls the "dissimulation" involved in the accrual of agency is always incomplete and contestable. Now consider such agency relations as a way to conceptualize delegated sovereignty in democratic republics. In democratic republics, there is, furthermore, a working expectation that each citizen is in some sense a rector, delegating to actors the tasks of politics through a process of representation. Under such conditions, we must ask: how is it possible that legitimate hierarchies persist in democratic republics where there are clearly many rectors (indeed, as many rectors as there are citizens) and numerous complex chains of power, such that hierarchical organizations dot the landscape of social life and give society its structure, yet also are somehow expected to act as actors for the "public" or the "people." Carole Pateman's (1988) retelling of the social contract myth, and Joan Landes' (1988) and Lynn Hunt's (1992) histories of the French Revolution, have excavated one way in which the stability of power and its representation is pursued and secured in a world of a multiplicity of citizen–rectors; namely, by constituting a civil contract founded in the domestication of women, the removal "feminine influence" from politics, and the masculinization of citizenship. Importantly, these accounts took as a departure point the symbolic politics of kingship and its replacement, enquiring how the "band of brothers" that constituted the male body politic of the republic was designed as a representational solution to the symbolic deficit created by the removal of the king as the "unmoved mover" of political agency (Hunt 1991, 1992; Pateman 1988; Landes 1988, 2001; Santner 2011), with the king as "ultimate rector." This does not explain the existence of hierarchical corporations in democratic societies for example, but it does explain how a specifically modern format of patriarchy could articulate the hierarchical family qua institution with equal citizenship *for men* qua institution, as examined in Reed and Weinman (2018).

In what follows, I take up this line of reasoning, extending and refining it as way to grasp the problematic of democratic sovereignty and its relationship to organizational power, beginning with (1) a recuperation of the ingenious device of the "King's Two Bodies" as analyzed by Ernst Kantorowicz (2016 [1957]), a mystical vision repeatedly deployed as a frame for the political solution of problems in the representation and delegation of power through long hierarchical chains. I then unpack the transformation of the King's Two Bodies in the emergent modern political theology of revolutionary France and the early American republic. Next, (2) Adriana Cavarero's (2016) critique of rectitude provides insight into the inconsistencies in the vision and practice of this modern political theology and how these tensions survived the transmutation of the king's second body into the second body of the people. I then turn to (3) Hannah Arendt's account of the difference between action and rule as an articulation of the inescapability of hierarchical relations for the delegation of power and the administration of society and how this irresistibly introduces tensions with popular sovereignty. Finally (4), I argue that Arendt's heterodox Augustinianism best answers the challenge of sovereignty in the liberal constitutional order because she analyses the continuing afterlife of the "early modern" problem of political theology and the impossibility of demystifying (disenchanting) the mysteries of state.

An Enchanted Band of Brothers, and their Others

It is well understood that Ernst Kantorowicz's classic study of medieval political theology addressed medieval and early modern jurisprudence so as to comprehend shifts in the *representation* of power; it is a study in the semiotics of the state (2016). If we mark the three great revolutions of the late eighteenth-century Atlantic world as one location for the critical interpretation of (political) modernity, what comes to light is how modernity involves a radical disruption, but by no means a discontinuation or disavowal of the semiotics of state earlier inherent in the "second body" of the king as a way of doing politics, constituting power, and endowing certain rectors and their actors with the aura of authority. So, what was this semiotics of the state that Kantorowicz investigated, and how did it work?

As a particular legal doctrine, the "King's Two Bodies" derived from an earlier understanding of Christ-like kingship, and in linking temporal and spiritual, it provided a frame within which to render both the relationship of individual kings to the succession of kings and the existence and persistence of the state. If God himself was eternal, outside of time, and the men who occupied positions of power were mere mortals, of this earth and destined to die, then the king's second body was sempiternal—it was understood to exist in time, but potentially "forever." This provided a logic for understanding the continuity of the state (a logic used, as well, by the Catholic Church in its understanding of itself as the earthly, time-bound representation of an eternal divinity).

The opening pages of Kantorowicz's text frame later doctrines, such as "the King never dies" as explicitly concerned with the "body politic" broadly understood. Kantorowicz (2016 [1957]: 9) quotes from Tudor jurists, who reached back to medieval articulations of the doctrine of the King's Two Bodies: "to [his] natural body is conjoined his Body politic, which contains his royal Estate and Dignity; and the Body politic includes the Body natural, but the Body natural is the lesser, and with this the Body politic is consolidated . . . these two Bodies are incorporated in one Person, and make one Body and not divers, that is the Body corporate in the Body natural, et e contra the Body natural in the Body corporate." Kantorowicz repeatedly found these kinds of convolution to express how the state and thus the "the polity as a whole," including the bodies of the people who lived as subjects of the king ("the body corporate"), belonged to the natural body of the king. As such, they articulated early modern sovereignty, incorporating the body politic into the leader, rather than the other way around. What has been perhaps less appreciated is the way in which this representation of kingship as legal doctrine and cultural representation provided a frame within which one could think, interpret, and conduct politics, and thus give meaning to agency and power. In other words, Kantorowicz elaborated a frame for what Robin Wagner-Pacifici (1986, 2000, 2005, 2010, 2017) has definitively analyzed as the process of political semiosis; specifically, this frame illuminates for us not only for understanding the funerals of monarchs and Shakespeare's Richard II, but also treason accusations and counter-accusations as a way of "doing politics" in early modern colonies of Spain, Britain, and France (Benton 2009; Reed 2020). Another way of saying this is that Kantorowicz's famous book was about not only royal ritual and state–church symbolics, but also building durable organizations through delegation.

But did this manner of meaning-granting and sense-making survive the political disruptions of the late eighteenth-century Atlantic world, with their various attempts at replacing the King's Two Bodies with other schemas for imagining power in the right? This question, we maintain, has not been adequately thematized in social theory. Consider, for example, how Michel Foucault (1991: 28–29) notes that Kantorowicz "gives a remarkable analysis of 'The King's Body'" and then argues that "at the opposite pole one might imagine placing the body of the condemned man . . . We should analyze what might be called, in homage to Kantorowicz, 'the least body of the condemned man.'" Foucault's text could be read as suggesting that the religious energies devoted to Christ-like kingship were redistributed into a new, in some ways also enchanted, order in which the moderns have invented happiness; yet Foucauldian literature, in its dispersions and connections, has hewed to the concern with discipline—the production of knowledge and subjects of knowledge—and with governmentality, neoliberal or otherwise, leaving the enchantments of modern condemnation to the side (Smith 2003). There is one strand of theory that has recognized the link between Foucault and Kantorowicz concerning what "remains" after the king, an intellectual line of thought concerned with "the people and the people," that can be traced from Foucault (1990: 135–59; 1991: 3–31; 2003: 239–63) to Giorgio Agamben (1998: 8–12, 15–29, 91–103, 119–53) and finally to Eric Santner's (2011) virtuosic discussion of "the royal remains." Here we do find a specific theory of the "people's two bodies": the disciplined, modern, docile subject that takes the soul as the prison of the body, and the population as an object of power politics, subject to manipulation, and thus as a location of productive power. Santner's theory, inflected not only by Foucault but also psychoanalysis, proposes an account of biopower as that which follows the irruptive event of the French Revolution; the "missing flesh" of the king's sacred body is the repeated, traumatic point of fantasy for a modern era that cannot come to terms with itself. Yet if Santner—like Burke and Robespierre before him, in their own ways—grasps the terror and fantasy that accompanied the shift to post-kingship society, his own interpretation of this traumatic break takes the emergence of biopower for granted, the understanding of which becomes an undisputable intellectual frame from which to grasp the modern politics. I am not so sure.

For, while there are modern power formations whose anonymous and capillary features deserve comment, my contention is that we must not allow their growth and dispersion to overwhelm our analysis of the repeated contestations in modern societies, over "who is in charge," a matter of recurrent concern in popular culture, highbrow political philosophy, and jurisprudence. Who manages to represent the body politic in the double sense of elected representative and figuration of the people?[1] Of course, one can develop a Foucauldian account of the figurations that discipline the bodies of the modern world: bodies are variously sexed, gendered, raced, and classed. But it is notable that Foucault's texts do not concern themselves with the fundamental shift in politics qua politics constituted by the French Revolution, whereas the now-classic feminist histories of the birth of modern France, of which we take Landes and Hunt to be particularly well-known instances, take up directly the question of how common understandings of "who is the decider" are embedded in mythological representations, both before and after the regicide.

Cavarero on Rectitude: Unmasking Liberalism as a Political Theology

Who gets to decide, who has the standing to rule (themselves, first of all, and then others) is the subject of Adriana Cavarero's (2013, 2016) richly sourced and wide-ranging study of the saturation of Western philosophy, literature,

[1] It is worthy of further comment how much Kantorowicz was concerned not only with the aesthetics of power, but with *figuration* in particular.

and art with the figure of the upright individual—the mature, adult, male. Crucially, Cavarero makes sense of the idiosyncratic distillation of Hobbesian individualism offered by Elias Canetti (1984 [1960]). Cavarero's reply to Canetti's Hobbesian view of postwar society clarifies the connection between rectitude (as the being a rector) and the production of abjected others, who are not merely unable to decide for themselves, but also are denied the agency of actors serving the projects of such rectors.

Cavarero (2013: 227–28) casts Canetti as a sympathetic critic of Hobbes, objecting to Hobbes' (2016 [1651]: 60–66) claim that "human life consists of 'a perpetual and restless desire of power after power, that ceased only in death,'" in stressing that social life "consists of a surviving featured as perfect verticality in front of the death of the other"; thus, unlike "Hobbes' natural individual, who is caught in the perpetual movement of his desire for power, Canetti's survivor is a static figure, immobilized in the moment of his verticalization before the dead body, a moment, for him, of unparalleled triumph." One can question how much difference there really is between the two; after all, Hobbes' natural individual is outside the Leviathan (the social order, the second body of the State (be it the People or the King)), while Canetti's survivor is within it. In this light, Canetti's picture, drawn in the aftermath of the Second World War, looks not so much like an updating or revision of Hobbes' as a retracing—substituting the horrors Canetti survived for those that Hobbes did. Be that as it may, the core of what Cavarero (2013: 228) wants us to learn from her engagement with Canetti–Hobbes underscores the lesson of our earlier discussion of the violent exclusion pursued coevally with popular sovereignty during state formation in both revolutionary France and the early American republic: "At the end of the day, thus, what is on display is not the mortal as such but, rather, the killable, that is, the individual who manages to survive his or her incumbent murder and the individual who instead does not."

Lest we think this is "merely" the dark side of the light ("*les misères des Lumières*"; Sala-Molins 2006), or a Hobbesian nightmare we can reject, Cavarero (2013: 230) next turns directly to Kantian moral perfectionism, reminding us that for all the real and apparent differences between the Kantian and Hobbesian traditions, the Kantian ambition for moral autonomy is illustrative of the same obsession with the upright posture within the philosophy of the subject, for: "verticality is confirmed as a structural paradigm allowing rubrication in the same agenda of either the aggressive I that comes from Hobbes or the autonomous Kantian I that belongs to the liberal-democratic tradition." Borrowing this key insight and shifting the focus of attention from the history of philosophy to the emergence of modern political life and in particular of modern state–society structures, we find that Cavarero is calling attention to a central trope of the dominant self-understanding of the liberal order in distinction from the medieval and early modern model of the king's second body.

We are thus well-equipped to address Walzer's (1993 [1973]: 15) classic argument about regicide and liberal power: in studying the speeches that attended the trial of Louis XVI, Walzer grasped the gap created by the elimination of the King's Two Bodies, and then argued that the dilemma or the modern republican politics was that "however one pictures God, he does not look like a council or a crowd." In this, Walzer was not quite correct because there are *repeated* attempts in the modern order to see God in a council or crowd; he is insightful because these attempts are often overwrought and full of difficulties. In the flurry of pamphlets before and after the American Revolution, and in the frequent, and sometimes bloody, emergencies that beset the making of the federal government in the early American republic, we trace early versions of seeing God in the "bodies of the people." But we must always ask: which bodies, interpreted in which ways? How are we to represent the chains of power that will buoy a new set of state–society relations, in this American "world turned upside down"? The King-in-Parliament, as John Murrin (2000: 4, 2) notes, had been replaced with the "empire for liberty" (that would turn out to be "for whites only"), whose projects of violent expansion, economic productivity, and a culture of self-rendering took as their ultimate rectors "ordinary citizens of the Republic."

The problem Cavarero poses for the tradition of rectitude, in both its moral and political guises, is this: the eradication of inclination in the body of the putatively upright, erect, self-sufficient subject is an essential element of what is meant to be an upright and forthright body politic that constitutes and represents the mystical, always right, second body of the people. But this great, "mystery of state," challenging enough for the theistic jurists of the medieval ages under conditions of divinely authorized royal sovereignty as Kantorowicz (1955) showed, is intensely paradoxical under democratic conditions. The emergence of the new republican form of state–society relations demanded not a "disenchantment" of political theology *per se*, but rather the reformation of political theology, which remains until today both necessary for the legitimation of the liberal order and an unfulfilled promise of the three great Atlantic revolutions.

Cavarero turns to Arendt (1994) to expose the limits of the reformulated subjectivity advanced by the great theorists of the emerging modern order; reflecting primarily on Kantian moral philosophy, Arendt points to the affective states that, for Kant, must under all circumstances, be entirely excluded from moral consideration: inclinations. Building from Arendt's etymological analysis of "inclination," Cavarero (2013: 226) concludes that: "inclination demands the self to incline 'toward others, be they objects or people,'" and that this bending self is precisely an "I" that, by assuming an oblique position, leans out of the vertical axis that allows one to stand erect on one's own basis "as a perfect autonomous subject." One's reliance on others and affection for them,

Arendt argues, makes one's rational self-reliance possible, to the limited extent it is possible. Inclinations make rectitude possible.

Cavarero's phenomenological analysis of the subject-that-inclines may seem distant from our intended object of analysis: the political semiosis through which the self-mythologizing citizen in the emerging order of popular sovereignty figures himself, and it is *him*self in that historical moment, with respect to the second body of the people. Prefiguring the way in which, for Arendt, the dynamics of willing (in terms of inclinations) are inextricably intertwined with those of judging (in terms of reflective judgments) as we will discuss at length in the coming chapters, Cavarero here quotes Arendt on the genius of jury trials as a democratic practice. Arendt (1994: 747) is moved by what she sees as "the undeniable greatness of the judiciary," the fact that the determination of the just result relies on the judgment of "the individual person," in all her frailties and peculiarities, and in her capacity for reason. For Cavarero following Arendt, citizens' self-determination, their rectitude, is not based on a rational agent itself-by-itself, free of all inclinations; rather, it is precisely their human wholeness with all its imperfections that is the basis of Arendt's search for what Linda Zerilli (2016) has figured as a democratic theory of judgment.

This is contrasted, for Arendt (1994: 749), to the rule by nobody of a rationalized bureaucracy; where "courtroom procedure would be superfluous," because "rulership is the rule by nobody." This sort of personhood, leaving the space for the pure eliminationism of the totalitarian regimes, is precisely the prospect that Arendt faces in her discussion of the Eichmann trial, which is the background for the essay ("Some Questions of Moral Philosophy") that Cavarero is quoting from here. In this light, it becomes clear that the impossibility of moral autonomy and the tendency to constitute oneself as part of a network of actors through the radical exclusion of some others, are not two different problematics. They are rather two aspects of the same set of significations through which it is possible, under conditions of popular sovereignty, for necessarily incomplete individuals to (mis-)recognize in one another that which constitutes their place within agency relations. The second body of the people, then, is precisely constituted by this enplacement within chains of rectors and actors, yoked together with those "others" who are both necessary for the agency relations to proceed and effectively excluded from chains of power and their significations.

In political science and sociology, the mundane state has dominated our conceptualization of transitions to modernity, with few exceptions, such as sovereignty in international relations theory, discussions of media events and state rituals. Even the "cultural turn" in the sociology of the state often retains the focus on the mundane state, emphasizing the naturalization of categories and the construction of bureaucratic logic; we do not find in Pierre Bourdieu much meditation on the trembling, ambivalence, and resentment provoked by the performance of domination that is the essence of the spectacular state. This tendency extends to accounts that focus on civil society, paradigmatically that of Honneth (1992 [English 1995], 2018), which attempt to fuse Foucault's historically situated critique of power within Habermas' analytic of social interaction as communicative action.[2] Indeed, following Honneth (2011: 402), there is an influential stream of work focusing on "recognitive power"; without denying the insights into the historical development of liberal civil society therein, nor the normative force of this speech-pragmatist perspective in political philosophy, we maintain that neither Honneth's attempt to reconcile Foucault and Habermas, nor Bourdieu's alternative to both Foucault and Habermas, can sufficiently cope with the paradoxes of distributed sovereignty.

My contention is that if we focus our attention on the transition to modernity conceived as a transformation within political theology, whereby relations between rectors, actors, and others are framed, we will be able to usefully rethink debates over redistribution and recognition. Here, we find that the "bodies of the people"—the political body, individual bodies, and grotesque, "stinking" bodies that are to be excluded at any cost—walk and talk as they are made concrete. We know from the complex history of the very term "political theology" that it encodes precisely the claims upon the individual made by states. But the hope is that by attempting to grasp the inner workings of the "mysteries of state," we can come to a better understanding of what modernity claims from the "body natural" of various persons. The question of *which* natural bodies of *which* persons come to form the body politic is the primary preoccupation of the politics of recognition and misrecognition. Debates about intersectionality and the politics of identity, then, show themselves as a symptom of our inability to come to terms with the political theology embedded in the People's Two Bodies. We need to develop a new understanding of liberalism as a political theology; Arendt's heterodox account of authority and power can help us.

Arendt and the Ineradicable Necessity of Hierarchy in Political Life

Arendt, in *The Human Condition* and elsewhere, is critical of the separation of *ruling and acting* in a way that would appear, at first, to put her work directly at odds with the (sociological) account of power on offer here. Indeed, insofar as, for Arendt, to engage in politics and to exercise *power* involves a mutual recognition of human natality, it would appear that her "politics" does not admit of the form of power in which actor becomes rector's agent-in-the-world.

[2] Honneth's recognition-based reconstruction of society is justly famous and influential. Honneth (2018) recently reconsiders how the concept of recognition developed variously in the English-, French-, and German-speaking contexts to form the foundations of a normative theory of society.

On closer inspection, however, her conception of action as embracing both rule and performance not only does not exclude a legitimate form of hierarchical agency relations; it actually demands it. Arendt's complaint is that *action*, as distinct from making and laboring as she wishes to understand them, is severed from human natality, creativity, and interdependence, when it is separated into two distinct moments of, first, ruling, and then acting. This separation, Arendt (THC: 189) argues, is best expressed in the Greek verbs *archein* and *prattein*, which she renders respectively as "'to begin,' 'to lead,' and finally 'to rule'" (*archein*), and "'to pass through,' 'to achieve,' 'to finish'" (*prattein*). What this shift in language represents, Arendt (THC: 189) argues, is the difference between what *was* "the original interdependence of action, the dependence of the beginner and leader upon others for help and the dependence of his followers upon him for an occasion to act themselves," and the (unfortunate) emergence of a *functional* differentiation of some into "command givers" and others into "command followers."

As Linda Zerilli (2005: 193 n.62) notes in discussing this passage, this relation of rule "was first introduced by Plato as an escape from action." This escape from freedom (as Fromm would have it) is integral to the preoccupation with sovereignty in the tradition, with disastrous consequences. While Habermas is pragma*tist* in his search for a normative and intersubjective basis for horizontal and democratic self-governance achieved through rational deliberation, Arendt, once we recover from her understandable but ultimately indefensible insistence that hierarchy is incompatible with power in her idiosyncratic sense of the term, is pragma*tic*. For this *pragmatic* understanding of reason and the claim of truth we derive from Arendt, there is no pretense to independent rational justification or to normativity through context independence.

To use the nomenclature developed by Reed (2017, 2020), Arendt distinguishes between a rector who listens and recognizes actor in the mutuality of a task undertaken by actor under the direction of rector, and a rector who does not. In the former relation, rector originates the project, and is hence superior, but recognizes as a condition of the development of said project and the recruitment of actor to it, conditions of mutuality, set by a larger set of actors who, in a democratic political culture, will set limits both on the content of projects and the conditions under which actors will carry out tasks in pursuit of the project's completion. This Arendtian account of leadership is very far from the rule in which Arendt sees the seeds of the destruction of the political in the contemporary catastrophic culmination of politics in the Western tradition. Here, contrary to true leadership, rector–ruler uses an initial superiority of strength or willingness to use force to condition a hierarchical relationship wherein rector misrecognizes actor as always already "on his side," and willing to mechanically follow commands (qua agent). In Arendt's terms, a bad rector or ruler brings about sameness, while a good rector or beginner/originator of actions brings about plurality, difference, and uniqueness as a condition for acting together.

What differentiates legitimate hierarchies, where rectors direct projects in which and for which actor–agents genuinely act in Arendt's sense, from those where rectorship decays into rule, into pure command? It is a matter of political culture. The question for a large, pluralistic society with some formal democratic mechanisms will always be how, beyond those mechanisms, membership in, and the ability to pursue self-actualization within, the society can be re-negotiated, particularly by those who are or have been excluded from the possibility of rectorship but recognize they must to be equally liable to accede to it. Any society that promises the capacity to author both one's own life and the conditions of living together to all of its members will always be confronted with the question of whether its basic norms and social structures allow or disallow an actualization of this process through the redistribution of power. I partially accept this Arendtian distinction between the form of rectorship that is either or both leading those who carry out a project and/or beginning it, and the narrower rectorship entailed in ruling those who do so, and partially do not. In power relations, which is to say agency relations, actors make themselves agents of a project's rector–ruler. This does not require direct functionality of command, but it does demand the appropriation of actors' efforts and capacities by rectors.

How, if it all, can this be made compatible with the Arendtian model just described? My contention is that there is a version of "leadership from the field" where agent–actors act "originally enough" to satisfy the Arendtian demand that we understand actors as directing as well as performing their actions. In other words, I suggest that these actors are both self-originating authors of their deeds, but also (contrary to the sense of originality inscribed in her definition of power) agents of another intentionality; namely, that *of* the rector *for the sake of* the project, of which the actor is not the originating author. The challenges are met—if they are met—with precisely the agency relations integral to "leadership from the field" of the sort that answers to Arendt's demand that acting and ruling remain sufficiently coeval so as not to succumb to the undermining of natality inherent to technocracy.

How Arendt's account of action and responsibility can be squared with this sense of leadership from the field can be seen through an example *in extremis*: Lieutenant-Colonel Helmuth Groscurth, staff officer of the 295th Infantry Division of the German Wehrmacht.[3] Groscurth played a crucial role in the

[3] Our account of the man and this incident are deeply indebted to the original archival research of historian Robert Kunath, and his interpretation of these sources (discussed in personal communication). I, of course, am responsible for any errors that might remain here.

ultimately failed attempt to prevent the execution of ninety Jewish children under the age of seven during what has become known as the "Bila Tserkva massacre." The essential details of the incident can be gleaned from a report written by Groscurth (1970: 534–42) during the events of August 1941. The picture of the events during the crucial ten-day period in which the execution of children was being deliberated and debated in the field by SS and Wehrmacht officers and at higher levels of central command show that Groscurth believed that he could "lead from the field" in the sense we have discussed. He took the initiative as the rector of a project (to save the lives of the children, who in the end were executed by Ukrainian militiamen on the orders of Einsatzgruppe C) to which, he believed, he could recruit as his actor a man who was effectively his highest superior, ignoring usual considerations of the chain of command.

On August 20, 1941, after visiting the house where the children were being held without food and water, Groscurth made two phone calls, with the intent of extracting a command to forbid the execution of the children, which he calls in the report an "atrocity no less bad than those of which we accuse the enemy of committing." The first call, usually overlooked in discussions of the incident, is to the highest authority he can reach, the HQ of Army Group South commanded by the doyen of the Prussian officer corps, Field Marshal von Rundstedt. Groscurth speaks to the operations officer at AG South HQ, who immediately refers him to the Sixth Army, commanded by Field Marshal von Reichenau, and then he makes a second call. The referral conforms wholly to standard procedure: the Army Group commanders had purely operational responsibilities, and it was army commanders who had authority for policies in the rear areas. But, as Oberbefehlshaber, Army Group commanders had the authority to intervene in anything they wanted to. Recognizing this, a clear understanding emerges: Groscurth thought that on the basis of a long personal connection through which he knew (he believed) that Rundstedt was as disturbed by Nazi excesses as was he, he would be able to prevent the SS from committing an atrocity the thought of which had so profoundly disturbed the Wehrmacht men serving under his command.

At the time, we should recall, Rundstedt's moral prestige in the German army was unrivaled. This would have made him the rector par excellence. Groscurth's efforts, then, make sense within our framework of agency relations. Groscurth, as an actor who had expanded Rundstedt's agency in the Wehrmacht and the Third Reich believed that, in the service of this limited project, he could "acquire" Rundstedt's authorship for this limited project, which Groscurth believed to fit within the logic of the larger project in which Rundstedt's rectorship reigned. This makes, for Groscurth, Rundstedt's lack of *Zivilcourage* shocking. All he risked by telling the SS to stop shooting Jewish women and children was getting fired. Be that as it may, we cannot but note how bitterly Rundstedt disappointed the hopes that were placed in him, and especially in him.

But why did Rundstedt disappoint Groscurth in this way? Stepping outside the narrow motivations of the two individuals, I believe that this incident provides an illuminating *negative* image of the sort of leadership that is not inimical to spontaneity and democratic life. Namely, it presents a format without which distributed sovereignty would be impossible, in which an actor in a large project becomes rector of a limited project within that frame precisely by enlisting the rector of said large project as an actor on behalf of the actor/would-be-rector's limited project. My suggestion is that at this crucial moment in August 1941, the Wehrmacht and its officers had just enough limited independence from the ideologically inflexible Nazi apparatus for it to be possible for a senior field officer like Groscurth (he was the "1a," or second in command, of his unit) to believe that he could skip the usual chain of command and make a direct appeal by telephone call to the rector-of-rectors of the Wehrmacht officer class. Enough independence of action, enough distribution of sovereignty, was enjoyed for this to be thinkable for Groscurth, but not enough, tragically, for him to succeed in saving the lives of those ninety children.

If Groscurth's failed attempt to reverse the agency relations between himself and Rundstedt provides a negative image of the format of distributed sovereignty and limited hierarchy we wish to evoke, then two limit cases seem to bookend the range of possible project formats where this model of legitimate hierarchy operates. At one end, there is the "nightmare scenario" behind Agamben's (1998: 174–80) account of the camp as the apparatus (*dispositif*) of the modern as such, where actors disappear altogether and we have a set of projects-in-the-world where there are only rectors and others. Here, rectors devise or extend projects, using one set of others who effectively run the apparatus to produce a set of results that are desirable for the project in and through another set of others, the object of the apparatus' performance. A real-world scenario close enough to this image illustrates how it provides content to one end of the spectrum of possible political semiosis within which agency relations as we account for them can function, namely, a political format such as Weber's analysis of illegitimate rule (*Illegitim Herrschaft*): rule that lacks popular legitimation through any of the three channels Weber identified as potentially providing such: legal–rational; traditional; charismatic. In this almost-nightmare scenario, we find an organization of effort toward the achievement of defined goals, but no socially salient mechanism whereby the would-be actors can recognize themselves as part of a project in which they have their own hierarchically defined position.

At the other end of the spectrum, we find what could be called the "dream of democratic republicanism," which we can recognize in Arendt's (OR: 164–78) rather distorted image of the American Experiment, discussed at greater length in Chapter 4. For Arendt, instead of the picture Agamben gives us, where the disappearance of actors leaves us with only rectors and others, we encounter the disappearance of rectors and others leaving us with only actors. To the extent that Arendt's "people power" is reducible to this dream, this model of agency relations as a central mechanism of distributed popular sovereignty is not Arendtian. I maintain, however, that in the wide swathe of social hermeneutic space between the Agambenian nightmare and Arendtian dream, legitimate hierarchical differentiation through chains of power and their representation embedded within the intentional framework of mutually recognized agency relations not only obtains, but also goes a long way to explain how distributed sovereignty *actually functions* under conditions that are more-or-less capitalist and more-or-less democratic.

Conclusion: The People's Second Body and the Tensions of Distributed Sovereignty

How, then, has—and how might—the second body of the people serve to answer the question of distributing or perhaps even eliminating sovereignty of the kind forged in the crucible of the king's second body? As we have seen, delegation is meant to derive from the people themselves as the ultimate rector, but the unresolved tension between the mysticism surrounding the king's second body as the fulcrum of the very material consolidation of state power has never left us. Where, then, are we to turn? Facing Chantal Mouffe (2005, 2018) and Wendy Brown (2010, 2016) who press the Schmittian case, and the debate about redistribution and recognition among Honneth, Fraser, and their followers, we see the very same alternative visions of popular sovereignty vying with each other today.

It was Albert Camus (1991 [1954]: 118, 119) who identified the opposition between the radicals and the liberals around the trial of the king as a matter not of law, but of "theology." He argued that in 1793 in Paris, "two different conceptions of transcendence meet in mortal combat." This combat was, clearly enough, a matter of violence. But it was also a matter of interpretation, and of political vision. The Gironde sought the performance of a legalistic republicanism for all of "the people" to see. The Jacobins sought an absolutist, undivided, and inviolable sovereignty of the people—that is, the people as inheritors of the king's second body upon the (literal) dismemberment of his first. As Annie Jourdan (2004) has pointed out, these are rather different interpretations of the general will. Francois Furet (1981) was correct about one thing, at least: Robespierre's performance of virtue was twinned with his paranoid style, obsessed with the corruption of the purity of the people's second body. This style is always available in politics framed by popular sovereignty, for it is built into the political theology of the people's two bodies. And hence Camus' (1991 [1954]: 120) insight: "the condemnation of the King is at the crux of our contemporary history." Isaac Arial Reed (2020) has developed out of this core insight from Camus a book-length analysis of power in modernity that, as the subtitle of the book makes clear, is born out of the distribution of power and authority through "agency relations" that first arose out of the "creative destruction of the King's two bodies" in precisely this way.

We seem to arrive, with Camus, at the conclusion that as with the old contest between the liberal Gironde and the radical Jacobin, politics of the left and center-left across liberal modernity is permanently stuck in an oscillation, or vacillation, between a Girdonist attraction to legitimacy (Habermas) and a Jacobin insistence on something more deeply grounded in the People (Brown, Mouffe). Yet this is inadequate to our contemporary moment, with the current crisis of the Republic that is in serious danger of either cooptation or destruction at the hands of a renovated (extreme) right. Put more narrowly, I have here attempted to provide an account of the second body of the people that provides a framework for addressing the problems of distributed sovereignty under conditions of popular rule that is more promising than the one on offer from Habermas, Forst and Honneth, or from Brown and Mouffe. But how can our apparent acceptance of the unacceptable thinness of Girdonist legitimacy coupled with outrage against Jacobin undivided popular sovereignty have any chance of actually advancing the debate?

Benhabib (2018: 190) names this dilemma the "Weimar syndrome": the condition in which we, like Kelsen, Schmitt, Strauss, Arendt, and Shklar before us, are "haunted by Weber's questions" concerning "how to defend, intellectually and institutionally, modern constitutional republics and liberal societies in an age of value pluralism as well as class conflict." Like Benhabib, I believe that Arendt offers the best response to this dilemma. Jacobinism, understood as a frame for representing power and doing politics, links equality to sameness—sameness of opinion via consensus decision; sameness of identity (Frenchness, whiteness); sameness in eschatological vision. In a well-known argument, Arendt traced the Terror to the politics of compassion and the explosion of *needs* into the space of revolution; this has been taken up as her fundamental denial of class politics, manifest in her negative judgment of the interruption of the political by the social.

But we can now see that this is, as it were, a red herring. Arendt's (THC: 175) response to the terror is contained, instead, in abstract form, in the tension between equality and distinction inherent to *The Human Condition*, in its manifestation in democratic society:

> human plurality, the basic condition of both action and speech, has the twofold character of equality and distinction. If men were not equal, they could neither understand each other and those who came before them nor plan for the future and foresee the needs of those who will come after them. If men were not distinct, each human being distinguished from any other who is, was, or will ever be, they would need neither speech nor action to make themselves understood.

Here, truly, Arendt throws the tragic error of Robespierre into relief. He was deeply complicit with the rector he was intent on destroying. For Robespierre—and, more broadly, if less exquisitely, for the Mountain—"the people" had to, somehow, exist in direct mimesis of unitary, unimpeachable, inviolable rule/kingship. We need only to turn to the historical sociology of the Jacobin dimension of modernity, with its careful reconstructions of the Russian, Chinese, and Iranian revolutions, to see that Jacobins continually prop upright sovereigns of their own, complete with second bodies, founded in the unalterable sameness of "the people" transmuted into the decisions and public performances of Lenin, Mao, and Khomeini (Eisenstadt 1999).

Jacobinism, however, is only one inheritance of the mystical afterlife of the king's second body. In the following two chapters, I aim to catalog the varieties of unexpected afterlives of early modern political theology that manifest themselves in different varieties of popular sovereignty in contemporary democratic life. In light of this catalog, I shall attempt (in Chapters 3 and 4) an Arendtian diagnosis of the three antinomies of liberalism as a political theology that rest beneath this variety. I will then argue, in Chapter 5, how it might be possible to resist further such slippage into an unmediated sovereignty of the People, construed as a metaphysical body within an inherent self-sameness as well as a concretely situated group of bodies that are ever constituting anew to the People as such a whole.

3

THREE ANTINOMIES OF LIBERALISM AS A POLITICAL THEOLOGY: FOUNDATIONS IN *WILLING*

As discussed in the preceding chapter, Arendt's account of action is based in her deep insight into the disastrous consequences of the separation of its two primary moments—*archein* and *prattein* (beginning and performing or ruling and acting)—from one another and into stultified and ossified positions of leader and follower (THC: 189). Arendt is profoundly right to notice an irresistible tension between the discipline required for statecraft, where rule must be permanently located in the machine of the state-system and in the person(s) charged with the operation of that system and the freedom required for democratic action. The question in this chapter is whether or not Arendt herself had, or in any case can provide us with, the resources with which to solve or at least resolve the problem of sovereignty under conditions of democratic self-rule, articulated in Chapter 2 through the figure of the "second body" of the people.

This problem has been variously analyzed as either: insoluble (Schmitt, Foucault, Agamben, Brown, Butler); pointing toward the need to overcome sovereignty with an accountable rule of law (Habermas, Honneth, Benhabib); or resolvable only within an agonistic (Fraser, Honig) or antagonistic (Mouffe) or judgment-based (Zerilli 2005) democratic politics based on a constant redefinition through competition of the people with themselves over what if anything can be taken as a stable basis for self-rule within democratic polities. Many of these accounts of the tension between rule and action, between founded law and unfounded freedom, appeal directly to Arendt as an authority or at least a singular voice on foundationalism and anti-foundationalism, with reference to either or both *The Human Condition* and *On Revolution*, sometimes with reference to *On Violence*.[1] Here, I turn to a different Arendtian resource, which happens to be the last finished written work she completed: the concluding chapter of part two of *The Life of the Mind* (*Willing*), titled "The abyss of freedom and *novus ordo seclorum*."

I turn to this less-traveled pathway in Arendt's *corpus* while following Linda Zerilli's (2005: 86) gesture to this chapter, yet also seeking to extend and intensify her discussion of "the difficulty of telling the story of the 'we' in non-necessary terms" as a fruitful place for us to labor with and against Arendt in trying to find a way through the tension between discipline and freedom, order and spontaneity. For sure, Arendt here addresses many of the same themes that bring readers and critics back time and again to especially *The Human Condition* and *On Revolution*. In this chapter, very much like in those canonical texts, readers of Arendt can find what Zerilli (2005: 16), quoting Arendt (THC: 234–35, 237), aptly describes as "rethinking freedom in terms of nonsovereignty" and, in this way, an attempt to "redeem" plurality from its abjected position within the tradition since, at least, Plato.[2]

What is unique to this less famous *topos* in Arendt's *corpus*, however, is the emphasis placed on the Roman and Hebrew foundation legends that are meant to but cannot underwrite the founding of the American Republic, insofar as each illuminates the gap between past and future, between the no-more and the not-yet in which we encounter the "abyss of freedom" that gives the chapter half of its memorable title. I discuss these two foundation legends in detail below; what is crucial for the moment is that Arendt here best addresses both the felt need for a link to the constative character of past actions in order for future-oriented *action* and democratic freedom to be possible and the self-contradiction inherent in such an appeal to the past in beginning something new. Zerilli (2005: 86) articulates well how Arendt correctly diagnoses the fundamental problem of "how to articulate the emergence of the 'we' as something constituted by a free act, that is, without naturalizing or predetermining its appearance in the possible," a problem the American founders left fundamentally unresolved because of their attempt to present "the new" as "the reestablishment of the old, a golden age when one was not a slave," making

1 As Bernal (2017: 5) puts this tension, as discussed by Arendt (OR: 193) "founding and constitutionalism have appeared to be in tension or conflict with democracy"; while Lucy Cane (2015: 66) examines the same problem, arguing that for Arendt political principles, derived from the Greek *archein*, while "not moral standards" do "serve as guiding criteria for political judgment." We return to this point in the conclusion of this chapter.

2 Richard E. Flathman (2003: 167) argues for "nonsovereign freedom" in the liberal tradition, concluding: "As regards pluralistic societies and polities, it is a mistake to think that order and stability are or could be maintained by someone omnipotent, some 'sovereign,' agent or agents, or agencies."

clear how the two parts of the title in the chapter of *Willing* on which we focus here are in tension with one another: precisely because the revolutionary founding is about the abyss of freedom, it cannot and will not do to seek a ground for that free act in the tradition. Yet beneath this intertwinement—one is tempted to say "bondage" or "yoking"—of the tension between freedom and law with that of natality and tradition, there is another dimension to Arendt's striking redeployment of Virgil's image of a "golden age when one was not a slave" that we cannot ignore: the clear reference to the institution of slavery.

The critical discourse—and often justifiable outrage—about Arendt's unsatisfying discussion of slavery generally focuses on the mere handful of pages Arendt devotes to the subject in *On Revolution*; about which see: Bernasconi (1996); Gines (2014)[3]; King (2012, 2015); and the extended discussion of these works in Weinman (2022) and Robaszkiewicz and Weinman (2022, ch. 9). Less discussed, as regards slavery in particular, are a few paragraphs from Arendt's discussion of the role of the Boers in the development of a racialized bureaucracy in British colonial South Africa. While the chapter in which these remarks are found contains infamous passages concerning African "savages" that are much discussed and rightly condemned in the literature on Arendt cited in the previous paragraph, less attention has been paid to what Arendt (OT: 192) says about slavery itself as an institution that was initially and remained throughout the late nineteenth and twentieth centuries "the basis for a race society"; namely, "slavery, though it domesticated a certain part of the savage population, never got hold of all of them, so the Boers were never able to forget their first horrible fright before a species of men whom human pride and the sense of human dignity could not allow them to accept as fellow-men." Here, indeed, we see one of those times that Arendt uses the term savages in describing Black Africans; in this case—and unlike others in the surrounding pages of this chapter where she clearly and indefensibly speaks of "savages" in her own voice—it is clear from the context that Arendt is using "free indirect discourse" and putting herself in the place of the Boers (or so she believes at least) and allowing them to speak through her text as it were. In work done together with Maria Robaszkiewicz (Robaszkiewicz and Weinman (2022, chs. 3 and 9 *passim*), I have reflected at greater length on this method of "representative thinking" as synonymous with judgment, and the perils and the promise of this method of and for "exercises in political thinking."

What I wish to call attention to here is how this discussion of how racialized bureaucracy is both grounded in the institution of slavery and never escapes

[3] I follow Kathryn Sophia Belle's suggestion of citing her work under the name she published it, even though she now goes by another name.

the basic phenomenology—the intersubjective experience—of slave-holding as its fundamental feature, even when a political system, like Apartheid in South Africa or the so-called Jim Crow Era in the United States, abolishes the practice of slavery in terms of legal instruments. As Arendt (OT: 193) concludes: "Slavery in the case of the Boers was a form of adjustment of a European people to a black race, and only superficially resembled those historical instances when it had been a result of conquest or slave trade. No body politic, no communal organization kept the Boers together, no territory was definitively colonized and the black slaves did not serve any white civilization." This conclusion, likely horrible in its own way to our ears, makes clear a few things. First, that Arendt clearly sees something like a hierarchical order of more and less bad forms of slavery, with the form of slavery practiced by the Boers—and then coopted by the British into their rule in South Africa—was "worse" than the institution of slavery in places where there was colonization, slave trade, and "communal organization." Second, that while other "comparisons" become possible in light of this hierarchy, the clear intended contrast—though the consequence is not drawn and the comparison not made explicitly—is with the systematic slavery in the United States. Third—and this is consistent with Arendt's misreading of the racial politics of the American republic as both Richard King (2012, 2015) and Kathryn Gines (2014), in particular, argue—is the implication that the social organization and political institutionalization of slavery in the United States somehow ameliorated or mitigated the extent to which slavery dehumanized slaves and masters there, in comparison with the absolute dehumanization she sees as integrated to South African race society both before, during, and after the British colonial period around the turn of the twentieth century.

Insofar as what we have just summarized is Arendt's point in speaking about slavery as constitutive for race societies and racialized bureaucracies, we have little to learn from her. But something else is clear as an implication of her line of thought here, even though Arendt neither pursued it here nor developed it in the brief discussion of slavery in *On Revolution*. Namely, that even after the abolition of slavery in either the "worse" case of South Africa or the "less bad" case of the United States, it remains the case that as Arendt (OT: 192) argues, Black people "were, as it were, 'natural' human beings who lacked the specifically human character, the specifically human reality, so that when European men massacred them they were somehow not aware that they had committed murder." In the immediate context, Arendt is thinking of the concentration and extermination camps that Europeans, namely, the British, first developed for the management of populations in South Africa and later exported for use in Europe itself—this being her famous "boomerang thesis" discussed in Robaszkiewicz and Weinman (2022: 183–84). Pulling back the lens, however, we can see that this applies just as well to what is often called "the Jim Crow Era" in the United States but which might better be called something like the "Era of Racial Terror," in which systematic judicial and extra-judicial killings were used for analogous policies of "administering" a race society.

This background of slavery as the basic structure of exclusion that is embedded in the tradition of modern revolution and republican founding, coupled with Arendt's unique understanding of slavery in perennial tension with freedom, is essential for understanding liberalism as a political theology; even if, disappointingly, Arendt herself never developed that account of slavery fully. What this, to my mind, leaves for us to expound more precisely in the rest of this chapter is the place of both biblical and classical "traditional authorities" in the political project of Republican modernity. In what follows, we will attend expressly to what was called in the previous chapter "liberalism as a political theology" in order to bring to light in a new way her incompletely developed answer to the "wrestling with the tradition" of political theology found in the work of thinkers taken to be basic the three alternative answers sketched above, principally those of Schmitt (and his followers), Kantorowicz, and Strauss. The chapter has three sections. In the first, I recast Chapter 2's depiction of popular sovereignty as a political mythology meant to move past the unappealing dead ends at which Weber's project of a value-free science and liberal, secular politics degenerated in the two decades that separate his vocation lectures and the disasters of the mid-twentieth century in terms of Arendt's account of the difference between political freedom and philosophical freedom in the first volume of *The Life of the Mind*. This brings us into dialogue with political theology as the term is deployed today.

In the second, longest section, I follow Arendt in discussing the three central antinomies of liberal politics as she presents them in the second volume of *The Life of the Mind* dedicated to the problem of the will. First, the antinomy of freedom and law, best captured in connection with the sense of political theology associated with Carl Schmitt; the study of political forms within the horizon of modern politics (first and foremost sovereignty) as "secularized theological concepts." Second, the antinomy of natality (spontaneity) and tradition, which is discussed in connection with the sense of "political theology" associated principally with Ernst Kantorowicz: a paradigmatically medieval and early modern phenomenon by which stability in politics and law, specifically the sovereignty of the monarch over his land and his people was secured through theological resources, specifically the analogy between the incorporation of the body politic into the monarch and the incorporation of body of the church into the godhead through the holy spirit. Third, and following from the first two, the antinomy of secular reason and theocratic faith, where in response to Strauss' reading of Spinoza and Hobbes as an attempt to address what Angélica Bernal (2017: 11–12) describes as "underauthorized authorizations," Arendt (THC: 235) articulates her own understanding of what others seek to understand as a truly democratic sovereignty and which she would have us understand as "the simultaneous presence of freedom and non-sovereignty" that is part and parcel of action.

In the concluding section I argue that taken together Arendt's cascading attempt to resolve the antinomies of liberalism as a political theology brings us, if not to a satisfactory solution of the problem of democratic sovereignty, then at least the closest we can get to that goal in reading her work; crucially, I will make the case that Arendt does better here than elsewhere in taking on the question of freedom as synonymous with power and action as the groundless ground of politics. This is so because in the *Life of the Mind*, read in contrast to *On Revolution* which is generally seen as authoritative for her account of politics, Arendt corrects Schmitt's ahistorical, or anti-historical, sublation of modern political concepts and institutions into a secularized theology with Kantorowicz's careful historical reconstruction of medieval political theology in its difference from early modern absolutist sovereignty. In this way, her related but not identical readings of the *Novus Ordo Saeclorum* in *On Revolution* and *The Life of the Mind, Vol. 2* make clear why and how the sphere of human plurality as the space of politics differs in a small but significant way from standard accounts of her view of politics.

Arendtian Political Theology: The Modern Afterlife of Roman and Hebrew Foundation Legends

It is not immediately obvious that or why the subject matter of *Willing*—individual freedom as a constituted by political rather than philosophical freedom—is an especially promising place to seek out Arendt's insights into the nature of liberalism as a political theology. After all, is she not here—as she had done earlier in *On Revolution* and *The Human Condition*—laying out an account of the nature of politics as life of action, performed in public by individuals who encounter and recognize one another as both equal and distinct? What has this to do with the afterlife of medieval political theology and the analogy between divine and earthly incorporation? Two pairs of passages, one from early in the last chapter of *Willing* and one from the Introduction to *Thinking*, will hopefully make this clear.

In the first passage of the first pair, Arendt (LOTM1: 195) condemns all *philosophies* of the will, the children of "Kant's 'professional thinkers'," as being incapable of enacting freedom insofar as they are "by nature more inclined to 'interpret the world' than to 'change it,'" and this with the consequence that among all the philosophers and theologians who took up the philosophy of the will, "only Duns Scotus . . . was ready to pay the price of contingency for the gift of freedom—the mental endowment we have for beginning something new, of which we know that it could just as well not be." The central importance of Duns Scotus to Arendt's account of freedom has been well remarked by

Zerilli (2005: 208 n. 30) who summarizes Arendt's reading of Duns Scotus as offering a theory of the "coincidence of causes" that "saves both freedom and necessity." This intervention in the theory of the will, insisting on the "contingent character of processes" (LOTM1: 137), will be of essential importance for Arendt's discussion of the abyss of freedom and the antinomies of liberalism as a political theology.

In the second passage of this first pair, Arendt (LOTM1: 197), quoting Kuhn (1962: 172), asserts that it is "hardly deniable that the reflections of the great founders of modern science—Einstein, Planck, Bohr, Heisenberg, Schrödinger—have brought about a 'crisis in the foundations of modern science' (*Grundlagenkrise*), and 'their central question' (What must the world be like in order than man may know it?) 'is as old as science itself and it remains unanswered.'" What links these two observations? What does the "foundations crisis" in twentieth-century science have to do with the philosophical obsession with necessity and the rejection of freedom incumbent in philosophers' rejection of contingency? Everything, Arendt contends. For, both are epiphenomena of the radical rejection of the immaterial and invisible that are integral to the project of philosophical and political modernity. That is to say, as Zerilli (2005: 75) notes while discussing how philosophical and political freedom differ: "If Arendt is right, we cannot eliminate causality from the telling of a story, but perhaps we can give an account of what has happened which, although touched, framed, and animated by causality, shows causality to be contingent." In other words, early twentieth-century and interwar attempts to, once for all, get past Kant's doubts about true and certain knowledge concerning the causes of physical phenomena show themselves in the end to be one more iteration of the self-contradiction inherent in the philosophy of the will.

To see this, let us turn to the second pair of passages, from the earliest moments of volume 1 of *The Life of the Mind*. Here, Arendt (LOTM1: 11) concludes a consideration of the history of the "sentiment: God is dead," which she traces not to Nietzsche but to Hegel, with the determination that these "modern 'deaths'—of God, metaphysics, philosophy, and, by implication, positivism—have become events of considerable historical consequence," because "they have ceased to be the exclusive concern of an intellectual elite and instead are not so much the concern as the common unexamined assumption of nearly everybody." The issue here, she believes, is primarily one of political authority and for this reason remains "outside our considerations" within the frame of Vol. 1, though of course political authority is very much *not* outside the scope of Vol. 2. Having thus named, but delayed, the question of how "modern deaths" can be answered only by political authority, Arendt (LOTM1: 12) goes on to note that "the possible advantage of our situation following the demise of metaphysics" is twofold: first, it allows us "to look on the past with new eyes, unburdened by any traditions"; second, we can thus "dispose of a tremendous wealth of raw experiences without being bound by any prescriptions." Put more directly in terms of the language Arendt uses in the first pair of passages our advantage is this: we are, and can acknowledge ourselves as, both contingent and free.

But there is a catch; for, along with our freedom and recognition of the unlimited contingency of the state of affairs into which we were born there has developed, with almost the same apparent ineluctability, a refusal of the invisible. For reasons perhaps internal to the anti-metaphysical commitments integral to thinking "since the death of God," Arendt (LOTM1: 12) bemoans how this advantage "would have been even greater had it not been accompanied, almost inevitably, by a growing inability to move . . . in the realm of the invisible" and the corresponding "disrepute into which everything that is not visible, tangible, palpable has fallen, so that we are in danger of losing the past itself together with our traditions." In other words, our free contingency might otherwise have been a true political freedom, if not for our determination to disallow anything beyond material determinism. As Lucy Cane (2015: 62–68) notes, the crucial interlocutor for Arendt in drawing out this missed opportunity to resolve better the tensions between tradition and spontaneity, between law and freedom, is Montesquieu, whose attempt to distinguish between laws and principles profoundly shapes Arendt's thinking. We will discuss this in further detail in unpacking the first of the three antinomies just below.

With both pairs of passages now laid out before us, hopefully, we can see why the discussion of political as opposed to philosophical freedom is in fact the right place to seek clarification of what liberalism as a political theology is and why Arendt can help us understand it. Namely, the foundations crisis in the sciences is of a piece with the incapacity of the philosophers precisely because of the disrepute into which "the realm of the invisible" has fallen. This is one aspect of a much deeper problem, which Arendt notes in introducing "Thinking" but only comes to address directly in the concluding chapter of *Willing*, and there only provisionally: the problem of political authority after the end of the tradition. To see what she has to say (incompletely) about this broader horizon of the limited problem discussed until now, we turn now to the substance of "The abyss of freedom and the *novus ordo seclorum*."

The Three Antinomies and their Theological–Political Residues

Antinomy 1: freedom and law

As we have seen just above, Arendt's (LOTM2: 198) attempt to distinguish philosophical freedom, the freedom of the will, from political freedom, power or action, begins with the observation that: "Professional thinkers, whether philosophers or scientists, have not been 'pleased with freedom' and its ineluctable randomness; they have been unwilling to pay the price of contingency for the questionable gift of spontaneity." For this reason, it is necessary to turn them aside and move, in the last chapter of *Willing* but with the third volume *Judging* very much in mind, to the consideration of "men of action." We will return, in the concluding third section of this chapter, to the salience of the intended argument of *Judging* for Arendt's conclusions about political as opposed to philosophic freedom in *Willing*. For now, let us note that the conclusion at which we will arrive in the present section is an inconclusive conclusion that requires further elaboration.

Drawing on what she describes as the only account of the distinction between philosophic and political freedom in the tradition, that of Montesquieu in *Spirit of the Laws*, Arendt (LOTM2: 198–99) argues that while "philosophic freedom, the freedom of the will, is relevant only to people who live outside political communities, as solitary individuals" in what we could call, following Richard J. Bernstein (1983), a Cartesian dream of self-reliant individualism, "political freedom 'can consist only in the power of doing what **we** ought to will and in not being constrained to do what **we** ought not to will [emphasis author].'" I emphasize the plurality of the first-person pronoun here because it is clear, by implication, that what Arendt wants to stress in quoting Montesquieu is precisely that political freedom is a result of principled (and thus customary) relations between persons who already see one another as fellows, and *not* an attribute of solitary individuals; while *philosophic* freedom, on the contrary, is an attribute of individuals. Cane (2015: 63, 65) points to three reasons why Montesquieu's view of political principles appeals to Arendt in this way: first, principles as Montesquieu understands them are not means–ends relations in which actions are directed toward the result or goal they are intended to bring about; second, "they are utterly *worldly*" in that the principles obtain not in the actor alone, driving them to act on the basis of a psychological motive, but in a manner like Montesquieu's spirit of the laws which exists, if at all, in the shared world in common; finally, principles are neither moral nor sentimental but rather properly political in that they orient action not through "the sentiment of pity" but through "the principle of solidarity."

This is as much to say, as Arendt (LOTM2: 200) does just after quoting Montesquieu, that "political freedom is possible only in a sphere of human plurality, and on the premise that this sphere is not simply an extension of the dual I-and-myself to a plural We." Here we see the great fault with the widespread view discussed above that in Arendt's view of politics speeches are deeds can be understood in terms of discursive democracy or communicative rationality along Habermas' lines. Arendt (LOTM2: 200) preemptively disputed this line of thought in a passage not taken into consideration in this regard: "An error rather prevalent among modern philosophers who insist on the importance of communication as a guarantee of truth . . . is to believe that the intimacy of dialogue, the 'inner action' in which I 'appeal' to myself or to the 'other self,'

Aristotle's friend, Jasper's beloved, Buber's Thou, can be extended and become paradigmatic for the political sphere." While Arendt is here concerned chiefly with Jaspers and Buber, and while Habermas is certainly not the *naif* either of these two about politics and contestation, the argument can surely be read as a critical response to Habermas' (1996: 147–51) assimilation of Arendt to his own project *avant la lettre*.

Be that as it may, the crucial bottom line for Arendt (LOTM2: 200) in distinguishing philosophic freedom (belonging to individuals, concerned with the I-will) and political freedom (belonging to us as members of political communities, concerned with the I-can, which is to say the We-can) is this: "Action, in which a We is always engaged in changing our common world, stands in the sharpest possible opposition to the solitary business of thought, which operates in a dialogue between me and myself." As such, as a feature of the I-can, which is always actuated in the We-can, political freedom is impossible without consent. That is to say, the problem of the freedom of the will—as a fixation of philosophy in its obsessive interest in the singular, more precisely, the *individual*, human being—turns out to be inextricably connected to the problem of the general will, as understood since modern social contract theory and its prioritization of the consent of the governed, be that consent understood a prior or posterior, as tacit or explicit, as constituted in law or in and by a (popular) sovereign.

But how is this consent to be secured and what are its conditions? Arendt (LOTM2: 201) elliptically argues that contrary to the *unlimited* character of "the mind's will power to affirm or negate" that constitutes the ultimate of philosophic freedom, "political power, even if the tyrant's supporters consent to terror—that is, to the use of violence—is always limited power, and since power and freedom in the sphere of human plurality are in fact synonyms, this means that political freedom is always limited freedom." Much is happening in this dense sentence, but two points merit mention here. First, we have to notice that "consent" has a wide range here and certainly cannot be reduced to rational consent based on the discursive discovery of shared norms or interests, or both. Second, notwithstanding this wide purview for consent, neither the object of the consent nor the subjective relation between those who grant consent and those who receive it, are absolute. Taken together, these two features point to something fundamental about how "legitimation" works under conditions of political freedom, namely, authority, the right to receive a grant of consent, depends on the recognition of the need to act in concert, whence derives the capacity for political leader to exercise power, even if this power is warranted only by violence, which for Arendt is the opposite of power. This sense of authority, as we will see, is crucial for Arendt's depiction of what can best be called liberalism as a political theology, and it is crucially different from other accounts of authority or domination that follow—as does Arendt's—from Weber's analysis of *Herrschaft*.

All of this is arguable, but let us set that to the side for the moment. More germane for us at present is that this is also familiar to those who have read the classical Arendtian discussions of these matters in her more frequently cited works. What Arendt (LOTM2: 201, 202) argues next offers an interesting twist on the conditions of possibility for this "sphere of human plurality" in which freedom and power "are in fact synonyms"; namely, "the predicament of not-knowing." With this predicament, which is in fact a special case of the old philosophical antinomy between freedom and law (or free will and determinism), Arendt is concerned with what she calls here the "In the beginning." This phrase, ineluctably calling to mind the first word of the Hebrew Bible (*be'reshit*), gestures toward the time and place within which the "We" first constituted itself as a salient entity. This search for origins—of the human race as a whole and of each people or nation as such—will forever remain with the realm of not-knowing; thus, some origin myth remains vitally necessary. Absent knowledge of the origin, at which we will never arrive, we must make do with an origin myth that can serve as an authoritative source of visibility and legitimation within a polity of free actors, regulated by law.

This first antinomy between freedom and order, contingency and determination, the I-can and the I-will, issues in the continuing and central importance of an origin myth and thus leaves us on the precipice of the second, between the spontaneity of I-can and the need for a grounding of the "We" of the We-can, in and through which alone the I-can, in fact, can. We are left with an unresolved problematic of how the power of individuals (their political freedom) can be enacted through the power of action-in-public which is both the product and the ground of individual action. We turn now to address with Arendt this second, perhaps even deeper, puzzle.

Antinomy 2: natality (spontaneity) and tradition

What, then, is or are the origin myth(s) relevant for us, for "We" who are gathered here today? We must already detect the influence of Augustine, again at least as Arendt reads him, when Arendt (LOTM2: 203) names "the two foundation legends of Western civilization, the one Roman and the other Hebrew," finding that what is first of all striking in taking up this pair of thought objects, is that they "are utterly different from each other, except that both arose among a people that thought of its past as a story whose beginning was known and could be dated." Arendt focuses our attention on this fact of dating because this, as it turns out, is of great moment for the fundamental problem of liberalism as a political theology: what, if anything, can bridge between the absolute freedom attending the spontaneous rupture of the old order—the *liberation from* the dominating/repressing unconstitutional regime—and the ordered and limited freedom of the new constitutional order. One crucial condition of the possibility of thinking, let alone making, such a bridge is that there is a moment of foundation. Both the Roman foundation legend and that of the Hebrews claims for itself knowledge of that moment, in relation to us in the present day. This accords to these two particular foundation legends a place of honor in the willing and the acting of the founding generation of the late eighteenth century.

Arendt (LOTM2: 203) next points to one other striking similarity between the two legends: they both "hold that in the case of foundation—the supreme act in which the 'We' is constituted as an identifiable entity—the inspiring principle of action is the love of freedom, and this both in the negative sense of liberation from oppression in the positive sense of the establishment of Freedom as a stable, tangible reality." Here, the vital importance and allure of each foundation legend for the authors of liberalism as a political theology is even more explicit: in each of the two legends, the act of foundation is cast precisely as an eventful act of liberation (from Pharoah for Moses and the Hebrews; from the ransack of Troy for Aeneas and the Romans) followed, through the course of a determined but contingent series events, by the establishment of a new rule in a new land.

The differences between two legends are numerous, and Arendt (LOTM2: 204) notes some of the essential ones; still, like her, we will not belabor them here because for the founding generation, as she argues, these differences were "not decisive": what was decisive was that "there was a *hiatus* between disaster and salvation, between liberation from the old order and the new freedom, embodied in a *novus ordo seclorum*, a 'new order of the ages' with whose rise the world had structurally changed." How, then, to fill this gap, to concretize in the series of events the radically uncaused spontaneous performance of the new order in such a way that it can fulfill itself in time and be efficiently causal within the horizon of that new order? This is the question that the founders of the would-be new orders in colonial America and monarchical France deployed these two legends to answer, in articulating the meaning of the constitutions so as to win consent for their revolutionary projects. How did they do so?

Speaking of the American experiment in particular, Arendt (LOTM2: 205–6) entertains the Lockean fantasy that "in the beginning all the world was America," with the implication that Biblical history was rewritten in European colonization of the so-called "New World," and the "colonial period would be interpreted as the transition period between bondage and freedom—the hiatus between leaving England and the Old World and the establishment of freedom in the New" before pointing out the obvious factual flaw of such a narrative: the colonists "had not settled there as exiles but as colonists" and "had no trouble recognizing the political authority of the mother-country" as they "prided themselves on being British subjects."

All this changed, Arendt (LOTM2: 206) argues, only when the practical maxim of "no taxation without representation" came to entail—as the result of pure contingency—a rebellion against a putatively unjust government that could be achieved only through a "change in the form of government itself and the constitution of a Republic as the only government, they now felt, fit to rule in the land of the free." This, Arendt (LOTM2: 207) continues, was "the moment when those who had started as men of action had been transformed into men of revolution" and "changed Virgil's great line '*Magnus ab integro saeclorum nascitur ordo*' (the great order of the ages is [re]born as it was in the beginning) to the *Novus Ordo Seclorum* (the '*new*' order), which we still find on our dollar bills."

Rejecting the millennialist, Protestant vision of the achievement of freedom across the globe as the ultimate victory of Christ that preceded by a century and more their political mobilization in the late eighteenth century, Arendt argues, the founders of the American republic turned instead to a revolutionized version of Rome's founding myth to lay out the dimensions of the political theology of the republic to be. Or, as Arendt (LOTM2: 207) puts it: "When men of action, men who wanted to change the world, became aware that such a change might actually postulate a new order of the ages, the start of something unprecedented, they turned to history for help." Not eschatology, not the Christian vision of the kingdom of ends and universal salvation, but the Pentateuch of the Hebrews and the Aeneid of the Romans were their guides, because they—unlike the millennialists—ground the order of the ages within historical time. As historicizing narratives, they teach us that the uncertain gift of freedom comes only with the price of contingency and the understanding that "what would be done now could just as well have been left undone" (LOTM2: 207).

Generalizing from the American experiment, Arendt (LOTM2: 207) concludes that "foundation legends, with their hiatus between liberation and the constitution of freedom, indicate the problem [of the "many-in-one"] without solving it" because they "point to the *abyss* of nothingness that opens up before any deed that cannot be accounted for by a reliable chain of cause and effect." At this general level, then, the problem of founding the modern republic opens back up onto the first antinomy: the unresolvable tension between the contingency of the free act and the determinism by which an act becomes an event and thus part of the logic of cause and effect, and therefore not free (in the sense of "radically undetermined").

This generalization also reminds us of the remaining unresolved tension at work here: the logic of the foundation myth works insofar as it is a contingent ground, it itself is the result of a now prior chain of causal events, but as a break from a prior chain it can nevertheless form the first link in a new causal chain. But what of the ultimate beginning? Is there not a major difference, at least from a theological perspective, between the Hebrew and Roman foundation legends, in that the former, unlike the latter, points back to the, as it were, original "In the beginning?" The beginning, that is, not of the Roman Republic or the People of Israel or the United States of America, but of the cosmos and time, that is the "absolute beginning" that Abrahamic monotheism demands and the classical tradition rejects? As Arendt (LOTM2: 208) says in concluding this consideration of the Roman and Hebrew origins of political freedom as enacted in liberal modernity: "The thought of an absolute beginning—a *creatio ex nihilo*—abolishes the sequence of temporality no less than does the thought of an absolute end, now rightly referred to as 'thinking the unthinkable.'" With this thought, we are confronted with the greatest self-contradiction of all: that of *absolute* contingency; not the contingency of what we will enact should we succeed but which could just as easily have never existed, but rather the contingency of the world as such, the conditionless condition of the possibility not of this or that sphere of plurality but of any at all.

This absolute contingency—the abyss of freedom—can be confronted, if it can at all, only by throwing off the disrepute into which the invisible and intangible has fallen and directly confronting the deepest of the three undecidable paralogisms at work here: that of reason and faith, of secularism and theocracy, of state and church. We turn to that now.

Antinomy 3: secular reason and theocratic faith

Provided that (1) some political authority or another guarantees consent from its subjects according to a non-rational but nevertheless legitimating process, and (2) the foundation myth whence such authority derives achieves salience within that consenting political entity, the first two impasses for liberalism as a political theology can be imagined to have been resolved. But what of the third—and greatest: the duel between the claim of reason and the demand of faith over the abyss of freedom?

Arendt (LOTM2: 208) begins with "the Hebrew solution for this perplexity," which "assumes a Creator-God who creates time along with the universe and who as legislator remains outside His creation, and outside of time as the One 'who is who he is . . . from eternity to eternity," and goes on to note that this picture provides one possible escape from the abyss, for: "[t]o the extent that the universe and everything in it can be traced back to the region of this absolute One-ness, the One-ness is rooted in something may be beyond the reasoning of temporal men but still possesses a kind of rationale of its own: it can *explain*, give a logical account of, the existentially inexplicable." Put more plainly, the solution is that any event, even an event that breaks the causal logic underlying the chain of events than makes each event an event, can be explained through an appeal to the Creator-God as both the ultimate One and the author of all subsidiary One-ness, including that of the event we are required to explain. (That event being, in this case, the act of founding of the political entity in question.)

Listing the examples of Locke, Jefferson, Adams, and Robespierre, Arendt (LOTM2: 208) suggests that it is precisely this capacity to explain the inexplicable that brings "men who were much too 'enlightened' to still believe in the Hebrew-Christian Creator-God" to turn "with rare unanimity to pseudo-religious language when they had to deal with the problem of foundation as the beginning of a 'new order of the ages.'" Indeed, it is quite remarkable to see Adams and Robespierre placed in fundamental agreement on anything whatsoever; it is also absolutely necessary to do so, if we are to understand liberalism as a political theology. Of particular importance is the way in which the founders of the new order of ages appeal to the "immortal legislator" (Robespierre) or "great legislator of the Universe" (Adams) actually function—as in medieval "mysteries of state" analyzed by Kantorowicz, it is by analogy. There is much more to say in order to make sufficiently clear *how* the immortal legislator is underwriting the revolutions for their practitioners, and we will unpack that in Chapter 4; for now, it suffices to see that for both Adams and Robespierre, there needs be this sort of underwriting.

In the case of Adams and Robespierre, who—quite remarkably given their crucial and myriad differences for Arendt and in fact—can be taken as two instances of the same type for present purposes, Arendt (LOTM2: 208–9) summarizes, the analogy runs thus: "just as God 'in the beginning created the heavens and the earth,' remaining outside His Creation and prior to it, so the human legislator . . . creates the condition for all future political life and historical development." This makes for a neat analogy and the parallelism is not without appeal. Yet Arendt (LOTM2: 210) immediately adds that these attempts to ground the modern republic on the foundation myth of the Hebrews proved to be both "a short-lived effort on the part of secular government to retain not the Hebrew-Christian faith but political instruments of rule that had been so very effective at protecting medieval communities against criminality." However sincere or insincere the appeal to the medieval political theological framework may have been, however confident Adams or Robespierre might have been in the ultimate cause as a universal legislator who (alone) could secure the consent of the political community to be ruled by a new order *on analogy not to the old political order, but on direct analogy to the Creator-God's rule of the universe*, that road quickly became a dead-end.

What, then, were the founders of liberalism as a political theology to do? Arendt (LOTM2: 210) encapsulates their method thus: "Wherever men of action, driven by the very momentum of the liberation process, began to prepare in earnest for an entirely new beginning, the *novus ordo seclorum*, instead of turning to the Bible ('In the beginning God created the heavens and the earth'), they ransacked the archives of Roman antiquity for 'ancient prudence' to guide them in the establishment of a Republic." What is of vital importance for this recapitulation of Arendt's argument about the authority of the Hebrew and Roman foundation legends is that whether or not it turns out to be the case that the influence of the Roman is more telling and momentous for the path that liberalism as a political theology came to take, this *emphatically does not entail* that there is something secular about the modern republic itself, or the vision of its founding that the "men of action" behind the revolutions performed into being.

A clear indication of this can be seen in the emphasis Arendt (LOTM2: 211–12) places on how important it was for the modern founders that "even the foundation of Rome, as the Romans themselves had understood it, was not an absolutely new beginning," but was rather the "re-establishment of a city-state that had preceded Rome," and specifically that was being renewed in Virgil's "*Magnus ab integro saeclorum nascitur ordo*" was the "ages of gold in Latium over the fields that once were the realm of Saturn." In this we see the political theological, in the reformed Arendtian sense articulated here, *par excellence*. Arendt's political theology is neither the medieval Christian version of the rule of Christ on earth through the king (a la Kantorowicz), nor a putatively secularized reformulation of that format (as Schimitt would have it); rather, it entails the establishment of political authority through the acceptance of a foundation myth that secures the consent of those to be ruled to the constitutional order under which they are to be ruled and which is imbued with content from an old religious order, supposedly irretrievably lost through the ages, that informs the present, modern (re-)founding.

This Roman residue then, according to Arendt, is the more abiding of the two foundation legends to which we turned to try to understand the nature of the political authority upon which the consent of the governed under liberal democratic conditions rests. All the same, this discovery (if such it is, and it can be argued, against Arendt, that there are good reasons not to be so sure) does not reveal the reward for which we began our search within the faculty of willing for which the faculty of thinking had nothing to offer because of its inwardness; that is, a notion of freedom as power. We failed, Arendt (LOTM2: 216) writes with some regret, herself calling the conclusion "frustrating," because the "abyss of pure spontaneity, which in the foundation legends is bridged by the hiatus between liberation and the constitution of freedom, was covered by the device, typical of the Occidental tradition . . . of understanding the *new* as an improved re-statement of the old."

This "covering-up" can be abided in terms of the antinomies of freedom and law and natality and tradition through the device of the Creator as that which explains. But the fundamental fissure cannot be healed: there is no device to mediate the claim of reason on freedom's behalf and the demand of faith in that which could secure that freedom. Thus, Arendt (LOTM2: 216) argues, returning to her old feud with Marx: "In its original integrity, freedom survived in political theory . . . only in utopian and unfounded promises of a final 'realm of freedom' that, in its Marxian version at any rate, would indeed spell 'the end of all things,' a sempiternal peace in which all specifically human activities would wither away." In other words, at the end of our tradition of political thought, announced definitely by Marx, we find that the only thinkable "founded freedom" is one in which the very act of foundation would spell the doom of the actors who would be the agents of its founding.

While principally responding to a different text by Arendt, the often maligned "Reflections on Little Rock," Ainsley LeSure (2021: 5) points to the same self-undoing that is a perennial inborn danger for constitutional democracies, whenever they understand themselves as stewards of either an unfounded, hence groundless, political freedom *or* as legitimated through one certain founding in the historical past; for Arendt, she argues, democratic institutions "cannot just be static entities that grant and protect rights" for such an understanding of liberal politics "is too susceptible to racial common sense." We will return to the particular problem of *racial* common sense and what it means for the possibility of a democratic people beyond the logic of exclusion in Chapter 5. For the moment, the crucial point here is that, as is often the case, Arendt leaves us in the closing moments of *Willing* (LOTM2: 217) with an impasse: "This impasse, if such it is, cannot be opened or solved except by appeal to another mental faculty, no less mysterious than the faculty of beginning, the faculty of Judgment, an analysis of which at least may tell us what is involved in our pleasures or displeasures." With these words, the second of the intended three parts of *The Life of the Mind* ends, and Arendt died less than a week after finishing this second part, and thus never wrote what was meant to come next. In the conclusion of this chapter, I offer an account of what I believe—irrespective of Arendt's plan but perhaps (who knows?) aligning with what she intended—follows as a consequence of the concluding chapter of *Willing*. For the moment, I want to conclude this chapter by indicating why the version of freedom's synonymity with power in and as the groundless ground of politics offered here at the conclusion of volume 2 of *The Life of the Mind* does better and goes further than the discussion of foundations in *On Revolution*. And perhaps, might even be preferable to, or more of a resource for contemporary democratic theory and practice than, the democratic theory of judgment that has been definitively described by Linda Zerilli (2016), which Arendt meant to derive from her idiosyncratic reading of Kant on judgment in that planned third volume, about which we have all learned so much from Ronald Beiner (1982).

Conclusion: Arendtian Political Theology as Neither Secular nor Theocratic

Much of the argument concerning the three impasses that torment attempts to yoke founding and freedom as two foundational, yet contradictory, sources of democratic legitimacy we have just traced through the final chapter of *Willing* appears in much the same form—in some cases, at the phrase- and sentence-level, in precisely the same form—as large portions of what had earlier appeared as Chapter 5 of *On Revolution*. Yet my argument here is that we find in *Willing*, and not in *On Revolution*, Arendt's most successful, if still incomplete and in any case not entirely successful, attempt to resolve one of the central dilemmas of "Weimar syndrome" (analyzed in Chapter 1), which we have diagnosed as the problem of distributed sovereignty as a feature of democratic peoplehood (discussed in Chapter 2). In what, then, can we see the superiority of Arendt's analysis of the three antinomies in the concluding chapter of *Willing*, such that the account here is indeed her best response to the foundational concerns about the self-constitution and self-rule of people that crystallize in her work as a response to the worries of her Weimar generation as framed, principally, by Max Weber? To see this, let us recapture, in brief form, the central argument of the relevant chapter of *On Revolution*, the work to which Arendt's readers usually turn when looking for her view of democratic foundations and the question of popular sovereignty.

For Arendt in *On Revolution*, it is the inevitable failure of the value judgments required for the truth of claims such as "all men are created equal" to carry the degree of infallible self-evidence as do "mathematical 'laws'" which brings Arendt (OR: 193) herself to place the "laws" of "mathematical laws" in scare-quotes of her own, showing that mathematical verities are not laws at all for the reason that laws are inescapably *less* rather than more certain than mathematical regularities. It is also the basis of Arendt's (OR: 193) judgment that such "self-evident truths" as the one Jefferson insists upon "possess a power to compel which is as irresistible as despotic power, they are not held by us but we are held by them; they stand in no need of agreement." A founding such as Jefferson's, or the one for which he wishes, then is *not* the solution to the problem of democratic founding for which Arendt is striving; it actually reintroduces, at the very heart of the democratic polity, the very despotic necessity that democratic revolution is meant to be replacing. As Bernal (2017: 4) rightly notes, drawing upon this same section of *On Revolution*, such political foundationalism "projects the founding event as the anchor of a foundationalist authority and legitimacy that is absolutist, beyond question."

How then, according to Arendt, might we arrive at an understanding of democratic founding as truly a project of freedom? As something ongoing and revisable? Paraphrasing and extending the analysis Arendt offers in the chapter of *On Revolution* just discussed, Bernal (2017) identifies three central concerns that haunt standard notions of democratic founding as *authorized* that she understands Arendt as trying to resist and move beyond in *On Revolution*. First, is the "*problem of original authority*," where Arendt demands to know what makes a "particular event as a 'founding' and point of origin," and what "supports present-day interpretations of the original meaning of the constitutional text," and in this way grants "superlative status granted to political and legal origins and the legitimacy of this status in a constitutional democracy"

(Bernal 2017: 14). Second, is the "*problem of the lawgiver and the people*," by which Bernal means tensions and contradictions inherent in "the interrelation between leaders and constituent publics" of precisely the kind highlighted at the outset of this chapter; as a practical matter, these questions surround whatever it is that that can serve as the right by which "a lawgiver can legislate and introduce such innovation' and most specifically the of where their "authority to constitute come[s] from" and "the unstable and uneasy relationship between founders and constituent publics" (Bernal 2017: 14–15).

Finally, and most stubbornly, as Bernal (2017: 15) rightly notes, there is "the *problem of democratic self-constitution*," which demands to know the source of "the people's legitimate authority as it manifests itself in real-world contexts of founding and refounding by connecting the theoretical problem of democratic founding with its political recasting"; crucially, this problem is where democratic theory meets democratic practice, revealing the contradictions in "asserting foundational claims in the name of the 'people,' with constructing the people's constituent power, and in reckoning with the persistence of exclusion long after an original founding event." In Bernal's capacious summary and defense of Arendt's view as we encounter it in *On Revolution*, we see much of what this chapter has discussed as the first two antinomies of liberalism as a political theology, that of freedom and law and of natality and tradition: the question of the groundless ground; the tension about the persistence of tradition after the introduction of the breach that separates modern political life from classical and biblical sources; most importantly, perhaps, the persistence of exclusion, specifically from a democratic future, on the basis of the past.

In the next chapter, which addresses the ways in which Arendt tries to resolve the problems of the liberal and putatively secular order that Bernal captures here, we will return to the details of chapters 4 and 5 of *On Revolution* as a starting point for Arendt's attempt to work out the problem of how to replace monarchical executive sovereignty with a government of, by and for the people: the problem of a distributed democratic sovereignty that can resist the impulse of popular, or populist, rule in the form of a strong and single executive. For now, however, let us note what—in its concluding paragraphs—Arendt's return to Virgil's *novus ordo saeclorum* in *Willing* possesses that its precursor in *On Revolution* lacks. What the former has and the latter lacks, most bluntly, is the literally epochal influence of Augustine. Arendt (OR: 217) actually notes the *necessary* absence of Augustine in the Augustinian influence in her account of the place of the *principium* as both the beginning and principle or rule in the American Revolution: he is missing there, because there she is telling the story of the American Revolution as the revolutionaries themselves were telling it, and they themselves arrived at their notion of a revolution born of mutual promises "certainly without any knowledge of Augustine and probably without any conscious notion of Plato." In other words, our conversation concerning what

Arendt has to teach us about freedom and foundation in modern democracies is looking largely to the wrong place; what Arendt most wants to say, I believe, is outside the bounds of her hermeneutic in *On Revolution* insofar as the latter remains with the horizon of classical liberal politics which is stuck in hopeless repetition of the three antinomies Arendt discusses and attempts to dissolve in *The Life of the Mind*.

And what, precisely, is it that she knows that the American revolutionaries did not? In the closing two paragraphs of *Willing*, Arendt (LOTM2: 216) speaks of "the only one alternative in our entire history of political thought" to the "frustrating conclusion" summarized in our discussion of the third antinomy just above; namely, Augustine's *City of God* in which "the only philosopher the Romans ever had" offered "what could have become a truly Roman or Virgilian philosophy of politics." Arendt (LOTM2: 216–17) argues that the cornerstone of this politics is temporality itself as a condition for the freedom to which created humankind is doomed "as a temporal creature, *homo temporalis*," as "time and man were created together" and for a specific purpose. As we know from her quotations of this line at critical junctures in *Origins*, *The Human Condition*, and *Eichmann*, and in other places too (discussed in Chapter 1 of this work in conversation with Stephen Kampowski's fine book on Arendt's reception of Augustine), Arendt (LOTM2: 217, quoting *City of God*, Bk XII: 20[4]) reminds us all the same: "The purpose of the creation of man" for Augustine, but crucially *not only for Augustine*, "was to make possible a beginning. 'That there be a beginning man was created, before whom nobody was.' The very capacity for beginning is rooted in *natality*, and by no means in creativity, not in a gift but in the fact that human beings, new men, again and again appear in the world."

We have encountered this idea of Augustine's—that each human being is a new beginning; not of *their* life, or their story, but of the world-in-common as an endless possibility, perhaps never to be actualized but nonetheless never extinguished either—before in this book, and we will encounter it again, and again. It is the last word of *Origins* and it is one of the first words of *The Human Condition*; it pops up in almost any text and context for Arendt. Why? As we noted in the conclusion of our discussion of the three impasses above, the chapter of *Willing* we discuss here ends in impasse, with a promise for a discussion of judgment that is—fittingly enough—forever delayed by Arendt's own death. Rather, it is in the sentence just before that conclusion of the chapter

[4] As Kampowski (2008: 50, 258 n.109) discusses, Arendt's numbering is consistently off by one from the standard numbering. His work on that page and in the surrounding two sections makes clear that this does not indicate that Arendt is misquoting or misattributing when quoting this chapter of *City of God*, here in *Life of the Mind*, or in *The Human Condition* or in other places where this chapter is discussed more briefly.

where Arendt (LOTM2: 217) makes clearest, once for all, what Augustine's legacy means for her, and for our (increasingly) lost tradition: "I am quite aware that the argument even in the Augustinian version is somehow opaque, that it seems to tell us no more than that we are *doomed* to be free by virtue of being born, no matter whether we like the freedom or abhor its arbitrariness, are 'pleased' with it or prefer to escape its awesome responsibility by electing some form of fatalism." In a provisional discussion of this sentence in a section of the Introduction devoted to showing that Arendt's Augustine is plausible, notwithstanding Mathewes' (2001: 196) argument that it is "incoherent" and a "failure," I argued that even as we must regret that *Judging* was never written, it is worthwhile to accept her return to Augustine's freedom as her last word. For even if it was Kant's "democratic theory of judgment" that was to be the hero of volume 3 of *The Life of the Mind*, it is Augustine who provides the ultimate rationale and the groundless ground of that iterative and unending practice. I want here, in concluding this account of Arendt's most considered attempt to resolve the three aporias of liberalism as a political theology, to argue why it is that we cannot look to Kant or any other "secular" Kantian: we must look, that is, to Augustine.

4

CONSTITUTING AND CONSTITUTED POWER: THE ANTINOMY OF THEOCRATIC FAITH AND SECULAR REASON IN *ON REVOLUTION*

The chapter grows out of the account of the first two of the three antimonies we confront in examining the contingent foundations of secular republicanism in Chapters 2 and 3: that between freedom and law, focused on the impossibility of deciding between the status of human beings as creatures of nature bound by nature's constant regularities; and that between natality and tradition, emanating from the deep sense of newness in the republican state making of the early modern period. This sits in awkward tension with the fact that these republics sought to legitimize themselves through appeals to classical antiquity; Arendt's focus on the "Novus Ordo Saeclorum" that became a motto of the early American republic neatly demonstrating both features. These antinomies themselves are an expression of a deeper tension, which could be called secular republicanism's permanent crisis of legitimation, as classically diagnosed by Jürgen Habermas (2015 [1976]) in the wake of Max Weber's theory of secular modernity and rationalization. As such, I want here to show how the third antinomy—between secular reason and theocratic faith as ungrounded grounds for a government "of the people, by the people, and for the people"—serves as both the *arhke* (beginning, rule, source, principle) and the unreachable *telos* (end, goal, purpose) for each of the earlier antinomies.

I will make my case through a reading of Arendt's reflections on "power" as both constituting and constituted in *On Revolution*. Arendt's perspective on power, as we have seen, differs radically from the usual senses of "power-for" (the enhancement of capacity via the act of authoritative delegation) and "power-over" (control and even domination). These senses of power, and the interpretation of power as constituted and constituting they imply, have been dominant in political thought since Weber, as discussed in Chapter 1. Disentangling the manner in which Arendt's sense of power, freedom, and action (understood as acting in concert) reinforce one another requires that we return to how she reconstructs the relationship of constituting and constituted power in the specific case of the American Revolution in *On Revolution* and why that account has shortcomings she attempts to address in returning to these issues in *Willing*, as discussed above in Chapter 3. In particular, this chapter explores how the representation of delegation in contemporary democratic societies comes to terms with the way in which the power of the executive is both growing exponentially and caught in a crisis concerning its legitimacy, which must be salient to the electorate that understands the executive as the delegate of a sovereign people, in much the same way that the natural body of the king was once understood as the second, physical embodiment of the divine sovereign who was the king's first, and sempiternal, body.

The chapter proceeds in three parts. The first examines Arendt's account of constituting and constituted powers in her analysis of the early American republic and its founding generation, finding that her appreciation of this historical formation is an expression of the unique resolution of the first two antinomies of liberal political theology she finds there. The second section discusses what Arendt misses about the early American republic, focusing on her all-too-limited discussion of slavery and her conscious silence about genocide of indigenous Americans. Both the promises and shortcomings of her analysis of the American republic's others bring us, in the closing section, to a comparison of Arendt and Schmitt as responses to Weber's fatalist and self-consciously irreligious account of democratic legitimation and why Arendt's rejoinder to Weber—what we can call her political theology—is the more compelling one.

Arendt on Constituting and Constituted Powers in the American Revolution

The scholarly conversation on Arendt's position on constituting and constituted powers primarily focuses on chapter 4 of *On Revolution*, *Constitutio Liberalis*, and with good reason: this is where Arendt offers her reading of the unique constitutionalism of the early American republic and what it still has to teach us. Lucia Rubinelli (2020) has recently discussed Arendt as key figure, in particular focusing on her response to the French Revolution. Her account builds on what Andrew Arato (2017) argues concerning Arendt's reading of American constitutionalism as essential for understanding the interplay of, and tension between, constituting and constituted powers. For both Rubinelli and Arato, Arendt (OR: 183) provides a unique lens on how eighteenth-century revolutionaries and republicans attempted "to find a form of government which puts the law above man." In this way, Arendt—on Arato's reading—is trying to rescue the notion of constituent power ("all power to the people") from its connection to what Arato (2017: 1) calls "a unitary, embodied popular sovereignty." As Rubinelli (2020: 5) argues following Arato (2017: 31–35), this yoking of constituent power to a single and embodied sovereign power is the hallmark of "sovereign constituent power" and "is problematic on many levels" but chiefly because to believe in it is to "fall prey to an ideological construct, which portrays constituent power as the normless, unlimited and unified source of all constitutions." This is so, for Arato, because of the paradox the people that make the constitution is in fact only constituted by the act of making a constitution: thus, to accept that this is a genuine paradox is ultimately an ideological construct. Here, for reasons that will emerge in our reading of the key fourth and fifth chapters of *On Revolution* in conversation with the interpretation offered by Paul Kottman (2012) just below, Arato presses Arendt's analysis into a condemnation of popular sovereignty that is not really hers, as she herself does see this problem (or paradox, or as I suggested in Chapter 3 above, this antinomy of freedom and law) as genuine.

For the moment, let us follow Arato's line of reasoning, suspending for the moment the question of whether or not it is Arendt's view. Arato, as Rubinelli (2020: 5–6) aptly relates, proposes a reading of Arendt as a constitutionalist in order to avoid this paradox, one that he describes as "post-sovereign constitution-making," the traces of which "can be found in the political practices of the English, French and American Revolutions, as well as in the political thought of Sieyès, some nineteenth-century French theorists of the state and Arendt." Arato's idea, as Rubinelli (2020: 6–7) succinctly relates, is that this notion of constituent power "escapes the paradox of constitutionalism while offering a truly democratic theory of legitimate constitution-making" because "it reveals the democratic essence of popular sovereignty and points at how it should be institutionalised in day-to-day political practices of popular participation inside the constitutional state. This view of Arendt as a constitutionalist who seeks to banish sovereignty is very influential, as evidenced by recent publications on constituent power.[1]

Yet, as Rubinelli (2020: 7) notes, for Arato no less than for Schmitt and the other democratic sovereigntists, it remains the case that "constituent power is defined in terms of sovereignty, and sovereignty in terms of constituent power," with the result that "the two ideas are seemingly equivalent." Rubinelli is correct about this and in effect is saying that what Arendt recognized as the genuine antimony of freedom and law pervades Arato's "post-sovereign constitution-making" no less than it does "sovereign constituent power" of the Schmittian

[1] For instance, Arvidsson, Brännström, and Minkkinen (2020), especially the editors' introduction and the chapters by Zakin and Lukkari.

persuasion. (Though, surely, without nearly so much ideological distortion.) In order to understand what is both deeply promising and deeply problematic about "founded freedom" for Arendt, we need to return to the interpretive moment with which we concluded the previous chapter and which is largely absent from the recent discussions of Arendt as a constitutional theorist. Namely: the aporetic tension between freedom and founding and how this haunts secular, modern, democratic politics as a theological residue of early modernity that emanates from the republican response, chiefly in Machiavelli and Montesquieu, to the Hebrew and Roman foundation legends with which Arendt concerned herself intensely in both chapter 5 of *On Revolution* and volume 2 of *The Life of the Mind*. While Arato turns to Siéyes, I am suggesting that we focus on Augustine, whose ideas in this connection are both promising, given his formative influence on her ideas of natality, new beginnings, and the world full of danger, given the millennialism that is not hard to derive from his "two cities" political theology.

As Paul Kottman (2012: 146) has noted, "the relationship in Arendt's analysis between freedom and foundation appears aporetic," pointing to the fact that in "*The Life of the Mind*, Arendt herself speaks of the "abyss of freedom and the *novus ordo seclorum*." Kottman, however, does not engage the details of that chapter in his account, following only *On Revolution* and what Arendt says there as a form of storytelling focused on the concrete circumstances of the American and French revolutions as attempts at political reformation: one more or less successful in her mind, the other an absolute failure. In this section, following Kottman but also dissenting on the key question of the degree to which, for Arendt or as such, the revolutionary tradition is in fact secular, I aim to reorient the analysis of Arendt on the question of founding and founded freedom in *On Revolution* as an expression of Arendt's response to what I am calling the antinomy of secular reason and theocratic faith. I will then point to how the findings of the previous chapter, which engages the material from *Willing* to which Kottman alludes here, ramifies this understanding of freedom and founding as two moments of democratic delegation that remain in permanent tension.

Arendt addresses this constellation of issues most directly not in chapter 4 of *On Revolution*, where we find her detailed discussion of constitutional order and freedom, but in chapter 5, titled "Foundation II: *Novus Ordo Saeclorum*," referring to the same phrase that serves as the focus of the final chapter of *Willing* discussed just above in Chapter 3. Here, Arendt (OR: 204) notes, in words very much like those used in *Willing*, "The very fact that the men of the American Revolution thought of themselves as 'founders' indicates the extent to which they must have known that it would be the act of foundation itself, rather than an Immortal Legislator or self-evident truth or any other transcendent, transmundane source, which eventually would become the fountain of authority in the new body politic." For Arendt, it is the act of foundation itself that serves as the source both American Revolution and the republic to which it gives birth and the legitimacy of this revolution and this republic. How is it possible for Arendt to assimilate the founders into a single collective with a single ultimate ground which is the act of founding itself, without ultimate warrant from either the "Hebrew-Christian tradition" or "ancient prudence" as she puts the two putative sources of historical and metaphysical legitimation to which the revolutionaries and later founders did in fact refer? Arendt (OR: 203) makes clear that her presentation of the constitution of the republic as a process and the constitution as a document and ruling order in which it terminates follows from the influential argumentation of Thomas Paine, who understood by constitution *not* what we "usually mean by it," namely, "the Constitution as a written document," but rather, "the constituting act, 'antecedent to government,' by which a people constitutes itself into a body politic."

This means that Paine's rationalist-religious, and later robustly secular, understanding of the revolutionary program simply carries the day in her analysis. For Arendt (OR: 204), Paine brings to awareness something that "in a way" has "always been known, though it was never fully articulated in conceptual thought" for the simple reason that "the beginning itself, prior to the era of revolution, has always been shrouded in mystery and remained an object of speculation." The time has come, for Paine and his ilk and—it would seem, for us following Arendt (OR: 204)—to recognize the "foundation which now, for the first time, had occurred in broad daylight to be witnessed by all who were present had been, for thousands of years, the object of foundation legends in which imagination tried to reach out into a past and to an event which memory could not reach." In this way, Arendt (OR: 204) concludes, the sheer act of founding becomes its own ungrounded ground: while the old foundation legends of the Hebrews and the Romans "attempted to solve the problem of the beginning, of an unconnected, new event breaking into the continuous sequence of historical time," the American founders resolve this impasse but casting the constitution not as that which is accomplished after the act of founding, nor as that which had been before and now is renewed or fulfilled, but as a self-generative act of beginning.

It is this understanding of the American Revolution that underpins what Kottman (2012: 143) quotes from Arendt as the epigraph of his chapter: "It may ultimately turn out that what we call revolution is precisely that transitory phase which brings about the birth of a new, secular realm." I would just stress, before turning to a reading of a key section of "Novus Ordo Saeclorum" in order to suggest a different reading of the (putatively) secular turn in the revolutionary tradition, that this claim with which Kottman begins reads that "it may ultimately turn out" that revolution is about the birth of the secular; I believe that Arendt pushes this suggestion quite far in her analysis but ultimately resists, if not rejects, the view that the revolutionaries were secular in this way. For Kottman (2012: 145), Arendt's "reflections on revolution thus unfold as the hard-won knowledge that a fully secular politics has no other content than the experience of such new beginnings out of our own past miseries, calamities, and failings." This reading stresses the conclusion Arendt (OR: 206) draws that "however carefully [the founders] may have followed Harrington's advice to 'ransack the archives of ancient prudence'—and no one spent more time in this business than John Adams—with respect to their main business, the constitution of some entirely new, unconnected body politic, these archives must have remained strangely silent." The point, and here I completely agree with Kottman, is that since there is no revolution absent the confrontation with the failures of the past purported revolutions, past experiences of attempting to resolve the antinomies of freedom and law and of natality and tradition, we cannot actually look to the past for a model of how to successfully resolve the aporetic tensions.

But neither can we look to the future for the security of freedom and natality as political values. This means that the only possible authorization to which founding and founders can appeal in acts of mutual promising in the present. To demonstrate this Arendt turns to a most unlikely source: the Mayflower Compact. As Kottman (2012: 148; quoting OR: 173) notes, "the English Puritans—in whom the "eagerness for experimentation, and the concomitant conviction of absolute novelty, of a *novus ordo saeclorum*, was conspicuously absent"—to have been the last people to act as revolutionaries; yet revolutionaries they were, and ardent ones, because (Arendt argues) they "'turned their minds to the matter long and intensely enough to discover, almost by inadvertence, the elementary grammar of political action': promising." For Arendt, as Kottman ably shows, it is the very actual of mutual promising in the present that secures the possibility of power as freedom through the future enactment, in the now-future/later-to-be-present, of the same promise. This, for Kottman's Arendt, is why "revolution is precisely that transitory phase which brings about the birth of a new, secular realm."

It is not lost on Kottman (2012: 148) that the Puritans "were themselves anything but secular"; nevertheless, he argues that in this reading of founding freedom as founded freedom, Arendt is able to "wrest a secular, revolutionary politics from the Puritans" by simply asking "us to think about lived human experience (revolutions, losses, traumas) as authoritative—instead of relying upon theories, doctrines, conceptual traditions, and so forth." In other words, the "may turn out" in Arendt's claim about revolution and the secular in the opening chapter becomes a definitive statement about revolution as secular through Arendt's phenomenological reading of the Mayflower Compact as being about the act of promising itself, rather than the content of the promise as grounded in theological principles. Kottman (2012: 148–49) argues that it is only their coming together in assembly that makes "the actual experience of human beings politically binding and authoritative" and "this very experience—if it is to really 'found' anything at all—must also become authoritative for the future." If it is not merely an event or performance, Kottman (2012: 149) concludes, then "this power needs to become politically *authoritative*"; for, if it is to be anything more than a passing moment, then somehow people—human beings—must themselves become or actualize the 'authority' that they already (potentially) are."

Kottman (2012: 149) regards this secular reading of the anything-but-secular Puritan form of mutual promise, stripped of its Israelite covenantal trappings, as an "achievement of such a political humanism, or secular politics," which, though it "may of course sound simple enough," actually "turns out to be the most intractable difficulty faced by the revolutionary tradition, by the secular ambition of the modern age." In so speaking he deftly announces what I claim to be the third and greatest of the three antinomies of liberal political theology analyzed by Arendt in *The Life of the Mind* and *On Revolution*. But whereas Kottman sees Arendt as offering a version of the American Revolution in which the antinomy is resolved through a secularization of Puritan promise-making, I hold that Arendt's view, especially as elaborated later in *Willing* tends the opposite way. I aim here to offer a reading of the chapters on constitutionalism and the secular age (*On Revolution*, chapters 4 and 5) that is more consistent with how Kottman (2012: 153) reads the title of the final chapter of *On Revolution*, "The Revolutionary Tradition and its Lost Treasure" than is his own reading of Arendt on secularization. Kottman (2012: 153), rightly, argues that "the 'loss of tradition' to which Arendt repeatedly refers does not merely indicate, as so many of her interpreters suggest, our separation from an irretrievable, ancient tradition for which we can only be nostalgic. Rather, the point is "*to recognize 'loss of tradition' as formative for whatever 'tradition' means in modernity*." The loss is double: it is not simply the gap or chasm that separates us from the past; it is also the gap or chasm that separates us from a *secure* future. To be modern, then, is to live in the gap itself, as Arendt argues in her opening to the essays collected in *Between Past and Future*.

This brings us back to the first two antinomies of liberal political theology, as I called them in the preceding chapter, following how Arendt diagnoses them in *Willing*. For Kottman (2012: 152), this aporetic faultline in Arendt's thinking manifests in two questions that bring together the antinomy of freedom and law with that of natality and tradition: "why does Arendt see in the *American* Revolution (and not, after all, in Rome or in Machiavelli or in the French revolutionaries) the crux and burden of the entire tradition of revolutionary spirit? . . . Why should the *novus ordo saeclorum* also presage the loss of revolutionary tradition, the loss of its 'treasure'?" If we follow Kottman (2012: 152), we ground our response to this question in an interpretation of Arendt where "the content of revolutionary spirit" is essentially the same as "the secular truth of its tradition," meaning that both the revolutionary spirit and the loss of its treasure are both to be found in the American founding. This is the meaning, Kottman believes, of Arendt's (OR: 212) claim that: "What saves the act of beginning from its own arbitrariness is that it carries its own principle within itself, or, to be more precise, that beginning and principle, *principium* and principle, are not only related to each other, but are coeval." On this account, Arendt's understanding of the self-understanding of the revolutionaries-turned-founders holds that the only legitimating force the act of founding has is its success (however partial) in actually founding freedom: there is no other referent in the past or the future to which the revolutionary claim can yoke itself.

This is how Kottman responds to Samuel Moyn (2008: 76) who reads *On Revolution* as arguing that "politics must have continuing recourse to an absolute of the kind that metaphysics in the form of religion provided far more plausibly and efficaciously than revolution could easily succeed in doing," and that it "is as if Arendt thought that it was easier for religion to fulfill its necessary secular functions than a fully secularist regime could by itself." Like Kottman (2012: 156 n.13), I find Moyn's claims "puzzling and wrong," specifically insofar as Moyn (2008: 75) argues that Arendt is defending a secularism where: "Secularization is precisely the attempt not to escape from the authority and the sanction with which the absolute provides politics but to find nonreligious versions of them." Here Kottman is right to object, and object most strenuously: Arendt is absolutely not making the argument about the slippery re-emergence of the absolute in the liberalism that Moyn holds her to have adopted from Heidegger and Heidegger's Nietzsche. Were Arendt's claims about the inability of the founders to purge their practice of founding freedom of all its metaphysics trapping truly to be in the service of an unmasking operation, what Ricoeur has called a "hermeneutics of suspicion," then Moyn would be right to assert that she, like Heidegger, sees liberalism as a politics of authority no less than the absolutist regimes it claims to oppose. Moyn (2023a) levels this charge still more robustly in his widely discussed reading of "Hannah Arendt among the Cold War liberals." But, as Kottman argues, Moyn was not right about that in 2008 and is not right in his more unambiguous charges against Arendt in his more recent work.

Yet Moyn *is* right that authority remains an important political keyword for Arendt. While she seems to consider it completely anathema in *On Revolution* (1963), and largely avoided it in *The Human Condition* (1958), it is nevertheless central to her reading of modernity and democratic politics, as is clear from "What is Authority?" (1954) and from *On Violence* (1969/70). The particular constitutive role that authority plays in a republic according to Arendt is not a matter one can easily find clarity about; determining what role it ought to play is even more ambiguous, as we shall see in the detailed discussion of authority in *On Violence* in the next chapter. For the moment, I want only to flag that while Kottman is, so to say, absolutely right to reject as Arendt's the openly paradoxical position on secularism and absolute authority that Moyn attributes to her, I do not believe that his own more properly secular reading of *On Revolution* can hold, either. For this reason, I propose a different, and perhaps differently unsatisfying, rejoinder to Moyn's approach, one grounded in a critique of the historiography of the American founding in *On Revolution* that hopes to "save" the central claim about founding/founded freedom in the key chapters of that text from its own ahistorical presentation of the American founding as self-consciously a break from the past. This is the task of the next section, devoted to unpacking (at last) the third antinomy of liberal political theology through an analysis of what Arendt misses, or perhaps consciously misrepresents, about the early American republic.

Arendt's secularization of the American founding, at least if read through Kottman's keen retelling of her approach to the Mayflower Compact and its function as a model version of promise-making and -keeping for the revolutionaries-turned-founders, is predicated on an understanding Americans of the revolutionary period as perfectionist in a recognizably rationalist way, but quite different from the moral perfectionism of Enlightenment Europe. Arendt (OR: 174–75) makes this clear in argument about the place of moral perfectionism in "American common philosophy" before during and just after the Revolution, in which "American faith was not at all based on a semi-religious trust in human nature, but on the contrary, on the possibility of checking human nature in its singularity by virtue of common bonds and mutual promises." Here we see the key features of the argument about the Puritans as Kottman unpacks it: an acknowledgement that the texts and tropes through which the new community is to be created draw on Biblical and Roman precedents, combined with a refusal to grant the seemingly natural reading of this intertwinement with tradition, in this case the "semi-religious trust in human nature" which others would see in promise-making, but which Arendt argues is not motivating this practice.

Having established, or asserted, this, Arendt (OR: 175) goes on to quite literally place her own principle of plurality (famously articulated in THC: 7) in the figurative mouths of the founders: "The hope for man in his singularity lay in the fact that not man but men inhabit the earth and form a world between them. It is human worldliness that will save men from the pitfalls of human nature." The grammatical insistence on the plural, one of Arendt's great rhetorical flourishes, signals a profound problem for democratic practice and (for that reason) for democratic theory as well: there must be a body politic if there is to be some singular popular authority charged with overseeing and adjudicating the promise-making and -keeping in which democratic freedom consists. But that body does not materially exist: many bodies of the people exist materially, but no single popular body, not even a legislative body, has that material existence in its singularity.

What Arendt Misses about the Early American Republic: The Antinomy of Secular Reason and Theocratic Faith

So how did (or do, or can) the people come to have a second body? The answer has to do with the figure Arendt insists played no role in the American common philosophy of the revolutionary period: Jean-Jacques Rousseau. For this reason, Arendt's nagging issues with replacing sovereignty (men/man) by authority (law) and with replacing theological religious codes by rational, secular principles both reemerge. We know well from the feminist historians of *ancien régime* salons and modern political publics that, in a world where the court, qua "household of the King," was the route to power and the king was the only public person, the pursuit of power, and attempts to construct and complete projects, required the acquisition of influence. This is to say, that the exercise of power in the Paris of the King's Two Bodies required a certain kind of persuasion, charm via aesthetic cultivation. It was just this "sociality" of power that infuriated the Jacobins and Rousseau, their intellectual touchstone. A society wherein the execution of power was linked to fashion was, for them, a horrifyingly corrupt society. This is the core of Landes' insight about the gendered politics of the making of the modern: there is a link, in the revolutionary imagination of the late eighteenth century, between the politics of "the people" and masculinity, for there is an association made between aristocracy, persuasion, and femininity. Landes (1988, 2001) shows quite clearly how resentment of the "powerlessness" of 'the people' in the ancien régime was inextricably bound up, in the revolutionary imagination, with the understanding of "influence" as feminine, seductive, and corrupt.

The enchanted second body of the king is replaced in the transition to modernity with the enchanted bodies of the band of brothers, which is (however hard Arendt tries to resist it) a profoundly Hebrew-Christian image of a theologically-informed republican politics of mutual promising; it is this image which, in liberal political modernity, seeks to provide the frame for doing politics. Transitions to modernity are *not*, in this rendering, transitions from myth to science, from religion to natural law, or from sovereignty to discipline (or sovereignty to government). They are, rather, transitions from one enchanted frame for political action to another, from the enchanted king as container of the body politic to an enchanted "people" that combines many bodies natural with a "body politic" that, as "the people" is an equally mystical entity—the *demos* composed by those who make and keep promises with one another through and in the very act of making and keeping those promises, as indicated by phrases like "the people have spoken." This is the fuller meaning of all power in the people as lived by the Republican revolutionaries-turned-founders.

This new frame—a democratic mysticism—is a quintessential instance of what Talal Asad (1993) influentially analyzed as "exclusionary inclusion."

Working in the sphere of secularization theory, Asad exposed the ways in which the development of comparative religion as an intellectual discipline included non-Christian "religions" precisely as it excluded the practitioners of those other religions from the domain of true religion. In the present context, those excluded by their inclusion are, most starkly, enslaved Blacks and the indigenous peoples who inhabited the American continent prior to colonization, are included in and excluded by the act of democratic founded simultaneously. The manner in which this democratic mysticism instantiates and incorporates itself, quite literally, in the bodies of those who "constitute" the newly founded republic can be seen with vivid and awful clarity in the infamous three-fifth clause of the United States Constitution. In the French context, and as Louis Sala-Molins (2006) argues, we see the same thing when reading the Declaration of the Rights of Man alongside the Code Noir. In both republics, democratic establishment is unthinkable without chattel slavery and colonial rule.

The exclusions from the story are notorious. Though Jean-Baptiste Belley was one of three representatives of Haiti at the Convention, the story of Black delegates in Paris is fraught with exclusion and silencing. Miranda Spieler (2009: 391) details how Black men were not well received at the Jacobin club, and had their demands suppressed by the *Journal de Montaigne*. Joan Landes (1988) makes clear that the Society of Revolutionary Republican Women shared a similar fate in the key "liminal" time between 1791 and Thermidor. These exclusions on the basis of the interpretation of the physical body were, simultaneously, interpretations of non-membership in the mystical, second political "body" that had "experienced" the French Revolution. And so, as the Terror, Thermidor, and royalist counter-revolutionary efforts proceeded, the colonies were repeatedly left as blank spaces on the French imperial map, lands containing bodies who could not be granted rectorship; simultaneously the public politics of the republic was constructed in opposition to the bourgeois domesticity of the "private sphere."

In the early American republic, the doctrine of American exceptionalism came to justify the same attribution of (non-)status to slaves and Indians. Here again, the double body of the band of brothers emerged as a mystical substitute for the King's Two Bodies. On this stage, a new candidate for the embodiment of the people's second body emerged: the violent edge-warrior as himself sovereign. The paradigmatic instance of this figure is Anthony Wayne, the general who successfully led the newly minted American Legions into a decisive victory against the allied Indians of the Ohio River valley in 1794 (inaugurating the push west of the "empire of liberty") and then negotiated the Treaty of Greenville in 1795 on behalf of the federal government and of "the People" of the United States (Knopf 1960; Gaff 2004; Reed 2017).

During the negotiations at Greenville, the gathered rectors of the allied tribes repeatedly posed a sovereign question to Wayne—what did the Great

Father George Washington think? And at a certain point, their most prestigious general—Little Turtle—manifested written promises from George Washington that his people would have hunting and fishing rights north of the Ohio River. These were all recognizable moves in the game of war and diplomacy that dominated the North American continent in the seventeenth and eighteenth centuries—the game of various kings, emperors, and chiefs manifesting their first and second bodies through their actors. But the Americans were playing a different game altogether, and there would be no secure rector–actor ties established between the new American state, as representative of "the people," and the Ohio Indians recently betrayed in battle by their erstwhile patrons, the agents of the British Empire. For Anthony Wayne saw himself as the direct representative of "the American public." When the defeated Indians manifested to Wayne, via a letter promising hunting rights, a small piece of Washington's second body (in a way Kantorowicz would have surely appreciated), they were playing the wrong game at the wrong time and in wrong place. Wayne did not care about letters from Washington, because he himself was the violent, pragmatic, and racist rector of a new band of brothers. He wrote the treaty as the avatar of the people's, not the president-king's, second body.

In the Indian policy of the U.S. government—and in the figures of sovereign edge warriors such as Wayne—we can see that there is a mirror-body to the two bodies of the people—the grotesque, "savage" body of the non-white other who must be eliminated, made dependent, kept in chains, or otherwise subordinated (Robinson 2000). If the King's Two Bodies is what is replaced by what Aziz Rana (2010: 5, 7, 120–31, 129–30) calls the "Two Faces of American Freedom," then we still must ask, how does this new formation work as political theology in Kantorowicz's sense? To understand this, we need to confront the third of the three antinomies of liberal political theology as they emerge in *On Revolution* and *The Life of the Mind*, the one with which Arendt most struggled: that of secular reason as expressed in inclusionary logic of humankind's universal self-emancipation, in its entwinement with the exclusionary logic of theocratic faith as expressed in American exceptionalism, a form of democratic nation-building as an apocalyptic Christian mission.[2]

[2] Also relevant on this point is "Founding Fathers," recently transcribed by Ursala Lutz from Arendt's notes for a 1963 lecture. This short text offers a thumbnail sketch of the arguments of *On Revolution*, chapters 4 and 5 together with ideas presented in other chapters and corroborates my suggestion that we can "reduce" Arendt's central claims in these chapters to a sort of melioration of the natality and the traditionalism in the "founding" rhetoric of revolutionaries. As in my retelling in this section of the present chapter as well as the one preceding, this short text features Thomas Paine as a central figure, the theorist-in-the-moment of differences between the American and French experiments with "revolution," and why that word deserves scare quotes for Arendt. I thank Siobhan Kattago for pointing me to this lecture.

Nothing can help us see this most starkly than coming to terms with the figure of Thomas Paine as influential thinker–actor implicated in both the practice of revolution and its theorization. Thomas Paine, for Arendt among others, represents the model of an eighteenth-century Deist and republican who serves a lynchpin in the secularization of theocratic republicanism. Ruth Bloch (2007: 49), meanwhile, offers a clear and straightforward diagnosis of what the focus on Paine's sense of American constitutionalism in *On Revolution* misses; namely, "some basic religious orientations defining early American Protestantism." Bloch (2007: 49) insists that while "exceptions can be found," there was "enough commonality among revolutionary American Protestants to justify a synthetic interpretation," more precisely "popular support for the American Revolution came overwhelmingly from Congregationalists, Baptists, Presbyterians, and southern lay Anglicans, almost all of whom can be loosely described as Calvinist." Arendt, as seen in our summary of her presentation of the genius of the American founding in *On-Revolution*, stresses the self-awareness of the revolutionaries-turned-founders as initiators, pursuing what Kottman (2012) describes as a secularization of Puritan promise-making as the practice of founded/founding freedom. In this way, the founders' eagerness to relate themselves to both the Hebrew-Christian tradition and Roman prudence, is marginalized in the service of emphasizing their embrace of Arendt's basic political principles, freedom and natality. Bloch (2007: 49), to the contrary, insists that while "the Revolution also enlisted the support of a number of religious rationalists, particularly among the urban elite and the southern gentry, [on] a more popular level, the religious faith of American revolutionaries was in the main Calvinist" and "typically Calvinist preoccupations underlay much of the development of revolutionary ideology." Arendt elides this whole concern, thus largely sidestepping the third and most challenging antinomy of liberalism as a political theology: that of secular reason and theocratic faith, as is clear from looking at the role of the Hebrew covenant and Protestant covenantal practices in the eighteenth century that Arendt is aware of but chooses to sideline.

Attending to the confessional specificity that Arendt ignores matters for reasons that Bloch (1985) established in much greater detail in her earlier monograph *Visionary Republic*. Here, against Arendt and a prevalent historiography of the American Revolution that Arendt shared with experts on the revolution and early American republic, Bloch (1985: xiii–iv) stresses that while the American Revolution "is inconceivable without the constitutional and social theories that developed out of the Renaissance and early Enlightenment," it is also the case that the "conviction that history was drawing to its glorious conclusion, when the world would be transformed into a paradise for righteous, predisposed large numbers of American Protestants to throw themselves behind the revolutionary cause with a fervency." That conviction, Bloch (1985: xi) contends, is grounded in millennialism, an unmistakably theocratic belief that teaches the "idea that human history is divinely ordained and will lead to a period of heavenly perfection on earth" that dates back at least to "the prophecies if Isaiah in the eight century B.C." Let us briefly take up three key manifestations of this joint marginalization of millennialism and overestimation of promise-making as a secular and modern basis for the legitimation of the revolutionary tradition: the critique of tyranny and call for republican rule; the importance of addressing poverty and deprivation (the "social question" as Arendt calls it) as a religious calling; and Thomas Paine's role in connecting the American and French revolutions and then the turn against this yoking after the Terror.

The first instantiation of the correction to the historiography Arendt shares with those historians of the American Revolution and founding of the republic, that marginalizes millennialism as a political force is in the very notion of freedom as an intrinsically secular form of promise-making and -keeping. After quoting from a series of pamphlets published not only in Boston, Philadelphia, and Providence (known for their radicalism), but also in places like Hartford, Connecticut, and Wilmington, Delaware (not known for its radicalism to say the least) in the late 1760s or early 1770s, Bloch (1985: 62) concludes that in the public opinion of the time "the meanings of liberty and grace" were "so interlocked that both religious and secular publications in various parts of the colonies implored Americans in the words of Galatians "to stand fast in the freedom wherewith Christ hath made you free." Indeed, as Bloch (1985: 63) pithily concludes concerning the opposition of liberty and slavery and of republicanism with tyranny being yoked to that of salvation and corruption in the pamphleteering of the early- to mid-1770s: "If religion was politicized, so was politics sacralized. Not only did ministers respond to the imperial crisis by preaching about liberty and tyranny in the language of the radical Whigs, but the very terms 'liberty' and 'tyranny' were deeply infused with religious, even spiritual, meaning." The former clause of that last sentence is where we see the politicization of religion in the revolutionary context: calling on a religious community to take up a particular political cause—this alone calls into question the putative secularism of the legitimation. More serious is the second part of Bloch's conclusion in which we see the very terms of political discourse as themselves imbued with and conveying a specific spiritual content, this presents us the picture of the centrality of millennial tropes and visions to the self-understanding of the political community in formation.

This same marginalization helps us to understand the second of the instances of Bloch's correction, which helps us to see through Arendt's general depiction of the American Revolution as properly about political freedom, while the French came to be focused on social equality of conditions. For Bloch (1985: 83) insists that "liberals' millennial visions also more frequently featured images of thriving agriculture and trade" while evangelical Calvinist millennialists "were geared less towards the expansion of commerce and more towards the provision of gifts from on high," while still others, often Free Baptists, "proclaimed that in the millennium an apparently spontaneous profusion of resources would guarantee that 'No more the labour'r pines and grieves, For want of plenty round.'" The deep connection between all these forms of millennialism and the Hebrew prophets is clear, for "pro-trade" activism of the Congregationalists in big harbor cities like Philadelphia and Boston as much as for the divine dispensation preached by more conservative Calvinists as again for the populist "rabble rousing" of the Free Baptists in the backcountry. It amounts, Bloch (1985: 83) summarizes, to a common "emphasis on the satisfaction of material needs" as an essential aspect of the legitimation of the revolution and the new republic in its wake. In seeing this, we correct Arendt's assertion that the American Revolution was not about the "social question" even as we correct her marginalization of the millennialist, and broadly the theocratic, underpinning of American revolutionary consciousness.

Finally, there is the question of the likeness and unlikeness of the two revolutions themselves, which once again foregrounds the role of Thomas Paine who, as we saw above, is a central figure for Arendt because of his ostensible secularism. Bloch (1985: 151) argues that here, too, as we shift from the comparatively moderate and nationalistic millennialism of the 1760s and 1770s, the "political millennialism of the [1790s] set its sights on the fundamental republican transformation of the entire world and projected an even more universalistic perspective on the future than the earlier revolutionary millennialism." In other words, and contrary to the secularizing tendency that Kottman follows Arendt in seeing in the shift from the Puritans' politics of covenantal politics to a Republican politics of promise-making and keeping, Bloch argues in her chapter on "Francophilic millennialism and partisan Republican ideology" American politics, at least for the Democratic-Republicans as an increasingly coherent partisan formation, were becoming *more* theocratic in the particular sense of the coming of an earthly age of paradise announced by the formation of republics. In this way, and related to the second point concerning material necessity and its presence as an organizing principle in American politics, Bloch (1985: 151) stresses that this 1790s millennialism was "more specifically egalitarian that the millennialism of the American Revolution, often incorporating an emphasis on equal rights similar to the thought of Thomas Paine." Whereas for Arendt Paine's centrality is integral to the emergence of a new secular republicanism, for Bloch, Paine's greater popularity in the early days of the French Revolution and its reception in the United States is at least in part attributable to Paine's *greater* emphasis on what Arendt sees as the "social" value of equality of conditions beyond the common republican cause of "political" equality before the law and his enthusiasm for the French Revolution.

This is no less true, Bloch argues, when American popular opinion turns against the French Revolution after the Terror in light of the constant bloodshed and havoc, domestically and in war with Britain and the rest of Europe. Reflecting on the shift in which the more overtly millennialist interpretation of the French Revolution was associated with advocates of its new order who saw it as a step toward the establishment of divine rule on earth up to the moment that Jacobin hegemony was replaced by the Francophobic millennialism in which the revolution was the work of a false messiah, Bloch (1985: 206) finds that "One index to the fundamental shift in the political mood in the late 1790's was the emergence . . . of a strongly catastrophic apocalyptic perspective on future events," in which "the French Revolution, the rise of infidelity, the false promise of political salvation, and the terrible bloodshed in Europe all seemed obvious signs of expanding satanic power." Here too, as with the earlier enthusiasm for the French Revolution—and just as in the advocacy of the new American republic as a divinely endowed paradise of plenty and the rejection of British rule as divinely ordained assertion of Christian freedom—we see the ways in which overtly theocratic millennialism informed the politics of the late colonial and revolutionary periods. Bloch's insistence on the importance of millennialist thinking, imagery, and values for understanding the mindset of the revolutionaries-turned-founders and its popular reception in the late colonial and early republic periods shows why we need to work "with and against Arendt" on thinking through the antinomy of secular reason and theocratic faith as integral to promise and the perversions of the American republic from pre-revolutionary times through the crises of the Nixon administration, and of course beyond that time horizon where Arendt's thinking ends as her life came to an abrupt end.

Taking this rejoinder on board allows us to correct the way Arendt elides the degree to which the institution of slavery pervaded life in the republic and undermined its claim to the secular prioritization of freedom as the basic principle of democratic legitimation. This is a lesson also emphasized by Niklas Plaetzer (2023) who discusses how Arendt's thinking, in particular in "Civil Disobedience," remains a unique resource for thinking about democratic founding as reconstruction notwithstanding the limitations of her discussion of the American founding in *On Revolution*. Plaetzer (2023: 961, 968–73), discusses the extent to which Arendt relied on Stanley Elkins (1976 [1959]) in her thinking about how the institution of slavery was, indeed, formative for the American experiment, pointing out, following Robert Bernasconi (1996), Richard H. King (2015), and Fred Moten (2018) that much of what Arendt gets wrong has to do with her over-reliance on Elkins' account. Yet the fact that her account of slavery in *On Revolution* was in the end far from adequate as King (2015) has demonstrably shown obscures the ways in which other of her works in the late 1960s and early 1970s addressed this in a more compelling way.

Indeed, as Plaetzer (2023: 968 n.12) writes, while King (2015, 361 n.57) "perceptively emphasizes the influence of Elkins," his claim that "Elkins's book is the only study of American slavery in Arendt's personal library" is incorrect:

she owned a copy of Du Bois' *Black Reconstruction in America*." More important than just the mere point that Arendt possessed more books on the topic of slavery than just the controversial work of Elkins is Plaetzer's (2023: 969) deeper claim that "Contrary to Bernasconi's (1996) criticism that Arendt failed to include the enslavement of Africans as exemplary of 'statelessness' and a 'loss of world,' her admiration for Elkins' *Slavery* seems to indicate that she herself did, in fact, allow for the comparison between modes of dehumanization in twentieth-century totalitarianism and Black slavery in America."

Once we take this correction into mind, we can look again at "Civil Disobedience" (1972), and in particular Arendt's discussion there of how Black actors' "open rebellion" against American institutions appears in a new light. As Plaetzer (2023: 960) says, "Arendt does not just condemn the 'general anti-institutional bias,' which she sees as the 20th century's Black movement's inheritance of 19th century's abolitionism; rather, she urges readers to recognize what she calls the 'simple and frightening fact' that Black and Native American people 'had never been included in the original *consensus universalis* of the American republic' (1972, 90). Indeed, Arendt (1972, 81) believed it was the practice of civil disobedience that 'brought into the open the American dilemma' and, perhaps for the first time, forced upon the nation the recognition of the enormity of the crime, not just of slavery, but of chattel slavery—'unique among all such systems known to civilization'—the responsibility for which the people have inherited, together with so many blessings, from their forefathers."

Reading this passage of "Civil Disobedience," Plaetzer (2023: 960) asks: "How did civil disobedience bring to light the *inheritance* of slavery?" and argues that "these passages stand at the edge of an insight that Arendt failed to spell out: Black movements had brought to light the limitations that America's racial order places on the augmentation of founding principles." This is an important corrective to the much more sanguine account of the revolution and early republic that Arendt presents in *On Revolution*. There, as summarized above, the founding instantiated and legitimized its own principles. Here in "Civil Disobedience," Arendt (1972: 91) argues "we need not be surprised that the present belated attempts to welcome the Negro population explicitly into the otherwise tacit *consensus universalis* of the nation are not trusted." As Plaetzer (2023: 961) concludes: "In Black rebellion, Arendt saw the breakdown of the dialectics of action and institution under the impact of slavery's afterlife," for the "spirit of the law remained indistinguishable from the specter of racial domination."

On this basis, Plaetzer (2023: 963) concludes that we ought to read "Arendt not as opposed to racial equality but as deeply pessimistic about its depoliticized forms allows one to recover crucial insights about the challenges that movements for racial justice continue to face." This, I am attempting to argue here, holds not only for the limitations of her account of the American experiment as regards the politics of race but also for the blind spots in her account of the secularity of American democratic legitimation. To see how this corrective improves not just her reading of the United States in *On Revolution* but also her attempt to resolve the third antinomy of liberalism as a political theology, let us now turn to the contrast between her response to the limitations of political liberalism and that of Carl Schmitt.

Arendt Contra Schmitt on Revolution and Freedom as Absolute or Contingent

If successful, the previous section has made clear two things. First, how and why the practice of exclusionary inclusion is foundational for republican citizenship and how it operationalizes a democratic mysticism that the American revolutionaries-turned-founders shared with their fellow republicans in France. Second, how this legacy informed the "Crises of the (American) Republic" as Arendt analyzed them in essays like "Reflections on Little Rock" and "Civil Disobedience" as examples of acts of willing as Arendt analyzed that faculty of the mind in *Willing*. In this section, I aim to show that despite Arendt's almost exclusive focus on an interpretation of the constitution of the republic as that which initiates an ongoing process of organizing the ordered freedom under which the citizens live, the argument of *On Revolution*, read together with these later works and with *Willing*, nevertheless presents an important step beyond Weber's disenchantment thesis for which political theory is still searching today, often turning down what seems to me the blind alley, or dead end, of Schmittian democratic sovereignty. It is true that her myopic misrepresentation of how slavery haunts not just the American founding and Constitution but also the life of citizens right up to the moment when she was writing *On Revolution*, during the Kennedy administration and just prior to the passage of the Civil Rights Act and the Voting Rights Act. Of course, the history of the institution of slavery continues to haunt American democracy since the time Arendt wrote that work as well. All this is serious enough. Yet another layer of occlusion, however, that remains to be exposed and unpacked, namely, the specifically Calvinist theological background to the revolutionary consensus in America. This closing section aims first to unearth this legacy behind Puritan promise-making and -keeping and then goes on to argue why Arendt's approach to the interweaving of antinomy of secular reason and theocratic faith with the revolutionary tradition, allows us to more successfully see beyond the limits imposed by the horizon of Weber's disenchantment thesis than the forms of "popular democracy" advocated by Carl Schmitt and his followers on both the right and the left today.

How does our largely critical reading of *On Revolution* in this chapter help us not just correct but also build upon Arendt's imminent critique of liberalism as a political theology? Why, specifically, does it hold the promise of thinking beyond the horizons imposed by Weber that is wrongly sought in the work of Schmitt. In following Paul Kottman (2012) in rejecting Samuel Moyn's (2008) argument that Arendt presents a notion of democratic sovereignty where the absolute remains as an unacknowledged but haunting presence after the secular revolution, we suggested that the full articulation of why Moyn's reading of the secular in *On Revolution* is especially misleading—even if, with Moyn, I doubt that Arendt's secular reading of Puritan's promise-making as model democratic behavior can be read as fully a break with the theocratic past as Kottman would have it—demands a return to Schmitt's political theology. Arendt presents an alternative that, for all its faults, remains a more promising view of the relationship of constituent and constituted power than the alternatives at hand. Lucia Rubinelli (2020: 216), largely following (yet deviating in one important particular from) Arato (2017: 30, 204–17), shows that Schmitt's theory of constituent power is "either a mythological conception without authority" or a "conception of constituent authority, relying on both state power and a combination of authoritarian and democratic-plebiscitary legitimation," which in either case "opens the way to the right of the stronger."

For this reason, Rubinelli (2020: 217) continues, "it is necessary to abandon Schmitt's theory of constituent power and adopt an Arendtian approach" in which "the legitimacy of a constitution depend[s] on the authority that created it, as opposed to the mere fact of its effectiveness; in this way, Arendt denies Schmitt's right of the stronger with a popular authority rather than a popular sovereignty, an authority that "is the people, in its flesh and bones." This is a powerful image, but as the use of the third-person neuter singular pronoun ("its") in referring to the "flesh and bones" of the people, Rubinelli calls attention to all the problems of "the second body of the people" analyzed in Chapter 2 and in the second section of this chapter: the people does not have flesh and bones, *people* do. How can we find in Arendt, or articulate through her reconstruction of liberalism as a political theology, an understanding of popular authority, rather than sovereignty, that does not replicate this form of exclusionary inclusion in the democratic body politic?

To do so, we must come back to the question with which we ended Chapter 3: why does Arendt return to Augustine in order to confront the abyss of freedom? Having traced how and why she cannot resolve the antinomy of secular reason and theocratic faith in the act of founding in the first two sections of this chapter, we come face to face with the absolute contingency of freedom that is meant to be both founding and founding that is both terrifying and liberating. It is this that leads to the leap of faith that Schmitt sees as the sovereign exception. For Arendt, on the contrary, it is the creative power of worldly love that brings her back to Augustine time and again. But how does Arendt's argument that Rome is the new Troy, following Augustine following Virgil, help us to see a popular authority that is embodied and non-mystical? We must see that, no matter how hard we try, we cannot completely break free from tradition because we are not born *ex nihilo* but into traditions and into the world; a democratic founding, even in revolution, acknowledges this as its groundless ground rather than as a paradox.

Arendt's reading of the *novus ordo saeclurum*, which she holds to be grounded in Augustine's appropriation of Virgil, undeniably runs against the deep anti-millennialism in Augustine's version of Christian eschatology that we have been arguing Arendt underestimates or ignores in her account of the legitimation of the revolution and founding of the American republic. As Bloch (1985: 6) notes, long before the American revolutionaries-turned-founders would turn to Augustine's redeployment of Virgil, Augustine's position "that the millennial prophecies be read figuratively, as referring to the perennial perfection of the City of God but not to the future of the City of Man" held sway. And, as Bloch (1985: 6) notes, it is true that "Luther and Calvin themselves had sought to establish a Protestant eschatology in keeping with Augustine" who "concentrated on the fallibility of humanity and the corruption of earthly existence," and for this reason rejected out of hand the notion that the world is the "arena for the expression of grace." Yet, Bloch (1985: 8) continues, the revolutions, rebellions, and popular uprisings of the sixteenth and seventeenth centuries had overcome this elite anti-millennialism for many Protestant sects and communities and the "definitive break with Augustine's and Luther's nonmillennial eschatology was made in the biblical commentaries published by German Calvinist Johannes Alsted in 1627 and, following Alsted, by the Cambridge Platonist Joseph Mede in 1632." In the view of Christian revelation as continuous with the Hebrew prophets favored by Alsted and Mede, the two-cities eschatology and the concomitant conviction of the irredeemable nature of fallen creation on which Augustine insisted was supplanted by a this-worldly eschatology in which revolution was not merely possible, but just, and not merely just, but necessary.

How does bringing this critique of Arendt's historiography of the American revolutionaries-turned-founders, in which she simultaneously invokes a secularized Augustine as a resource for the constitutionalism of the new republic and ignores the millennialism to which many of its supporters subscribed help us to see beyond Weber, working with and against Arendt in her appeal to Augustine–Virgil in *Willing*? Does this not rather, only give us reason to hold her thinking about the United States in lower esteem? So as to see why not, it is helpful to return to the debate staged above between Schmitt and Arendt on revolution and founding, now with the added dimension of the millennialism of a significant portion of the devout Protestants responsible for the making, and the public reception, of the revolution and the new constitution.

In order to properly orient ourselves in the debate between Arendt and Schmitt, we first need to correct a common picture of Schmitt as simply and problematically a fascist ideologue, or, if not that, at least as an advocate for populist, rather than popular, democracy. Montserrat Herrero (2023: 2) argues that contrary to such judgments of his views, the main focus of Schmitt's major works on parliamentary democracy, on dictatorship, and on political theology is a factual, rather than normative, claim; namely, the view that it is impossible for "political modernity [to be] anything other than authoritarian populism," irrespective of its use of "democratic or autocratic procedures." Herrero (2023: 2) insists that this is "not normative" but rather "descriptive of a de facto political situation" because "modern politics, born out of the French Revolution, cannot be anything else." Where the common critique of Schmitt's critique of liberal constitutionalism sees him as intentionally obscuring, Herrero (2023: 2) follows Andreas Kalyvas in holding that "Schmitt's interpretation of constituent power of the people can be practically developed . . . in the direction of constitutional democracy." Contrary to the common critique of Schmitt as a normative, or ideological, opponent of liberalism, Herrero (2023: 3) advances a reading in which "Schmitt is more a genealogist of the idea of the constitution of the political subject 'people' than a normative theoretician, defending a position."

This repositioning of Schmitt in debates about popular sovereignty and the difficulty for thinkers—and, more importantly, for political actors—to uncover and persuasively convey some legitimizing ground for the constitutional order is at work when Herrero (2023: 6) addresses the argument Schmitt makes about what we have discussed throughout the past three chapters as the impasses surrounding the second body of the people; namely, that under modern conditions, sovereignty is undying "not because the prince is eternal, but because the people are." This Hobbesian idea is at the very center of Schmitt's critique of liberalism, and its descriptive accuracy is why John McCormick (1999) and William E. Scheuerman (1999) follow Schmitt in insisting on the importance of the constituent power for a theory of democracy, even if they reject Schmitt's thesis about the exception as constitutive for the normal order insofar as they hold Schmitt as irredeemably affiliated with dictatorship. As Herrero (2023: 3) insists, Andreas Kalyvas (2008) shows that Schmitt's theses on the political identity of the people, in combination with the principle of representation, are salient for constitutional democracy because Schmitt's "differentiation between normal and extraordinary cases, Schmitt's constitutional theory resolves the aporias of liberal constitutionalism."

For Kalyvas in particular, but for all three of these influential accounts Herrero is drawing on, the picture of Schmitt as a mystifier and ideologue advanced by Arato among others as discussed above comes across as itself normatively motivated. If persuaded by the view of Schmitt as a critical theorist offering a historically grounded account of constitutionalism as founded in a paradoxical structure that can be overcome through the distinction between extraordinary and normal moments that the revolutions of the seventeenth and eighteenth centuries evidences. As with Arato's quite different approach to constituent power, Herrero (2023: 7) focuses on Schmitt emphasis that "Sieyès's notion of constituent power postulates that there must be a power that is the actual giver of the constitution and that, in principle, is unlimited because it is not subject to the constitution and does not disappear with it. It is never left behind," this power is truly "constituent because it aims to create law from antecedent juridical nothingness," and for that reason it "must be a revolutionary concept capable of destabilizing the established order at any time." If we accept Herrero's gesture and reject Arato's picture of Schmitt and his appropriation of Sieyès, what does this mean for our discussion of Arendt and the attempt to resolve the antinomy of secular reason and theocratic faith as integral to liberalism as a political theology?

The crucial point, as Herrero (2023: 11) puts it, is that for Schmitt, "A people are primarily without authority or state magistracy and are made up of those who, in principle, are not organized, do not exercise organic functions of authority and do not govern. In this sense, the people is a "negative" concept, defined by that which it is not." Here is where we see the difference that makes a difference between Arendt and Schmitt. Contrary to the picture of the debate between the two that is staged by Arato (and, relatedly, by Rubinelli and Kottman), the point is *not* that Arendt offers a vision of secular constitutionalism as self-legitimizing while Schmitt embraces either a mythological conception without authority or a conception of constituent authority. Instead, what we see is that Schmitt and Arendt *alike* see that political modernity, operating in the wake of revolution, is born of an unbridgeable gap between constituted and constitutive power; they differ, however, in that Schmitt's conception of the people is negative, while Arendt's is positive, and this itself points to how each of the two view the relationship between power and authority.

When we read Arendt as in one sense like and in another sense unlike Schmitt when she insists on the revolutionary character of republican constitutionalism, we find that—as Yotam Hotam (2023: 149, 150) argues—"Arendt's retort to Schmitt does not dismiss but rather revises political theology," especially considering how "Arendt integrates this close association between theology and political emergency into her discussion of modern revolutions." Hotam is absolutely correct in reading Arendt thus, and bringing his presentation of the Arendt–Schmitt debate into conversation with Herrero's recontextualization of Schmitt on revolution and constitutive power allows us to see Arendt as closer to Schmitt's critique of liberal constitutionalism than she is to many opponents of Schmitt who see her as a liberal critic of his critique like them (perhaps Arato being the paramount instance here). We can see this as well when Hotam (2023: 152) argues, correctly I think, that for Arendt "the decline of theology" embodied in the *novo ordo saeclurum* brought about by the eighteenth-century revolutions "also means, conversely, a redeploying of traditional theological concepts." These points are connected; for, as argued in the Introduction above, the reading of Arendt as a secular Jew is mutually reinforcing with the reading of her as a fairly standard liberal. These mutually reinforcing readings undergird the picture of Arendt's debate with Schmitt where she is the secular liberal and he is the theocratic authoritarian (or the mystical–mythical populist). Hotam helpfully destabilizes this picture of their debate.

At the same time, I believe Hotam (2023: 154) is mistaken when arguing that, for Arendt, secularization "also encompasses the recapturing of a theological tradition that cannot be revived," and for this reason "demonstrates the same problem of holding on to the unholdable object of tradition" that bedeviled Adorno and Benjamin. While this view of the "tragic" character of the theological treasure that is "lost" along with the revolutionary tradition makes possible Hotam's (2023: 156–60) interesting reading of Arendt's "secularization of evil" in *Eichmann* in particular, I believe that it overstates the degree to which Arendt takes on, or aligns with or at least resembles, the ostensibly mystical and negative-theological character of Benjamin and Adorno as dialectic thinkers. To see why, let us turn to Arendt's central statement on secularism, the seldom-read essay "Religion and Politics" (1953).

Following Hotam (2023) and Herrero (2023), we have seen that Arendt like Schmitt, attempted to challenge Weber's claim that there could be no legitimation of constitutional government beyond the commitment to constitutionalism itself. But, also like Schmitt (and this is not emphasized by either Hotam or Herrero), Arendt struggled mightily to articulate a coherent account of liberalism as neither a break from the past nor a continuation of it. For Arendt, the incoherent and inconsistent interweaving of tradition and the modern age means that constitutional republicanism is neither a new and secular order founded on rational principles, as Habermas (1996) among others would have it, nor an adaptation ("secularization") of the theocratic principles that held from late antiquity through the early period, as Schmitt (2005) argues. How then, to understand the antinomy of secular reason and theocratic faith as it is left unresolved in modern constitutional arrangements?

As argued throughout this chapter and unlike the first two antinomies, Arendt does not bring this antinomy to anything like a satisfactory resolution in either of the places it gets the most sustained discussion: *On Revolution* and *The Life of the Mind*. There is, however, the kernel of a more successful resolution in "Religion and Politics," written around the time she was still trying to write her "Marx book," which was meant to be a statement on "The Modern Challenge to Tradition." As Barbara Hahn and James McFarland (2018: 854–56) relate in their Editor's Note to volume 6 of Arendt's collected works, Arendt abandoned this project, for practical reasons, eventually publishing certain parts of it as essays, such as "Tradition and the Modern Age" and "What is Authority?"

before moving on to what became *The Human Condition* instead. We can see how these ideas returned after the publication of that work, resurfacing in chapter 6 of *On Revolution* in particular and then in the entire conception of *The Life of the Mind*. But the specific question of secularism and secularity never gets a direct scouring in these works, because they each have their own topical and argumentative foci which is not this antinomy.

Here, Arendt (RP: 226) comments directly on "two quite distinct trends of thought" in addressing what she notes is the increasingly common habit of referring to communism, socialism, or liberalism as either an ideology, or a "political or secular religion," with the implication that an ideology is a secular religion. One group of thinkers speaking this way, Arendt (RP: 226) notes, follow an historical approach—here she foregrounds Eric Voegelin's focus on "immanentist heresy"; while others, operating in the social sciences, follow in the wake of Marx as they "treat ideology and religion as one and the same thing." While Arendt (RP: 226) finds that the historical approach has a "great advantage" on the social scientists insofar as it understands that neither "totalitarian domination" nor liberal democracy is an "accident in Western history" that must be understood in its long historical context, she also argues that Voegelin and others like him—Schmitt comes to mind but he is not named here—present "a double misunderstanding of the nature of secularism and the secular world."

The first misunderstanding is that, contra the historicists, Arendt (RP: 226) argues that "the long alliance between religion and authority does not necessarily prove that the concept of authority is itself of a religious nature." This matters because, as we saw in unpacking Arendt's reading of Augustine following in the wake of Virgil, Arendt (RP: 226) is of the view that authority "is of Roman political origin" and is not Christian or religious at all; indeed, while she allows that "our present crisis is the breakdown of all authority and the broken thread of our tradition"—and here she sounds very much like the author of "What is Authority?" and "The Crisis in Education"—she insists that this does not entail "that the crisis is primarily religious or has a religious origin." What is at stake most deeply, Arendt (RP: 227) believes, is not "a crisis of traditional faith" but rather "the authority of churches insofar as they are, among other things, public institutions." This last point makes clear why Arendt is—for all her criticism of a view like that of Voegelin (or Schmitt or Strauss)—closer to what she here calls the "historical approach" to discussing so-called "secular religions" than she is to the social scientific discourse that identifies religion with ideology.

This becomes clearer when she articulates the second misunderstanding in the approach of Voegelin among others, which Arendt (RP: 227) says, is "more obvious and more relevant"; namely, "neither Christian equality nor Christian freedom could ever have led by themselves to the concept of 'government of the people, by the people, for the people.'" Here, indeed we get at the heart of the dispute with Voegelin, and with Schmitt, as Herrero reconstructs his position quite compellingly, even as we see why she is much closer to both Voegelin and Schmitt than to those who analyze religions and political value systems equally as ideologies. For, as Arendt (RP: 227), continues, the "very fact that we, as far as our public life is concerned, care more about freedom than about anything else proves that we do not live publicly in a religious world." This, for Arendt, is the rock-bottom sense in which liberalism is, indeed, secular—albeit a very particular sense of the term secular that she is working with here and which we she brings to her limited and ultimately unpersuasive reading of the American Revolution as a secular revolution.

This revolution and the republic it made it possible to found are secular not because it was the work of people who were atheist or pan-confessional or ecumenicist or any such position theologically or anti-theologically; the secularism consists precisely in the subsumption of public life under the sign of freedom itself: an individual and this-worldly freedom in which, Arendt (RP: 233) insists, "the separation of the public and religious spheres of life" did not actually serve to "sever politics from religion in general but very specifically from the Christian creed." Yet, Arendt (RP: 240 n.28) is well aware that Marx's indictment of religion as an opiate of the people does not mean that "religion was *invented* as an opiate for the people, but that is was *used* for such purposes" by specific, repressive and revanchist, rulers subsequent to popular uprisings in the wake of the French Revolution. In this light, Arendt (RP: 233) wonders, how it could be that a largely secularized monarch could see in Christianity—which is—a resource that "could be called upon for the preservation of political life." Arendt (RP: 236) insists here that the desperate appeal to Christianity to buttress a repressive monarchy lacking political legitimation in the wake of the failed revolution of 1848 is indicative of the "outstanding political characteristic of our modern secular world," which is that "more and more people are losing their belief in reward and punishment after death while the functioning of individual consciences . . . has remained politically as unreliable as ever."

This argument about the loss of hell and the corresponding crisis of moral reasoning about evil resonates with her discussion of evil and the belief in hell in *Origins* and *Eichmann* discussed in Chapter 1. Here, it is mobilized to support the conclusion Arendt (RP: 236) stresses: "if secularity of the world involves the separation of the religious and political realms of life," then public confidence in "the fear of Hell" as one of "the motives which would prevent or stimulate the actions of the majority . . . seems inevitable." Yet, while she is clearly quite disturbed by the loss of hell as a motivation for being moral, she is not about to "throw in" with Voegelin or Schmitt or anyone else that would, as Arendt (RP: 236) puts it, "forge an alliance between throne and altar." For, as Arendt (RP: 237) argues in the closing sentence of this article, "If we try to inspire public-political life once more with 'religious passion' or to use religion as a means of political distinctions, the result may very well be the transformation of religion into an ideology and the corruption of our fight against totalitarianism by a fanaticism which is utterly alien to the very essence of freedom." In a moment where fully one-quarter of Americans identify with Christian Nationalism as a political program, Arendt's warning seems all the more distant from attempts, like that of Samuel Moyn (2023a/b), to brand her a Cold War liberal for whom the fight against the Soviet Union was paramount. Rather, she comes across much more like a prophet warning against the adoption of forthrightly Christian politics of the kind advocated by Eric Voegelin, or the sort advocated by Carl Schmitt or, if Herrero is right in her redescription of his work as descriptive and genealogical rather than normative, by followers of Schmitt.

5

THE *ESCHATON* OF LIBERALISM AS A POLITICAL THEOLOGY: POPULAR SOVEREIGNTY WITHOUT EXCLUSION

In the Introduction, I advanced the idea that Arendt's heterodox liberalism is perhaps best understood as an equally heterodox form of "New Augustinianism." In this framing, we see Arendt as a thinker both inspired by the concept of love in Augustine, and its concomitant politic of hope, faith, and love—of God's grace as a gift, given equally to all—and alive to all the violence, and let's face it, evil that the Church has done here on Earth. As we saw then, there is a deep paradox in thinking of such an Augustinian at all: how can Augustine, who was not just a thinker of Christian imperialism, but also a chief agent of its worldly works, possibly serve us in trying to make good on what we can call the challenge of thinking in and through decoloniality? More starkly: can we seriously consider Augustine, however mediated by Arendt, to be a resource for thinking and achieving a political theology that is not just liberal but liberatory? Despite all the tensions, and perhaps even because of them, I want to show in this chapter that Arendt engages Augustine in just this way. Whatever Augustine's limits, and whatever the limits of Arendt's Augustine, and Arendt herself, this chapter will show that engaging this thread offers us the best hope for finding or founding a situated yet non-parochial democratic politics that is not based on exclusion and enmity.

I have earlier (Weinman 2016; Weinman and Vormann 2020) articulated this as a "non-parochial politics of place" in conversation with what David Roochnik (2016) calls Aristotle's "topological politics." In this chapter, I hope to peel back a further layer of the onion, engaging Arendt's reading of Augustine and its limitations to further uncover both the cosmopolitical character of any liberal political theology that escapes practices of exclusion and how different such a cosmopolitics is from the globalist theories and practices that seem synonymous with being cosmopolitan or espousing "universal values" in current discussions. This account sets out from the discussion of Arendt's unique perspective on constituted versus constitutive power in Chapter 4 as a lens on the third antinomy of liberal political theology, secular reason, and theocratic faith. For this, we must read Arendt's unsatisfying analysis of the place of both race and slavery in the America republic (in *On Revolution*, discussed in Chapter 4) together with her complicated engagement with the anti-colonial uprisings in the Global South and Black Power movement of the 1960s and later (in *On Violence*), which is the aim of the opening section. In the second section, leaning on the insights gained from exploring the limits of Arendt's outlook through an engagement with the unique account of the prophetic tradition as a mediation of Black Protestant political theology and social democratic coalition politics offered by Bayard Rustin (whom Arendt was following at the time of writing *On Violence*), we open up a comparative reading of *On Violence* alongside her responses to the Civil Rights movement in essays and letters from the 1960s, which helps us to understand Arendt's willful blindness as regards the depth with which anti-Black racism is, just like antisemitism, embedded within European modernity. In the closing section of this chapter, we can see more fully both the extent and the limits of her underlying insight regarding the temptation—on both the political right and the political left—to discover in irrationality or mystical depth the true politics that can deliver us from "Weimar syndrome."

Arendt on the End of Authority and the Blindness of Liberation Movements in *On Violence*

Much can and has been said about the putative wrong-headedness of the central argument of *On Violence*, which—perhaps surprisingly—is written in large part as a response to what Arendt (OV: 80 n.109) perceives as an attack on the authority of the university through "the student rebellion [that] is a global phenomenon." This focus on authority, and its ever-growing absence in the postwar restoration of a liberal order, is essential for understanding the main argumentative aim of *On Violence* as an Augustinian heritage. It is often missed, though, not just because Augustine is only discussed briefly, but also because the argument focuses, at first obliquely but then obsessionally and profoundly unhelpfully, on the Black Power movement in key moments. In this section, I want to do three things, each through a pair of focused readings. First, reading part I of *On Violence*, I will show how the student rebellions of 1968 prompt Arendt's analysis in the direction of the autonomy of the university in the first section of the text and why this involves a discussion of Black Power. Next, in a reading of part II, I aim to help resurface the submerged Augustinian commitments that motivated Arendt in articulating the critique of the student protest movement. Finally, I offer a critical reconstruction of the place of Augustine's understanding of authority in part III of the text to show how and why Arendt's discussion of authority and what she figures as "the crises of the republic" in the Vietnam era point to a need to rethink her rejection of Baldwin's call for a politics of love as offering the best hope for addressing the broken promises of the American experiment with truly representative democratic governance as the expression of popular sovereignty.

We begin, then, in part I of *On Violence*, with the student rebellions themselves and how engaging them brings Arendt to a discussion of Black Power. Any discussion of Arendt's highly controversial position-taking on the student protest movement in the 1968-and-just-after moment must begin with one of the more infamous statements in her corpus, namely, the long first sentence of appendix VIII (OV: 94):

> Bayard Rustin, the Negro civil-rights leader, has said all that needed to be said on the matter: College officials should "stop capitulating to the stupid demands of Negro students"; it is wrong if one group's "sense of guilt and masochism permits another segment of society to hold guns in the name of justice"; black students were "suffering from the shock of integration" and looking for "an easy way out of their problems"; what Negro students need is "remedial training" so that they "can do mathematics and write a correct sentence," not "soul courses." (Quoted from the *Daily News*, April 28, 1969)

This quotation of Rustin's judgment—just who Rustin was and why Arendt is quoting him is important, and we will discuss this at length in the third section of this chapter—is meant to serve as an explanation or justification for an only slightly less infamous claim that Arendt (OV: 19) advances in her own voice in the body of the text; namely, that "it seems that the academic establishment, in its curious tendency to yield more to Negro demands, even if they are clearly silly and outrageous, than to the disinterested and usually highly moral claims of the white rebels, also thinks in these terms and feels more comfortable when confronted with interests plus violence than when it is a matter of nonviolent 'participatory democracy.'"

[1] For a longer discussion of these controversies and a full bibliography of them, see: chapter 9 of Robaszkiewicz and Weinman (2022) and Weinman (2022).

Both her claim in her own voice, and her endorsement of Rustin's judgment have proven most controversial or intolerable for her readers, especially her American readers, in recent decades.[1] For those critics of Arendt, and I suspect that most readers will agree, both the sentence in the main body of Arendt's text just quoted, and perhaps even more so the sentence quoted from the appendix above, are far from Arendt's best moments as a practitioner of "exercises in political thinking."

That said, we are remiss in judging the claim in the second half of this long sentence if we do not attend to the context in which Arendt (OV: 19) introduces this claim in the first clause of the sentence, namely: "Black violence can indeed be understood in analogy to the labor violence in America a generation ago; and although, as far as I know, only Staughton Lynd has drawn the analogy between labor riots and student rebellion explicitly." Just before Arendt offers the rather indefensibly staged false comparison between the "highly moral claims of the white rebels" and the "clearly silly and outrageous" demands of Black students, Arendt pauses to note just how infrequently commentators in her time—and in the time since, one can add—noted the very real connections between the class-based labor agitation of the 1930s and the race-based Black Power movement in the late 1960s. Indeed, however perspicuous or dull we find her judgment here, what is really of the moment is her singular inability to hear the claims of Black student dissidents as the expression of self-assertion in the face of attacks on their personhood and indeed their very right to exist. In this light, it is important to remember that unlike with antisemitism, which Arendt studied carefully and systematically in part one of *Origins*, we can find in her corpus no sustained analysis of anti-Black racism in America.

What perhaps comes closest to such is the analysis of slavery in *On Revolution* (61–66), where Arendt's claims are highly debatable and perhaps ought more justly to be described as self-serving for her larger historiographical and political theoretical aim of broadly vindicating the actions of the revolutionaries in colonial America while castigating those of the revolutionaries in France. In short, we must acknowledge that Arendt's presentation of the American Revolution in *On Revolution*, as discussed in Chapter 4 above, is of a piece with her refusal to recognize the deep resonance between her own practice of solidarity in civil society as a Jew and on behalf of other Jews and the activism of Black Americans struggling both to eradicate the enduring legacies of slavery and at the same time to make the white majority in the United States recognize the deep enmeshment of the constitutional order and the legally enforced inferiority of Black and other non-white Americans.

If, however, we are willing to dig a little deeper, we will see that the story is more complex. For, what is most remarkable about the way in which Arendt "misses" this relationship is the fact that her too-brief account of slavery comes in the context of her examination of why the *social* need to end poverty and achieve freedom from want did not consume the revolutionary demand for *political* freedom in America as it did in Jacobin France. We find the same basic analysis in part III of "Zionism Reconsidered" written almost two decades earlier than *On Revolution*. Here Arendt becomes increasingly critical of the mainstream Zionist movement in its then-current form, on very much the same grounds as those which lead her to condemn the place of social needs in the revolutionary tradition in *On Revolution*. Concluding her historical reconstruction of how the Zionist movement devolved over the half-century from the first Zionist Congress (Basel 1897) to the Atlantic City convention, Arendt argues that while the movement "started half a century ago with ideals so lofty that it overlooked the particular realities of the Near East and the general wickedness of the world," it ended up supporting "not only national but chauvinist claims." Her critique of the Black Power movement and its claims for the unification of the Third World and for the destruction of the institutional academe draws on normative resources that are quite similar to those she calls upon in her critique of Zionism here.

This deeper engagement with the details of Arendt's views about Zionism demonstrates how unfair it would be to accuse her of judging the self-actualization of Black people and peoples negatively while positively judging the self-mobilization of Jewish people and peoples. We may very well come to different judgments than those of Arendt when it comes to the Black Power and Zionist movements; we ought, however, to recognize that her judgments are founded on the same convictions that run much deeper than the question of her being a Jew who understands Jewishness as a legitimate basis for politics, and a white European who fails to see Blackness in the same light. We might well disagree with Arendt's judgments, expressed in *On Revolution* and *On Violence* read comparatively with "Zionism Reconsidered" and we must, in any case, attend to the crucial if narrow issue of Arendt's inability (or refusal) to recognize the political agency of Black Americans as a minority mobilizing itself, very much along the lines which she herself participated in Jewish movements, Zionist and otherwise, in her youth and early adulthood.

To come to the second of three points that we need to discuss with respect to *On Violence*: what, precisely, does this have to do with Augustine? Everything, actually. The Augustinian background is both very deep and very buried. It surfaces explicitly only in a footnote in the center of the first of the two quotes from part II on which I will focus here. At the outset of a famous section of this text, where she presents what is widely known as her idiosyncratic theorization of power and violence as absolutely opposed to one another, Arendt (OV: 43) bemoans "the present state of political science that our terminology does not distinguish among such key words 'power,' 'strength,' 'force,' 'authority,' and, finally, 'violence'—all of which refer to distinct, different phenomena and would hardly exist unless they did." Following from this impetus to better understand the phenomena behind the conceptual jumble, Arendt (OV: 45) argues that of all these crucial concepts that contemporary political science fails to understand in distinction from one another, authority is "the most elusive of these phenomena" and "therefore, as a term, most frequently abused," explaining that it "can be vested in persons—there is such a thing as personal authority, as, for instance, in the relation between parent and child, between teacher and pupil—or it can be vested in offices, as, for instance, in the Roman senate (*auctoritas in senatu*) or in the hierarchical offices of the Church."

The difficulty of disentangling the personal from the institutional dimensions of authority is a familiar challenge, which we have come across already, dressed so to say in Augustinian garb, in a variety of contexts: the discussion of Arendt's struggle to find in Augustine a justification for neighborly love in *Der Liebesbegriff* (Chapter 1); the problem of the second body of the people as a source of democratic legitimation (Chapter 2); the three impasses of liberal political theology discussed in light of the discussion of *Willing* (Chapter 3); and the appeal to ancient authorities in the modern democratic revolutions explored in *On Revolution* (Chapter 4). Now, in the discussion of the complex interaction of personal and institutional authority, we see Arendt turn to Augustine again—albeit obliquely, as a ramification of an offhand reminder of something she argues at length elsewhere: that neither the totalitarian form of government, nor the tyrannical and dictatorial forms it resembles and with which it is sometimes confused, have anything to do with authority, either personal or institutional. She does not have the time to address the issue but, in the explication of the claim quoted just above in a footnote, Arendt (OV: 45 n.66) writes: "There is such a thing as authoritarian government, but it certainly has nothing in common with tyranny, dictatorship, or totalitarian rule"; recognizing that this bald formulation is likely not going to suffice for itself, she continues: "For a discussion of the historical background and political significance of [authority], see my 'What is Authority?' and part I of Karl-Heinz Lübke's valuable study, *Auctoritas bei Augustin* (Stuttgart, 1968), with extensive bibliography."

Two points are worth stressing here: first, that as she continues to puzzle through the paradoxes of the question "what is authority?"—or, remembering the first sentence of her essay, what it *was*—Augustine continues to be a touchstone about whose works she continues to revise and sharpen her views. Second, that this ongoing working-out of her agreements and disagreements with Augustine can profoundly help us to understand the positions that Arendt took on matters of public concern in her "American" years. The confounding nature of Arendt's appearance in public debates—as a "child of the German left" who is seen as a maverick or hidden (or not hidden) conservative—can perhaps best be understood as a sign of how hard it was, and is, for people to take to heart that and why Arendt is advocating for the restoration of authority in universities, that is, for what we might call "academic governance" in contemporary higher education.

Part II of *On Violence*, with its critical and even outraged response she offers to many aspects of the politicization of the university in the late 1960s can be hard for her interlocutors to accept as her real line of thought, let alone something with which to agree, because when confronted with the judgments that Arendt (OV: 45) advances, such as "The greatest enemy of authority, therefore, is contempt, and the surest way to undermine it is laughter," her readers think of this a good basis for a handbook for a *Selbstdenker* (someone who thinks for themselves, unswayed by authorities either personal or institutional), whom Arendt should lionize, while Arendt—who surely loves a good laugh—is rather on the side this time around. But why is Arendt on the other side in this case? With typical irony, we might say that one reason why Arendt's readers, both in the wider reading public and specialists in political theory, struggle so greatly to come to terms with the position she stakes out in part II is because she actually sees Augustine on *both* sides of the debate she is staging between the protesting students and the universities that are failing to assert their authority and instead turning either to the state to supply violence or to other parts of civil society to supply power in order to keep the university system viable.

Augustine is figured as, on the one hand, the authority on the sort of authority that intellectual leadership in the university ought to have but does not; yet Arendt (OV: 56) also sees Augustine lurking in her contemporaries' great trust in the redemptive power of violence: "Hegel's and Marx's great trust in the dialectical 'power of negation' . . . rests on a much older philosophical prejudice: that evil is no more than a privative modus of the good, that good can come out of evil; that, in short, evil is but a temporary manifestation of a still-hidden good. Such time-honored opinions have become dangerous." In other words, even if Augustine rests beneath a decent and compelling sense of authority that can withstand the assaults of the contemptuous laughter and worse from the leaders of the student movements on the one hand and the zero-sum calculations of think-tank culture and increasingly bureaucratized establishment, his neo-Platonic insistence that evil is just the privation of the good undergirds the radical anti-establishment politics of both the traditional Marxist–Hegelians and the increasingly non-Marxist new Left.

We are now in a position to assess both the political theological core of Arendt's defense of the independence of the university as a vital site for the preservation of a *res publica*, a public thing, in and as America. We begin with *On Violence* and what Arendt (OV: 73, 74) sees as "the strange revival of the life philosophies of Bergson and Nietzsche in their Sorelian version" which purport to offer a "seemingly so novel biological justification of violence." Importantly, Arendt puts Bergson in a completely different light when she returns to him a few years later in *Willing*; in the later text, not only is Bergson not to blame for this new embrace of violence as creative destruction, he is actually something of the intellectual hero of the whole second volume of *The Life of the Mind*. This will be a central focus of the Epilogue to follow; for now, let us attend to the withering critique that Arendt (OV: 74) levels against this *seemingly* new Bergsonian–Sorelian line stresses that the "combination of violence, life, and creativity" that figures so prominently in "in the rebellious state of mind of the present generation," and how this "new phenomenon" is actually quite old.

Arendt (OV: 74) allows that "the emphasis on the sheer factuality of living, and hence on love-making as life's most glorious manifestation, is a response to the real possibility of constructing a doomsday machine and destroying all life on earth"; nevertheless, she insists that while there is *something* new in this, and the existence of nuclear weaponry and the slow climate catastrophe do motivate these movements in some way, "the categories in which the new glorifiers of life understand themselves are not new." Wherein, then, does this glorification of life ultimately rest? Digging deeper into the putatively new biological justifications of violence, we can see that they point back to Marx and through Marx to the eschatological vision of early Christianity. Arendt (OV: 74), noting that "to see the productivity of society in the image of life's 'creativity' is at least as old as Marx" and that the belief "in violence as a life-promoting force is at least as old as Nietzsche," while thinking "of creativity as man's highest good is at least as old as Bergson," presses on these proximal sources for the "seemingly novel" biological justification of violence in order to show what rests beneath them. In doing so, Arendt (OV: 75) focuses on "the tradition of organic thought in political matters by which power and violence are interpreted in biological terms," which she considers to be the most "theoretically dangerous" tradition of all. This tradition, Arendt (OV: 75) avers, sees "life and life's alleged creativity" as the "common denominator" of power and violence—that is, what yokes them together—such that "violence is justified on the ground of creativity," giving rise to "organic metaphors with which our entire present discussion of these matters, especially of the riots, is permeated," like "the notion of a 'sick society,' of which riots are symptoms, as fever is a symptom of disease—can only promote violence in the end."

Arendt then concludes her analysis of, and her normative warning about, the biological justification of violence with a claim that sounds very much like the description of biopolitics in the sense of Foucault and Agamben. Arendt (OV: 75) first notes that political debates in America in 1968/69 "sound ominously like a discussion between two physicians who debate the relative advantages of surgical as opposed to medical treatment of their patient"; she then generalizes from the particular valence of the yoking together of violence and power in biological terms at the dawn of the Nixon administration to a more general, even universal, point concerning the entire tradition of thinking in terms of a body politic:

> Moreover, so long as we talk in nonpolitical, biological terms, the glorifiers of violence can appeal to the undeniable fact that in the household of nature destruction and creation are but two sides of the natural process, so that collective violent action, quite apart from its inherent attraction, may appear as natural a prerequisite for the collective life of mankind as the struggle for survival and violent death for continuing life in the animal kingdom.

It is here, I would contend, and not in *Origins*, or *On Revolution*, and surely not in *The Human Condition*, that Arendt defines most precisely the deepest of the three antinomies at the heart of liberalism as a political theology. Beyond even the impasses surrounding (i) the interpenetration of freedom and law, and of (ii) spontaneity (or natality, the creation of something truly new) and tradition, that always arise in a liberal polity that attempts to give shape to founded freedom and a constitutional order, there is this deeper one about human society as the site where (iii) theocratic faith and secular reason-giving concerning the justification of that order are bound together. The irresolvable tension between faith and reason ultimately resides in the valuation of life itself. This is what makes the biological justification of violence so incredibly and inherently dangerous for Arendt: it runs the risk of dissolving the antinomy by reducing the purpose of the constitutional order to the elimination of the disease responsible for the sick society, of whatever it holds responsible for the "illness" in the "body politic."

This biopolitical program, for Arendt—and this is profoundly to her credit and not generally recognized—is essentially, not historically and accidentally, related to racism. For this reason, I would argue that it is here in part III of *On Violence*, arguing against the biological justification of violence as such and in general and not in the discussion of race and racism in *Origins* or any other text explicitly about anti-Black racism that Arendt (OV: 76) makes her most powerful anti-racist argument:

> Racism, as distinguished from race, is not a fact of life, but an ideology, and the deeds it leads to are not reflex actions, but deliberate acts based on pseudo-scientific theories. Violence in interracial struggle is always murderous, but it is not "irrational"; it is the logical and rational consequence of racism, by which I do not mean some rather vague prejudices on either side, but an explicit ideological system.

The anti-Black violence of the criminal justice system run for and by the white majority, Arendt is arguing, does not arise accidentally, as a matter of convenience or as a response to acts of violence by Blacks. Rather, it is a biopolitical project of *some* powerful, government actors in the United States who share a vision of the American body politic; in this light anti-Black violence ("policing") is best seen as what Arendt (OV: 76) calls a "logical and rational consequence" of "an explicit ideological system."

This means that, in some cases and in some places, the backlash against the successes of the civil rights movement—in particular, of course, the *Brown* decision (1954) and the passage of the Civil Rights Act (1964) and Voting Rights Act (1965)—gives proof positive to a general, even universal, danger in (even) liberal politics: a tendency toward to the yoking of violence and power grounded in the biological justification of violence as the means by which to preserve the vitality of the body politic. Yet it could be worse, Arendt continues. In a rare example of her stepping into the role of the prophet or prognosticator, Arendt (OV: 77) allows herself to imagine how the increasing prevalence of violence in the streets of America's cities—and it is crucial to remember that she is living in upper Manhattan, where there are acts of arson and clashes with police quite literally every weekend outside her window—will lead to "a really violent white backlash, whose greatest danger would be the transformation of white prejudices into a full-fledged racist ideology for which 'law and order' would indeed become a mere façade"; in this "still unlikely case," Arendt imagines, "a majority of [American] citizens would be willing to pay the price of the invisible terror of a police state for law and order in the streets."

Northern liberals, in their self-serving responses to increasing friction surrounding the methods of non-violent resistance in Black communities, particularly in urban centers outside the American South, Arendt argues in the third part of *On Violence*, created a right mess for themselves. In their own adoption of the biological justification of violence they have quite literally empowered, in Arendt's sense of the term "power," Richard Nixon and the Republican Party's frankly and robustly ideological turn to quasi-Fascist "law and order" politics that many whites (often prejudiced but *not* racist in her sense of those two terms) found appealing, or even necessary. Arendt (OV: 75) finds that:

> while boycotts, sit-ins, and demonstrations were successful in eliminating discriminatory laws and ordinances in the South, they proved utter failures and became counterproductive when they encountered the social conditions in the large urban centers [for, all] this mode of action could do, and indeed did, was to bring these conditions into the open, into the street, where the basic irreconcilability of interests was dangerously exposed.

Once this basic irreconcilability of interests became clear, the hollow worthlessness of Kennedy-style technocracy by liberal elites was clear to everyone, regardless of race. Such an environment, coupled with a popular discourse in which violence and power share a biological justification as a common denominator, proved very fertile ground (to use a biological metaphor of precisely the kind Arendt decries) for the very worst tendencies of even a liberal order, when it adopts the language of the body politic non-metaphorically.

It is here, in her response of vitalism and appeals to nature as a political principle in *On Violence*, that Arendt comes closest to offering a resolution to the third of the three antinomies of liberal political theology (as discussed in Chapters 3 and 4 above). Specifically, in rejecting the notion that power (and hence action) is related to natural growth, Arendt also resists the image of a body politic as an organic community whose health and livelihood must be defended at all costs, and with whatever degree of violence. In so doing, she offers a window on the prospect of a form of popular sovereignty in which the "we" of the people is grounded in neither ethnic nor confessional sameness. Such a peoplehood, it is just about imaginable, would be on in which power, rather than violence or force or authority, would be the self-organizing principle of collective organization, along the lines of Arendt's (OV: 51) famous claim in part II of *On Violence* that power, like peace, is "absolute" and thus "an end in itself."

That said, while Arendt—with the help of Augustine—was able to find some sort of resolution for the first two antinomies of liberal political theology, a workable response to the third of these impasses eludes her. While her critique of what, precisely, goes wrong when the attempt to resolve the antinomy brings about a "great compromise" in which violence and power are interwoven is unimpeachable, to my mind, it does not yield a positive politics of power divorced from violence. Nor does she have anything to offer in terms of a vision of what ground, contingent or otherwise, could possibly serve as a basis for such a popular sovereignty without a body politic. For that reason, in facing the deepest source of what I will figure as the *eschaton*—both the limit and the end—of liberalism as a political theology, which is the sacred status of that which is by definition excluded from the second body of the people, we must set Arendt's Augustine in conversation with a related, but quite distinct, form of engagement with Augustine as a source for transformative change for the better in the here and now; namely, the presentation of and mobilization around Augustine's doctrine of love in the Black Protestant tradition of theology and political self-organization.

Arendt (RLR: 53) herself, I hope to show in the coming section, recognizes this when she argues that the

> only public force that can fight social prejudice is the churches, and they can do so in the name of the uniqueness of the person, for it is on the principle of the uniqueness of souls that religion (and especially the Christian faith) is based. The churches are indeed the only communal and public

> place where appearances do not count, and if discrimination creeps into the houses of worship, this is an infallible sign of their religious failing. They then have become and are no longer religious institutions.

This point only becomes more explicit in her response to Ralph Ellison's damning, yet sensitive, critique of her argument in which she acknowledges that, in particular, she missed the ways in which "the ideal of sacrifice" was so integral to the efforts of the NAACP and others during the high-water days of the civil rights movement.

Before attending to those exchanges from the mid-1960s, let us note one other key piece of evidence that shows that Arendt herself came to see that, at least in the United States, something else was needed, something connected to the religious sources of political claims from the Black minority in particular, in order to resist what we could call the rise of the biopolitical championed by the technocratic elite and the ethnonationalist elements of the white majority. In "Introduction into Politics," Arendt (2005: 103) argues if "we want to dispel prejudices, we must first discover the past judgments contained within them, which is to say, we must reveal whatever truth lies within them." Here, in an entirely underdeveloped aside in "Reflections," she crucially acknowledges that churches—and, tacitly, the Black church in particular—have an essential and inescapable role to play in correcting the obvious and profound failure she understands legally sanctioned segregation to be. Sadly, this promising thought is not brought out in any kind of detail in the rest of the essay, nor in her "Reply" to critics; a key to understanding it, however, can be found in Arendt's exchange about "Reflections" with Ralph Ellison and in particular their discussion there about "the ideal of sacrifice" that Arendt recognizes she "missed" in her argument concerning the Black parents who, in her judgment, wrongly sent their children to schools that were forced to integrate by Federal troops, as we will examine through Danielle Allen's (2004) acute analysis, with which the next section—in which we will shift from trying to understand the limits of Arendt's Augustine to seeing the ways in which another appropriation of Augustine, namely, that of Black Protestant thought in the nineteenth and twentieth centuries, can help us move beyond her own limits.

Augustine and the Politics of Love in the Black Protestant Tradition

Danielle Allen (2004) has offered the definitive statement on what, precisely, brings Arendt to misread the desegregation of schools as a site, even the central site, of political activism during the highwater mark of the civil rights era. By contrasting Arendt's argument about the desegregation of Central High School in Little Rock, Arkansas with that of Ralph Ellison, Allen (2004: 27) shows that Ellison, who had "developed the concepts of ritual and sacrifice at length in his 1952 novel *Invisible Man*, and amplified his accounts of both terms in his many essays" offers these concepts "as the foundation for a provocative account of democracy," in which ritual and sacrifice are integral not only to the civil rights movement, but also to "democratic citizenship" as such.

In what, precisely, does this sacrificial (and ritualistic, but this will be less important for us here) aspect of democratic citizenship consist, which Ellison sees and Arendt missed, at least until Ellison insisted upon it, prompting her to change her mind—in some respects—regarding her argument in "Reflections"? Allen (2004: 29) puts it this way: "The hard truth of democracy is that some citizens are always giving things up for others. Only vigorous forms of citizenship can give a polity the resources to deal with the inevitable problem of sacrifice." Note that, in this formulation, there is no express religious connotation to the term sacrifice and no theological underpinning to its use as a keyword for democratic theory. On this level and in this usage, describing a citizen as making a "sacrifice" would be interchangeable with that citizen accepting some sort of "trade-off" or absorbing an "opportunity cost." Yet, clearly, there is more to this term than just that, and this "something more" is integral to why Ellison uses it and why Allen adopts it from him in her own corrective to Arendt, while broadly and openly operating in an Arendtian vein in her democratic and political theory more broadly.

What is this something more? Undeniably, it is a certain Christian legacy and in particular a legacy that is essential to understanding the Black Protestant tradition that is at the core of not only civil rights activism but also American politics, especially since the rise of Abolitionism and the Civil War in particular. Crucially, it requires abandoning Arendt's impossible to maintain wall of separation between the social and the political. As Allen (2004: 29) insists, the "site of sacrifice is between the social world—of custom and of mental, physical, and economic harm from other citizens—and the political world of institutions and practices," and for this reason, it is "no wonder, then, that Ellison, in powerful contrast to Arendt, so frequently uses the term 'socio-political.'" When we look a bit more deeply into that social world, whose distinctive features for Ellison involve both custom *and harm*, and which Arendt so ardently wants to keep as separate as possible from the political world, we begin to see the religious and theological background that is implicit in the choice to use the term "sacrifice" rather than explicitly secular (at least putatively) term such as "cost" or "trade-off."

We can see this, Allen (2024: 30) notes, when attending to the fact that, for Ellison, the "sacrifices of African Americans living in a segregated polity were sufficiently extreme to constitute scapegoating rather than legitimate sacrifice." It begins to become apparent here because scapegoating has an inescapable theological undertone; the very meaning of the word, and the name of the animal hiding within the compound note at the root of that usage as a verb, points to a religious ritual that goes back to the pre-Temple traditions of the Israelites. Importantly, a religious ritual that remains part of the liturgy of Yom Kippur, the Jewish Day of Atonement, and through that incorporation and preservation, is part of the Christian heritage lurking in the figure of the Black students integrating Central High School as scapegoats. Not figuratively speaking, but quite literally: this is the political theological underpinning of the ideal of sacrifice that Ellison is adumbrating and Arendt acknowledges she initially missed entirely.

Allen does not bring out all these dimensions in her excursus on Ellison as a rejoinder to Arendt, but she does draw the lesson for the discussion of the inability to divide the political from the social in the way Arendt wishes to both in "Reflections" and in *The Human Condition*, which she was writing at the same time. As Allen (2004: 30) puts it, the sacrifice was really the scapegoating to which the parents of the Little Rock Nine and many other civil rights activists exposed themselves which "revealed a truth that applies to all democratic citizens"; namely, that "the political world cannot be entirely separated from the social world," and "learning how to negotiate the losses one experiences at the hands of the public is fundamental to becoming a political actor, not only for minorities suffering political abuses, but for all citizens." The ultimate inseparability of the social and the political matters deeply, because for Allen (2004: 31) following Ellison, "the figure of Elizabeth Eckford brought before the public eye not only the truth about then existing modes of citizenship but also the glimmerings of a new account of democratic agency." That is to say, Arendt is mistaken in the argument about the irresponsibility of the parents and the NAACP representatives in being absent, or "invisible" in the photograph of Elizabeth Eckford that so disturbed her initially because she is mistaken about ideal of sacrifice that was motivating them to be present there in the manner in which they were: a present loss, an exposure to further harm. As Allen (2004: 34) stresses, the point is not that Arendt, individually, was not able to understand how and why the social and the political are bound together but that "this invisibility was not merely the failure of one theorist to see individual sacrifice," but the way that "democratic practice" lacks "a language to comprehend sacrifice, or the losses and disappointments people accept" to make both the society and the polity work.

But what happens when we correct this myopia? What can we see more clearly when we account for the persistent presence of sacrifice in democratic life? This requires us to take a turn more directly and frankly into political theology, which Allen does in her chapter on "Sacrifice and Citizenship." Allen (2004: 37) begins with how "Thomas Hobbes, John Locke, and Jean-Jacques Rousseau all draw on the same Old Testament story in grounding their accounts of consent and political obligation." While the story of Isaac, where Abraham is willing to sacrifice his son for the Lord might come to mind, it is actually the story of Jepthah in Judges 11 to which they turn. Jepthah's story was instructive for Hobbes, Locke, and Rousseau insofar as its model of military sacrifice in order to earn citizenship is integral to modern republics—another instantiation of the inability for liberal orders to ever express themselves in terms of secular values. Allen's (2004: 38) focus, however, is different; she reminds us of how Ellison insists that while "Jepthah thus gains his citizenship among the Israelites through military heroism," he "cements a system of promise and consent only on the basis of his daughter's self-sacrifice." Even when theorists and the tradition see the political theological sources, they mistake both the core of the sources, at least as read in Black churches; this is as true today as it was true when Ellison was responding to Hobbes, Locke, and Rousseau.

Indeed, today's political theory and analysis, and also ordinary political reporting and public discourse remain just as blind to these everyday sacrifices that are, for Allen and Ellison, the real lesson of Jepthah's story as a foundational text for promise-making and -keeping in a democratic society. As Allen (2004: 39) argues "the story of Jepthah's daughter's self-sacrifice" has much to teach us "about the experience of women in democratic polities" if we are able "to look beyond the battlefield to other moments of sacrifice." While it is common enough, Allen (2004: 39) continues, to identify the work of "soldiers, firemen, and policemen" as exemplars of Jepthah's military sacrifice, his "daughter's self-sacrifice, however, is the model for a whole other range of anonymous loss in democratic politics, which, as it happens, democratic citizens generally do not see clearly; nor do they honor it." Here we see the deeper meaning as well as the broader context of Arendt's failure to understand the ideal of sacrifice that motivated civil rights activists, individually and through organizations like the NAACP to pursue court-enforced integration. It is not just Arendt, or theorists in the 1950s failing to understand the motivation of integrationist policies; rather, as Allen (2004: 39) concludes this part of her analysis, "just as the political theory of the 1950s was not equipped to acknowledge the sacrifices of Little Rock, neither do our present terms of political analysis come to grips with this kind of sacrifice." Now, as then, in other words, the ideal of sacrifice and the everyday heroism of those who make sacrifices for the sake of democratic life remain largely invisible both in democratic theory and in public discourse.

In short, Allen expands on Ellison not primarily to correct Arendt but to help us see today how the grounding of civil rights mobilization in the Black Protestant tradition is of a piece with the fuller reading of the story of Jepthah in which it is his daughter's act of sacrifice that cements the new bond with the Israelites and not the military service of the heroic father. This, in its fullness, is the "ideal of sacrifice" that Arendt acknowledged (in her July 29, 1965 letter to Ellison) she had missed in "Reflections," leading her to describe the issue of public schooling as non-political. If, however, we focus on the civic dimension of ritual and sacrifice, we run the risk of minimizing its political theological character and thus leave something still present in Arendt's own thinking as a possibility behind. In the rest of this chapter, building from Allen's insights into the political theology behind the legal and political activism of the NAACP and its fellow travelers, I aim to demonstrate what, precisely, are those resources in Arendt's thinking that remain to be harvested should we wish to understand better than she did.

This holds not only in "Reflections" but throughout her writings on Black political mobilization in America in the 1950s and 1960s, as there is a political theology behind Ellison's rebuke of her argument in "Reflections." For this, I suggest we turn to Bayard Rustin's writings on the importance of non-violent methods for Black political mobilization and his conceptualization of Black political action as a civil rights revolution. Rustin here presents civil rights activism as politics and therefore action in Arendt's sense, rather than as a social movement as people tended to see it at the time of Rustin's writings as well as now. When we do so, we will find that the politics of love—which Arendt rebuked so forcefully—is an integral piece of the revolution Rustin sees and tries to support, one that carries, yes, a Pauline legacy through the theology of Augustine but is ultimately grounded in the Hebrew prophets in a way that links the political activism of Jews and Black Americans in a manner that Arendt, for whatever reasons, never accepted.

What precisely is this theological legacy with which Arendt is deeply embedded and but which she always kept at arm's length? To understand it better, we turn to the work of Bayard Rustin—a figure much more thought of recently than in the past decades, especially with the release of a major motion picture bearing his name (with Barack and Michelle Obama named as executive producers) in November 2023. While generally seen as a strategist, activist, and organizer, Rustin was also a crafter of policy and a political thinker in Arendt's sense (of "thinking what we are doing"). In a series of essays and speeches written and delivered in a pivotal moment of American history (1964–1968) when he was at the peak of his powers, following his reception as one of "the leaders" of the March (as *Life* magazine put it while placing him on the cover on September 6, 1963), Rustin lays out what I think we can consider the central tenets of his political philosophy.

This political philosophy, not often recognized as such, is drawn from a number of sources and is very much in contact with the main debates of that time; it remains, however, a unique and original reflection on how the normative weight of internationalism, non-violence, integration, and labor-friendly industrial policy are mutually reinforcing and, in fact, why none of those values can be actualized absent the others. In a time when: international and transnational institutions are the least popular they have ever been since the Second World War in both more and less perfectly democratic societies;

the efficacy and moral superiority of non-violent resistance is more doubted by social movements across the ideological spectrum; the politics of identity and identification is celebrated by everyone from white nationalists to Christian nationalists to large portions of the political left; and membership in labor organizations remains at or near historic lows, even if unionization drives have gathered much attention and popular support since the Covid pandemic—in such a time, we surely need to hear and understand Rustin's unique perspective, which valorizes all those aspects of an internationalist, non-violent, integrationist, and solidaristic worldview that seem less than ever persuasive for the political left, let alone the center and right of the ideological spectrum.

Before turning to these essays from the mid-1960s, let us first call to mind the fundamental principle motivating Rustin's thought and direct action: the commitment to non-violence, as he articulated it in the 1940s and 1950s. In one especially stark formulation, quoting from the statement drafted by "sixty beleaguered Negro leaders from across the South [who] voted to establish a permanent Southern Negro Leaders Conference on Nonviolent Integration" that Martin Luther King, Jr. had invited Rustin to organize and educate, Rustin (2003: 106) admonishes: "Nonviolence is not a symbol of weakness or cowardice, but, as Jesus and Gandhi demonstrated, nonviolent resistance transforms weakness into strength and breeds courage in the face of danger." This position, taken here from Rustin's 1957 "Even in the face of death," a statement on non-violence and the politics of love, informs how Rustin understands segregation. For, Rustin believes, only non-violence can guard against a propensity for self-love and self-interest that are incompatible with seeking justice for all and rejecting injustice against any. This is the deep fount of the oft-quoted conviction that one must be, in oneself, the change that one wishes to see in the world.

This principle of non-violence is also why integration requires, as Rustin puts in "Some Lessons from Watts" (1965), a revolution and not a social movement or a protest movement. Rustin (2003: 130) argues that in order to speak about the unrest that was called "riots" by the white establishment, it is "necessary for me to talk first about the nature of the revolution through which we are moving." Rustin goes on to stress that it is hard for Americans—and even harder for Europeans (remember this is in the summer of 1965; by the spring of 1968 the Europeans he was thinking of would likely not have had any trouble conceptualizing the revolution that Rustin was naming years earlier)—to understand that this "civil rights revolution" is a revolution because of a "common assumption" that revolution requires or involves three features that are rejected by what is generally called the civil rights movement but Rustin wants us to think of as a revolution: first, an attempt to seize political power, likely by force; second, a commitment to constitutional change; third, and most important for Rustin, "revolutions as we have known them invariably have used any form of power and in any degree—whatever it can get into its hands for the accomplishment of its aim, the achieving of power. By and large, the Negro revolt has denied that it is interested in, nor has it used, violence. It has limited itself in tactics and stratagems to nonviolence." Since the civil rights revolution does not display these characteristics, Rustin says, it is hard for white Americans and even harder for Europeans, he believes, to believe that it is, in fact a revolution. For this reason, he argues, they find the violent and destructive—at least of property and goods—nature of the uprisings ("riots") in American cities so unfathomable.

How are we, then, to understand the revolutionary character of the demand for equality and freedom? In an essay written in the immediate wake of the passage of the Civil Rights Act (July 2, 1964) and some months before the uprising and violence in Watts, called "From Protest to Politics," Rustin (2003: 116) notes that the increasing street agitation apparent at the time "were outbursts of class aggression in a society where class and color definitions are converging disastrously" and asks "how can the (perhaps misnamed) civil rights movement deal with this problem?" In noting that the passage of the Civil Rights Act is just the beginning of the revolution that is required in order for the goals of Black Americans to be met, Rustin (2003: 116) links his commitment to integration with the importance of just economic development, arguing that the "widespread assumption that the removal of artificial racial barriers should result in the automatic integration of the Negro into all aspects of American life" is a "myth fostered by facile analogies with the experience of various ethnic immigrant groups, particularly the Jews." Rustin's insistence that the experience of Black Americans cannot be compared with that of other—often initially unwelcome—migrants to America is something we still need to hear today.

This is evident from the fact that while still president and speaking during a naturalization ceremony at the National Archives in December 2015, Barack Obama said: "It wasn't always easy for new immigrants. Certainly, it wasn't easy for those of African heritage who had not come here voluntarily, and yet in their own way were immigrants themselves." Then-President Obama struggled, speaking less than a decade ago, and many observers of all nationalities and political persuasions today struggle, to sufficiently distinguish the legacy of slavery and being descended from people who were kidnapped and sent unwillingly to the United States from all other origin stories underlying "the American experience" today.

Still more relevant is the point Rustin (2003: 116–17) makes in laying out the rationale of his denial that the Black American experience can be meaningfully compared with the Jewish American experience, finding three "simple but profound reasons" why their place in America is so fundamentally different. First, while "Jews have a long history as a literate people, a resource which has afforded them opportunities to advance in the academic and professional worlds, to achieve intellectual status even in the midst of economic hardship, and to evolve sustaining value systems in the context of ghetto life," Black Americans, "for the greater part of their presence in this country, were forbidden by law to read or write." Second, while "Jews have a long history of family stability," Blacks found their "family structure was totally destroyed by slavery and with it the possibility of cultural transmission." Third, while "Jews are white and have the option of relinquishing their cultural religious identity, intermarrying, passing, etc. Negroes, or at least the overwhelming majority of them, do not have this option." Acknowledging that the Jewish population in America was never entirely white and is more diverse today than when Rustin made this argument nearly sixty years ago, all three of these grounds for the *incommensurable* and ultimately *incomparable* forms and degrees of exclusion to which Black Americans and Jewish Americans have been subjected in their country very much bear the test of time. Even when faced with the greatest degree of prejudice and discrimination, the American state—at whichever level of governance—neither directly forbade nor subtly obstructed the capacity for Jews to educate themselves in their literary and cultural–religious traditions nor to build and maintain their families and their property in and through those families. And, whenever popular sentiment locally, regionally, or nationally is least sympathetic to American Jews, it was—and is—possible for them to "pass" as white in a relatively straightforward way, without ceasing to identify as Jews in "safe" spaces; an option absolutely closed off to Black Americans as Black Americans.

This, quite precisely, is why the ("perhaps misnamed" as Rustin wrote) Black civil rights movement was—and is—a revolutionary practice and site of ongoing political mobilization. As Rustin argues, and unlike other ethnic minorities, including other non-white ethnic minorities, Black Americans have never been granted the equal access to educational and familial structures, nor the putative color-blindness, that make it possible to reconstitute their communities as productive and sustaining socially, culturally, and economically. As Rustin (2003: 117) concludes on this theme in this piece from 1965, if "Jewish and Negro communities are not comparable in terms of education, family structure, and color, it is also true that their respective economic roles bear little resemblance" and no just and equitable society can be formed while the economic deprivation of the Black minority remains so stark.

For all these reasons, Rustin claims, justice and equality for Black Americans requires nothing short of a revolution. Why, then, is it just as necessary that this revolution be non-violent? For this we need to turn to the expressly theological underpinnings of Rustin's thinking in these essays and speeches. Let us hear Rustin answering this question not during the decade of mobilization from the *Brown* v. *Board of Education of Topeka, Kansas* decision (1954) until the passage of the Civil Rights Act (1964) and Voting Rights Act (1965), but in two texts written in the immediate aftermath of the assassination of Martin Luther King on April 4, 1968. In the first, speaking to one of the central Jewish civil rights organizations in the United States (the Anti-Defamation League) in May 1968, Rustin (2003: 153) argues that in order to understand why non-violence is necessary for the social revolution, notwithstanding and even because of then-increasing polarization and the widening popularity of the Black Power movement and Black separatism more generally, we must first understand what he calls "the anatomy of frustration," which itself requires asking hard questions about "the Jewish problem." Rustin (2003: 153) continues by insisting that we cannot go around "apologizing for or explaining away Negro anti-Semitism," which "is dangerous" and "must be rooted out."

Crucially, Rustin (2003: 159) points out that while Black antisemitism is inextricably linked with the failures of the civil rights movement to produce meaningful change where it was felt most needed; the Hebrew Bible provides a resource where Black and Jews can come together to confront Black frustration and root out antisemitism: "To hear these young Negroes spouting material directly from *Mein Kampf* must bring terrible memories, shocking inner turmoil. But in times of confusion, I recommend to Jews what I do for myself in times of confusion. I go back and read the Jewish prophets, mainly Isaiah and Jeremiah. Isaiah and Jeremiah have taught me to be against injustice wherever it is, and first of all in myself." The books of the prophets bring Rustin and us back to the politics of non-violence: while Jesus and Gandhi are the names one hears the most when it comes to the philosophical and theological resources at the heart of the civil rights movement, Rustin is clear that the doctrine that a failure to create an equitable and just society (often called the "social gospel" in Christian theology) can best be redressed through each individual's recognition of the moral imperative to enact justice in oneself and one's community that rests at the heart of his vision of the civil rights revolution and "the work that needs to be done." And, he stresses here, this ethic originates in the Hebrew prophets who are the source of inspiration for the call to achieve change through non-violence.

Why so? Why are the Hebrew prophets the best source for assistance in times of confusion and doubt? Rustin (2003: 159) concludes:

> Isaiah and Jeremiah would be the first to point out [that the] issue never was, and never can be, simply a problem of Jew and gentile or black and white. The problem is man's inhumanity to man and must be fought from that basic principle regardless of race or creed. . . . White fear, Negro frustration, and anti-Semitism will disappear not because we rail against them but because we bring about a social and economic program to neutralize them.

In their recognition that injustice anywhere is a threat to justice everywhere and their coeval demand that all people of conscience commit to a "social and economic program" to create an equitable society, Rustin argues, Isaiah and Jeremiah as model Hebrew prophets make clear that the principle of non-violence is not just a moral principle but also a principle of action that brings about transformative change. Rustin's analysis of Black antisemitism and his call for solidaristic action between Black and Jewish Americans grounded in their shared inheritance of the Hebrew prophets as a necessary aspect of the civil rights revolution was delivered as a speech fifty-five years ago; they remain directly pertinent to the divided and polarized America of today, where Kyrie Irving's thoughtless repetition of antisemitic tropes can still monopolize airtime and popular debate for months and where the latest round of violence between Israel and Hamas is dividing American opinion more than ever.

In the second of these two pieces written right after King's assassination, addressed to those who would consider themselves his followers and admirers, whom Rustin frames as "the Negro–labor–liberal coalition," Rustin (2003: 189) bemoans that "a process of polarization" is taking place not only between liberal and conservatives, between the north and the south, and between whites and non-whites in 1968 America, but also "within the Negro community"; he worries that "with the murder of Dr. King, it is likely to be accelerated." This, of course, very much proved to be case with the intensification of the "Southern strategy" during the Nixon administration—Nixon was elected months after Rustin composed these two texts—and the increasingly bleak experience of life in America's cities during the period of white flight, economic recession, and the disinvestment of state and federal governments in urban areas throughout the 1970s and 1980s. What is even more telling in Rustin's writing from this particular period is his prescient awareness that non-violence, already very much doubted in the Black community, would only come to be more and more discredited with King's assassination. Rustin (2003: 189–90) warns that "young militants will tell you, 'this country was built on violence. Look at what we did to the Indians. Look at our television and movies. And look at Vietnam. If the cause of the Vietnamese is worth taking up guns for, why isn't the cause of the black man right here in Harlem?'" Rustin's (2003: 194) reflection on King's passing and his call for the Negro–labor–liberal coalition to use the 1968 election to carry out soon-to-be-former President Johnson's call to "build a 'second America' between now and the year 2000" are an unheeded call for the true civil rights revolution, which still remains as the work to be done.

It is this unique political theology, in which theory and practice and thinking and action are interwoven, that makes Rustin a still-untapped resource today. The recent media attention he is now deemed to merit demonstrates a desire to "restore" Rustin to his rightful place as a central figure in the uneven and incomplete struggle for equality and freedom. If so, we would do well to channel that energy *not* into a hagiography of him as a man with intersectional identities but rather into efforts to understand his unique advocacy of a "politics of love." Rustin's view of love-as-reconciliation, reconstructed very briefly above, connects with the mainstream of the Black Protestant tradition as represented by Martin Luther King, Jr. and discussed critically but sympathetically by James Baldwin, especially in "Letter from a Region of My Mind" (*New Yorker*, November 9, 1962, which became the bulk of *The Fire Next Time* (1963)). But it also crucially differs from that mainstream. As terrance wiley shows in his contribution to the newly released volume edited by Michael G. Long (2024: 162–63), Rustin came—during the increasingly febrile period we are discussing here (from the passage of the Civil Rights and Voting Rights Acts in 1964–1965 to the assassination of Martin Luther King Jr. in April 1968)—to "question love as an appropriate ethic, emotion, or motive in the political domain." In so doing, Rustin makes very much the same arguments that Arendt does in her rejection of love as a political principle in both her major work and in her letter to Baldwin on the occasion of reading "Letter" in the *New Yorker* in November 1962. As wiley rightly emphasizes, Rustin is at pains in his major written work of this moment ("The Lessons of the Long Hot Summer" (*Commentary*, 44:4, October 1967), not collected in the 2003 volume of his writings) to reject *both* the embrace of violence *and* the Gospel-based embrace of loving one's enemies.

In "Long Hot Summer," Rustin insists as he would as well in "The Anatomy of Frustration," that even though white society "keeps providing the ghetto communities with evidence that unless they riot, they will get nothing," all the same he is sure that violent resistance will "almost certainly reap only resistance and repression." What wiley stresses less, though, is that Black civil rights and economic democracy are linked, for Rustin in these pieces at this moment no less than over the prior twenty years of activism and writing, precisely in Hebrew prophetic tradition of love-of-neighbor-as-self. For wiley, Rustin's skepticism about love as a principle orienting Black citizens toward the white majority as a rejection of the politics of love as such—a sort of siding with Malcolm against Martin. I believe that Rustin's insistence on the continuing practice of non-violent activism and the need to implement the Freedom Budget for All Americans proposed by A. Philip Randolph shows rather that Rustin is offering an alternative vision of the relevance of what gets called "the Judeo-Christian tradition" as an alternative to both Martin Luther King, Jr. and Malcolm X.

Rustin knew and understood better than anyone, I have tried to show, the contradictory dynamics of coalition-building in a late modern, capitalist and multifaith democracy like the United States. He understood, from painful experience, that to fight for social and economic equality will lead you into conflict with figures sympathetic to the call to end civil inequality who really are not bothered by social and economic inequality. That to stand up not just against violence but for non-violence will lead you to be thought of as countercultural, unpredictable and unreliable, even within your own minoritized community. And he knew well and theorized cogently about, how advocating both those positions while also representing in your person an alternative sexuality will make you an outcast. In short, he both lived the life of what Hannah Arendt calls "a conscious pariah," of which Richard J. Bernstein (1996: 14–45) has given a definitive account. Rustin, moreover, lived that life in an examined way; the fruits of his life, and his examination of it, are still very much relevant for us today.

Moving Arendt Beyond her Inability to Understand the Black Protestant Tradition

We have just seen why, if my reading of his essays and lectures of the 1960s are on point, Bayard Rustin presents a political analysis—explicitly grounded in theological resources from the Black church but deriving ultimately from the Hebrew Bible rather than Paul and Augustine's appropriation of Paul—that offers a positive response to the third of the three antinomies of liberal political theology that Arendt's own work lacks. In this concluding section, I aim to show why Arendt was never able fully to see why Black Protestant appropriations of Augustine were not merely very close to her own expressed values but actually extended and improved upon her own findings and judgments in key ways. Rather, in her private and public statements she repeatedly rejected, or at least pushed back against, views put forward by Ellison and James Baldwin that resonate with and further develop the kernel of a truly emancipatory and radically democratic political theology without exclusion Rustin lays out. Specifically, I hope to show why on the basis of her own reconstruction of her analysis of the three antinomies of liberal political theology, this is a mistake.

As we saw in our discussion of Arendt's doctoral dissertation on Augustine's concept of love in Chapter 1, Arendt began her intellectual career deeply skeptical of neighborly love as a basis for political solidarity, even as she was very attracted to certain central aspects of Augustine's approach to temporality and each human being as the, and not one kind or species of, temporal being. This skepticism informed her responses to the civil rights movement in general and to Black Protestant thought and political activity in particular. This manifests itself, above all, in Arendt's unconvincing response to Baldwin's "Letter from a Region of My Mind" (November 17, 1962).

Arendt wrote to Baldwin almost immediately after the article's publication, in a letter dated November 21, 1962 and on file at the Library of Congress.[2] As Sean Butorac (2018) relates, the heart of Arendt's response to Baldwin is a version of a central argument of her dissertation on the concept of love in

[2] Retrievable from HannahArendt.net, first published September 2006, at: https://www.hannaharendt.net/index.php/han/article/view/95/156.

Augustine. Butorac (2018: 711) succinctly summarizes Arendt's position, her argument—both in *Liebesbegriff* and in expressing her reservations to what she figures as Baldwin's "gospel of love" in the 1962 letter—thus: neighborly love, or *caritas*, is not just apolitical but actively antipolitical "because it sublimates our uniqueness, that dimension of plurality that distinguishes us." Why so? Given how fundamental Augustine's insight about the human being as that form of life that introduces the possibility of beginning, the ultimate source of the principle of natality that together with plurality constitutes the spring of action and hence of politics, how can it be that the same thinker, in the same text, expresses a view that is actively in contradiction to that other principle of plurality?

Butorac (2018: 711, quoting from the English translation (LSA: 43)) claims that the reason for this is that, for Arendt, Augustine's *caritas* requires "that one loves their neighbor with a 'sublime indifference of what or who he is.'" Paraphrasing both the central claim from Arendt's letter to Baldwin and the critical pages from *Liebesbegriff*, Butorac (2018: 711) holds that this conception of *caritas* "sublimates our uniqueness," making each living and breathing human being a mere cipher of God's power of creation—we are each God's creature, and thus we are each *only* that; this is the ground of neighborly love, of loving one's neighbor as one loves oneself. For this reason, as Butorac (2018: 711) ably puts it, "emulating God's unconditional love" is absolutely and irredeemably opposed to what might be the single most inviolable principle in Arendt's works: the conviction that plurality is "the condition of action, and therefore the precondition of freedom."

But as we have seen, however compelling Arendt's reconceptualization of liberal political theology through the basic building blocks of natality and plurality may be, and in particular however successful she might have been in pointing a way forward through the first two antinomies of classical liberalism as a political theology, there is a fundamental aporia in her work that reemerges here. As Butorac (2018: 711) puts the matter: "For Arendt, who refuted the title of philosopher and posited herself as a theorist because men not man inhabit the earth, *caritas* sublimates the plurality that gives politics both purpose and form." So far from being the means by which Black Americans in particular, because of the unique circumstances of their highly constrained status citizenship, can call American democracy to account and transform it into something if not consonant with its stated values of freedom and equality for all, for Arendt this politics of love is actually an antipolitics. So far as she can see, Baldwin's call—were it to be heeded—would serve only to compound, rather than address, the manifest faults in American democracy when it comes to finding or founding a democratic polity without exclusion.

Arendt is wrong about this. While, as Butorac (2018: 713) notes, Arendt's critique of love as a political principle is "not without merit," and in particular

Baldwin himself allows one of Arendt's central concerns: that love *can* unite and mobilize in a political way, but only among those who are oppressed and marginalized and only "the moment of liberation." Here, she is insisting on her point about conscious pariahs, discussed above, a role that she as a German Jew has played and which she recognizes as at least a possibility for Black Americans. In this respect, at least, Arendt here has pressed beyond the limits of her horizons in "Reflections" where she denied that the Black mobilization against school segregation was a political matter at all, insisting this was a social question. This is a marked advance, but it also makes clear where Arendt cannot follow Baldwin and, I would argue following Butorac, needs to go in order to come more satisfactorily to terms with Augustine as—for her—the source of natality as a basic principle and norm and the enemy of plurality as its coequal.

For Baldwin, just as love works politically, so does the absence or refusal of love. Indeed, integral to Baldwin's diagnosis of love as central to political mobilization of Black Americans as Black Americans is his corresponding and quite compelling account of whiteness in America as the condition of lovelessness, a lovelessness that is not merely a lack but an active principle of destruction; something like an antimatter that has a centrifugal effect on America as a society and a polity, especially given the power of whites as a newly racially conscious majority in the wake of the notable, yet limited, successes of the Civil Rights Era. As Butorac (2018: 714) argues, it is precisely in casting this love-less politics as increasingly the politics of the white majority that Baldwin is able to "prescribe love as a way to resolve those pathologies, reclaim an uncorrupted sense of oneself through self-examination and a restoration of one's capacity for sensuality." In the most subtle and helpful gesture in his fine essay, Butorac (2018: 714) is here able to show that "contrary to Arendt's concerns, love does not suppress human uniqueness, but, rather, fortifies that uniqueness"; it does so "by restoring white Americans' sense of positionality and history." In other words, not only does a politics of love in Baldwin's sense not reduce or sublimate the uniqueness of each human being, it actually corrects the tendency to ignore difference and pluralism; in particular to ignore race in the tradition, a tradition with which Arendt identifies, even if she claims it ended with Marx and bemoans it as "lost" or "buried." By naming and calling out the "sublimation" that Arendt also rejects and interprets as a legacy of Augustine as actually a lovelessness and denial of sensual vitality that is integral to whiteness as a political principle in 1960s America, Butorac argues, it is Baldwin and not Arendt who preserves politics as the "in betweenness," the space of appearance, that natality and plurality make possible.

I do not dissent in any way from Butorac's conclusion regarding Arendt's unconvincing rejoinder to Baldwin; indeed, as Robert P. Crease (2022) aptly puts it, there simply was a "missed connection" here between Baldwin and

Arendt. It also seems right to me, if one so wishes, to place the responsibility for this missed connection with Arendt. At the same time, the central point now, six decades on, is that we should aim to push Arendt beyond her own failings here. In the same way that I argued in the previous section that we ought to move beyond Arendt's inability to answer Ellison's critique of her argument in "Reflections" by noticing the underlying compatibility of Arendt's discussion of the Hebrew foundation legend with Rustin's appeal to Isaiah and Jeremiah in his writings of the 1960s.

For, as it has been the central aim of this entire study to argue, what I take to be Arendt's unique and never-completed project to rationally reconstruct what is still viable in the liberal promise as classically formulated through a recovery of the revolutionary tradition comes too close to giving us a language about and practice of democratic citizenship for us to give up on it because she was unwilling to come to terms more completely with her mistaken account of love as a political principle. In the remainder of this chapter, I suggest that it is possible to continue in Arendt's wake while refusing her refusal to see neighbor-love and the ideal of sacrifice as an integral mechanism of that love as a political principle. In the Epilogue that follows I go a step further, arguing that, if we are to truly find or found a popular democracy without exclusion, it might well be necessary to push Arendt's thinking further in this way.

What would it look like if Arendt's argument concerning the three aporias of liberalism as a political theology, analyzed in Chapters 3 and 4 above, came into contact with Baldwin's politics of love as Butorac defends it from Arendt's critical response and did not take recourse to the arguments against love as a political principle that we find in *Liebesbegriff*, *The Human Condition*, and the 1962 letter to Baldwin. To answer this question, I turn to a figure whose writings on love, Butorac (2018: 715), unfavorably compares with Baldwin but who I think offers a particular lens on the question of neighbor-love in relation to the figure of "The children of Israel." I turn, that is, to Howard Thurman, whom Butorac, I think wrongly, accuses of "primarily" linking "love's political power to deliberative reasoning."

In his most influential work, *Jesus and the Disinherited* (1949), Thurman stresses the fact that Jesus was a Jew, not a Roman, and moreover that Jesus was a poor Jew. Thurman (1996: 16) is emphatic that "The Christian Church has tended to overlook its Judaic origins," and this is quite problematic given that "Jesus of Nazareth was a Jew of Palestine when he went about his Father's business," and in particular was a man who in this particular positionality (as we might put it now) "was the perfect instrument for the embodiment of a set of ideals." That set of ideals, of course, center on neighbor-love and sacrifice, the very motivating principles we have been discussing throughout this chapter. Indeed, Thurman was a primary source for Rustin, as he was for King, in making the arguments described in the second section, above.

What is most remarkable, given Arendt's critique of Baldwin, as a follower of Augustine essentially, in advancing a politics of love that undercuts the uniqueness and distinctiveness of each human person to which she is beholden as the source and expression of human plurality is that Thurman (1996: 19) casts the lesson of Jesus as a Jew of Palestine precisely in terms of human uniqueness, which is "after all, the most important question, since the thing which makes him most significant is not the way in which he resembled his fellows but the way in which he differed from the rest of them. Jesus inherited the same traits as countless other Jews of his time . . . yet he was Jesus, and the others were not." In what closely resembles an argument that Arendt makes in *The Human Condition*, Thurman argues with respect to the historical personage of Jesus that two mistakes are possible: we can make the Pauline and standard Christian error of ignoring the historical specificity of Jesus as a *poor*, working-class (we could say) Jew of Palestine; or we could make something like the chiasmically opposite error of reducing Jesus to his historical circumstances, losing his uniqueness and thus, paradoxically, his universal appeal.

But what if we do not make either of those two errors? What if we embrace Jesus of Nazareth as a historical personage in his uniqueness? What, then, do we learn about love? Thurman (1996: 104), meditating on the similarities between Jesus' mission in Palestine during a period of great economic and political turmoil and serious repression by Roman and Jewish authorities alike and the recent history of the decade during which he was writing, writes that "many experiences of the last war" were the source of the "primary discovery" Jesus tried to share: that when put under pressure by natural disaster or extreme political distress each human being, even the enemy, "stood in immediate candidacy for the profoundest fellowship, understanding, and love." This seemingly high-minded sentiment gets a very grounded, material sense when Thurman (1996: 104) states a central example: the realization that since "an army is a part of the pretensions of the modern state, the state's using it to perpetuate the system of segregation is mere stupidity," and in the desegregation of the U.S. Army—which had happened only in July 1948, months before his composition of this text—Thurman finds "a public activity of the state in which the raw material of democracy can be fashioned into an experience of that personality confirmation without which there can be no lasting health in the state." Leaving aside his choice of metaphor ("health of the state"), which it must be said is indicative of the "organic metaphor" increasingly prevalent in political talk that we saw Arendt abjure when analyzing part II of *On Violence* above, it is striking just how resonant this is with Arendt's insistence that we only ever act in concert, that individuals require what Thurman here calls "personality confirmation" in order to enter and engage in the space of appearance.

This connection is all the more striking when we read the next words Thurman (1996: 104) utters in this connection: "It is not merely coincidental that this same experience is that out of which the ethical promise of love can find fulfillment." What I particularly wish to call attention to here is that, for Thurman as for Arendt, plurality and natality are the fundamental principles of a democratic polity that is pushing itself toward the perhaps impossible goal of a community not founded on exclusion. Yet, for Thurman unlike Arendt, this is precisely united with the ethical premise of neighbor-love that Jesus, as a Jew of Palestine and not as Christian universalist, taught. But is it, in the end, possible to reconcile Thurman's reading of the July 1948 desegregation of the U.S. Army as a moment that displays in its fullness what I am trying to think through here as an Arendtian political theology that rejects her rejection of love as a political principle as related to but distinct from the ultimately personal and intimate character of love?

In concluding the chapter on love, which we have been reading together here with his chapter on the interpretation of the historical personage of Jesus, Thurman (1996: 106) argues that "merely preaching the love of one's enemies" cannot call society to account for itself when it fails to recognize the unique and equal value of each person; yet he argues that at what we are here describing as a politics of neighbor-love has as its center "a core of painstaking discipline" and an "ethical demand upon the more privileged and the underprivileged" that is "the same." Here, I think, we see the real difference between Baldwin and Thurman on the politics of love and it is not about sensuality and reason at all, notwithstanding Butorac's important intervention. Like Rustin and unlike Baldwin, Thurman believes that the project for self-improvement through self-restraint advocated by Jesus, the Jew of Palestine, following Isaiah and Jeremiah among others, is not just a lesson but the central political lesson for Americans trying to reconstruct the American republic one more time in the wake of a cataclysmic war.

If the Arendtian line developed in Chapters 2 through 4 as a response to Weber's impossible call for a truly disenchanted politics as discussed in the Introduction and Chapter 1, could take on this legacy from Thurman, overcoming its opposition to love as a political principle, then perhaps we might find a resolution to the third of the three antinomies of liberal political theology that is Arendtian in spirit if not in letter. That such a resolution is at least in principle possible I hope to have shown in the common ground between Rustin and Arendt on the need for a civil rights revolution rather than a civil rights movement and the common ground between Thurman and Arendt on the salience of Jesus' uniqueness for understanding the desegregation of the U.S. Army as a case study of the resolution of the antinomy of tradition and spontaneity. If I have earned the right to suppose that such a political theology is out there to search for, then I hope in the Epilogue that follows to outline and gesture at its contours and possible content.

EPILOGUE: ARENDTIAN POLITICAL THEOLOGY AND NEIGHBOR-LOVE AS POLITICAL PRINCIPLE

Our journey through Arendt's nearly five decade-long writing career, from *Liebesbegriff* (published in 1929) through the two-volume *Life of the Mind* (posthumously published in 1978) and then back through her major and minor works of the 1950s, 1960s, and early 1970s, has brought us to two major conclusions. First, that running through all of Arendt's work is a critique of liberalism as a political theology (as argued in the Introduction and Chapter 1) that is also an incomplete attempt to rationally reconstruct the liberal promise to found a polity that practices democratic citizenship (as argued in Chapters 2 and 3) without also practicing inclusion through exclusion (as argued in Chapter 4). Second, that Arendt's project remains incomplete not so much because she never finished the intended volume 3 of *The Life of the Mind*, and therefore never formalized or finalized her defense of Kant's unwritten political philosophy, but rather because she was unwilling to come to terms more completely with an error in her attempt to reject, outright, love as a political principle (as argued in Chapter 5).

In this Epilogue, through a reading of Augustine as he appears in the early chapters of *Willing* to an extent against Arendt's purposes (much as Arendt herself read Augustine), I hope to show how we can continue in the wake of both Arendt's critique and her reconstruction of liberalism as a political theology while refusing her refusal to see neighbor-love, and the ideal of sacrifice as an integral mechanism of that love, as a political principle. I do so in order to substantiate the claim that if we are truly to practice democracy without exclusion, it will be necessary to follow Arendt in her attempted resolution of liberalism's antinomies but to part ways with her when it comes to neighbor-love as a political–theological principle for plural, liberal democratic life.

But why, ultimately, is Arendt's Augustine worth uncovering and dissociating from some of the commitments with which it comes along that are intrinsically problematic as explored in Chapters 4 and 5 above? An answer has, perhaps, already been suggested back in Chapters 1 and 3, where we focused on how and why Arendt's reading of Augustine, in theory, offers the promise of a liberalism that can stand up to both the secular "disenchantment" thesis we find in Weber and others and the apocalyptic response to that secular liberalism we find in Schmitt and others. But now that we have seen just how awry Arendt's views about people-power and social democracy often were in practice, it is hard to see why we should be listening to her at all. The discussion of chapters 4 and 8–10 of *Willing* I present now are meant to offer us a reason to continue working "with and against Arendt" in trying to find an horizon for popular democracy without exclusion.

We begin with a familiar theme when it comes to what brings Arendt back to Augustine: "the problem of the new" as she titles chapter 4 of *Willing*. We already know—from her discussion of natality as connected to the creator/creature relation in, principally, *Liebesbegriff* and *The Human Condition*—that Arendt is concerned with the problem of creation from nothing. Here, however, Arendt (LOTM2: 29) emphasizes that the real problem with "the creation of something new" and hence with the will arises "only if one adds that God's creation is *ex nihilo*, and of such a creation the Hebrew Bible knows nothing; it is an addition of later speculations." Arendt attributes this insight to her old friend and intellectual sparring partner Hans Jonas, and it is highly important and relevant that in returning to this subject, and hence the first two antinomies analyzed in Chapter 3 above (law/freedom and spontaneity/tradition) we hear here of the innocence of the Hebrew Bible as regards "the problem of the new." That is, we only see natality (or spontaneity) in irresolvable intellectual tension with tradition if we conceive of the new as "entirely new"; insofar as the creator-god of the Hebrew Bible does not create in this fashion, the seemingly insoluble problem of the freedom of the will simply does not present itself in the Jewish tradition. This refinement of the picture of "the problem of the new," absent in her *corpus* until now as it is something she has learned from Jonas in ongoing conversations about these issues over the intervening decade-plus since she published *The Human Condition* and *Eichmann*, will prove of vital importance when it comes to neighbor-love a political principle.

But first, let us reflect on the immediate significance of this insight from Jonas, which becomes clearer when we notice that the thinker to whom Arendt turns next—of whom she had earlier only written about with derision (in part III of *On Violence*, as discussed in Chapter 5)—is none other than Henri Bergson, whose philosophy of life is of paramount importance to Jonas, and who had served as a foil, perhaps even an enemy, in part III of *On Violence*. What, above all, Arendt (LOTM2: 31) aims to adopt from Bergson is the observation that in "the perspective of the willing ego, it is not freedom but necessity that appears as a delusion of consciousness," an insight that she holds to be "both elementary and highly significant," and all the more so because "despite its simple plausibility" this insight "never played any role in the endless discussions of necessity and freedom." From here, Arendt (LOTM2: 31) goes on to discuss the history of the will and offers the analysis of the first antinomy as presented in Chapter 3, beginning with the role (emphasized in our discussion of those passages there) of Duns Scotus as the "lonely defender of the primacy of the Will over the Intellect." What is crucial for us in the present context, though, is *not* how Arendt frames and then resolves the antinomy but rather the conviction that this antinomy, which is foundational for liberalism (understood as a political theology that is continuous with, if always trying to extricate itself, from paradoxes about the free will of individuals that ultimately spring from Pauline theology, need not have arisen at all: its seeming necessity, here interpreted with Bergson as a "delusion of consciousness," is in this way the very picture of our imagination being held captive by a picture of our imagination being held captive.

The importance of Paul—prefigured by the brief discussion of his unparalleled influence on conceptions of freedom in Christendom in *The Human Condition*, among other places—erupts to the fore in *Willing*'s eighth chapter on "the impotence of the will." Here the constitutive-yet-adversarial role that Paul plays for Arendt's history of the will, and hence for her rational reconstruction of liberalism as a political theology that *does not* take Paul as its source, rule and origin (*arkhē*) is most explicit. For this reason, it is here that we come closest to a clear statement from Arendt of how she is, in her *corpus* as a whole, wrestling with Augustine to try and derive from his work a politics that is ultimately not Pauline, however close Augustine might (sometimes) have brought his political theology to elements of Paul's antipolitical, apocalyptic vision. We see this, above all, when Arendt (LOTM2: 64) partly quotes and partly paraphrases Paul, in Letter to the Romans (7:7–15), as arguing that the "function of the law is equivocal" in that "it is 'good in order that sin might be shown to sin,'" but also "since it speaks in the voice of command, 'arouses the passions' and 'revives sin.'" Paul frames this equivocality paradoxically and willingly, saying that when he willfully follows the law, in order not to sin: "I do not do what I want, but I do the very thing I hate" (Romans 7:15; quoted in LOTM2: 65). What he means, Arendt (LOTM2: 65) argues, is that to follow the law dutifully (as an observant Jew, and Paul had been, he claims an "extremely zealous" one) is itself sinful; one does not commit the sin that law forbids be done, but in one's very *not* sinning, one sins, as the avoidance of sin is grounded one's own (itself sinful) hubristic quest for righteousness (*dikaiosunē*).

It is, as Arendt (LOTM2: 65) next shows, a short journey from this conviction to the conclusion that "this inner conflict can never be settled in terms of obedience to the law or submission to sin; this inner 'wretchedness,' according to Paul, can be healed only through grace, gratuitously." Here we get directly to the heart of the debates surrounding the extent to which Arendt's Augustine is Augustine at all; for, as we will see in a moment, her central proposition when turning to Augustine's place in the history of the will that she began with Jonas' insight into the difference between the Hebrew Bible on God-as-creator and the Creator from nothing invented by Christianity, later analyzed by Bergson as a delusion of consciousness by means of a phenomenological reading of necessity, and then issuing in the conclusion that this putative necessity comes into irresistible tension the with freedom through Paul's doctrine of original sin. But we can already anticipate—having read (and read again many times) that central insight from Augustine that Arendt wishes us to keep front of mind concerning the human being as that which is created in order to be a creator of something new—that her Augustine cannot possibly accept this notion of a wholly gratuitous grace. Human freedom, for Arendt's Augustine, must somehow rest in accordance with law and willful acceptance of that law's authority.

The positioning of Augustine as importantly a rejoinder to, rather than a continuation of, Paul's position on law is only one half of the story, though. As Arendt (LOTM2: 65) next stresses, "Paul became the founder of the Christian religion not only because . . . he was 'entrusted with the gospel to the uncircumcised' (Galatians 2:7), but also because wherever he went, he preached the 'resurrection of the dead' (Acts 24:21)." Here we see the fusion of the antinomian element of Paul's doctrine of grace with his particularly apocalyptic vision of Christian eschatology, in which, as Arendt (LOTM2: 65) stresses, the center of concern, "in sharp and obvious distinction from that of the gospels, is not Jesus of Nazareth, his preachings and his deeds, but Christ, crucified and resurrected." One can argue with Arendt—and those Christian commentators on Augustine who hold her depiction of Augustine in relative degrees of contempt have argued, as discussed in Introduction and Chapter 1—about the extent to which Christian Scripture relatively emphasizes Jesus' moral teachings, which are clearly in the tradition of the Hebrew Bible, especially the books of the prophets, or the glory of crucifixion and resurrection. What is clear, however, is that Paul's way of framing the theological problem of law and grace predetermines how anyone following in his wake would frame and seek to resolve the antinomies of law/freedom and spontaneity/tradition.

Equally clear, then, is why Arendt would seek to distance Augustine from this Pauline account. It is no accident, then, that the last word of this chapter on Paul is actually given to Augustine. Specifically, Arendt (LOTM2: 72–73) quotes from *Confessions* (Bk. 11, Ch. 30) in the service of an argument that in giving his "logically correct and existentially unsatisfying answer" to the question "'What did God do before he made heaven and earth?'" (namely, "'He must have created time when He created Heaven and Earth, so that there could be no 'before' prior to the Creation'"). Here, Arendt (LOTM2: 73) argues, Augustine offers a "faint echo of the faithful awe" that is recorded in the Book of Job, where the focus is on the sovereignty of the one God, not grace. Arendt (LOTM2: 73) closes the chapter with Augustine's conclusion ("Let them see that there could be no time without a created being") without any comment, but the implication is clear: Augustine, on her reading, is siding with a Hebrew tradition in remaining silent on the mysteries of God's will in creating time together with the heaven and earth against an apocalyptic messianism focused on the resurrection as a necessary and known end of time. This is not an anti-eschatological vision, of course, but Augustine is (for Arendt) muted when it comes to the future destination of this world and emphatic about the past origin.

The political implications of these theological debates are clear, both in Augustine's time and, as I believe Arendt is arguing here, in our own. To see this, we need to address Arendt's chapter on Augustine's place in the history of the will and how she understands his philosophy of the will as both Roman and Christian. The first thing to note in this regard is that what Arendt (LOTM2: 83) figures as the abyss of freedom, discussed above in Chapter 3 as one half of the title of the last chapter of *Willing* and thus as a core feature of the most intransigent of the three antinomies of liberalism as a political theology, first arises as a feature of the "feeling of omnipotence as well as of human freedom" that belongs to this philosophical will, which she identifies with Epictetus and locates in what that author characterizes as "the Will's power to assent or dissent, say Yes or No" which, the Stoic insists, is an absolute and utterly unqualified power. It is Augustine, Arendt (LOTM2: 84) suggests, who first notes the abysmal character of this absolute, philosophical, freedom, arguing that *if* it were true, then "Man in that case would have been given a truly 'monstrous' faculty" in which we find "the 'abyss' which, according to Augustine, lies hidden "in the good heart and in the evil heart." It is in naming this abyss—which gives us half of the second half of the title of the closing chapter of *Willing* ("the abyss of freedom"), discussed in Chapter 3 above—that Augustine, as I put it in the subtitle of this book, invents modernity. Arendt here quotes Augustine from his sermon on Psalm 134, suggesting as she closes the chapter on the "omnipotence of the will," which itself is an answer to the previous chapter on the "impotence of the will" that it is Augustine as "the first philosopher of the Will" (as she titles the next chapter) whose thought offers the best resolution of the debate between the Stoics and the Paulines concerning the impotence or omnipotence of the will.

The crucial point for Arendt (LOTM2: 89–90) arises in *Of Grace and Free Will*, chapter 44, where "Augustine comes to interpret the scandalous side of Paul's doctrine of grace." Arendt (LOTM2: 90) quotes Augustine's version of the scandal thus: "Law came in to increase the trespass; but where sin increased, grace abounded all the more"; a position that she argues is tantamount to saying: "Let us do evil that good may come." With that restatement of Augustine's position regarding what can be called Paul's antinomianism as Arendt reconstructs it, we return directly to the debates about Pelagianism and Augustine's place in modern debates about grace, divine election, and the possibility of one meriting the reward of divine grace. This is the very feature discussed just above in our reading of Arendt's discussion of Paul in chapter 8 of *Willing* and, as you may recall, also anticipated in the Introduction when we addressed the arguments of Kiess (2016) and Mathewes (2001) regarding Arendt's heterodox, or partial or simply incorrect, reading of Augustine on grace and original sin.

Augustine's answer, and correction, to Paul—as Arendt (LOTM2: 91) understands it—hinges on the goodness of the creation as created, in a version of the argument we followed her in advancing in the *Liebesbegriff*: "In short, 'all things by the very fact that they *are* are good,' evil and sin included and this not only because of their divine origin and because of belief in a Creator-God, but also because your own existence prevents you from either thinking or willing absolute non-existence." On the basis of this conviction, quoted and paraphrased from Augustine's "On the free choice of the will," which is a trace of Augustine's Platonism that stands in direct contrast to Paul's apocalypticism, Augustine (again being quoted from book III of the same treatise on the free choice of the will), according to Arendt (LOTM2: 92) advocates "not Will but Praise: 'Give thanks that you are'; 'praise all things for the very fact that they are'"; for, to do otherwise—to imagine that anything is out of order or that a better world is possible—is to act like "'a man who grasped by his reason perfect roundness' but 'became disgusted' because he could not find it in nature. He should be grateful for having the idea of roundness." This gratefulness for having the idea of perfect roundness despite the frustration of never being able to experience and the inference that this and other like convictions offer us the great consolation of knowing that this imperfect world is indeed entirely good and the best of all *possible* worlds, undeniably, resonates in modern ears with Leibniz and thus with the problem of theodicy discussed in the Introduction and Chapter 1. And, while she does not draw the connection to Leibniz in this passage, Arendt (LOTM2: 36–39, 133, 149, 195) does trace the lineage of this argument from Plato through Augustine and Duns Scotus to Leibniz.

What Arendt wants (and needs) from this lineage and what she wishes to distance herself from emerges as we turn to that which is both the principle or source (*arkhē*) and the end or goal (*telos*) of this basic gratitude for everything that is as it is (as Arendt puts it in her famous 1964 letter to Gershom Scholem regarding her being a "daughter of the Jewish people" on the occasion of his critique of *Eichmann in Jerusalem*): namely, love.[1] Arendt (LOTM2: 95) makes this explicit in drawing the consequence of her reading Augustine as offering an important rejoinder and revision to Paul on God's grace rather than espousing the latter's view is that this thankfulness must be grounded in love as a political, as well as theological, principle:

> But the healing of the will, and this is decisive, does not come about through divine grace. At the end of *Confessions* he returns once more to the problem and relying on certain very different considerations that are explicitly argued in the treatise *On the Trinity* . . . he diagnoses the ultimate unifying will that eventually decides a man's conduct as *Love*.

This sense of love as the fundamental mover (or "efficient cause" as this sense of causation in Aristotle came to be understood in Scholastic physics) is no metaphor for Augustine. As Arendt (LOTM2: 95) argues, Augustine "holds that the end of all movement is rest, and now he understands the emotions—the motions of the soul—in analogy to the physical world"; this may be only an analogy to locomotion "out there" in the physical world, but it is no metaphor, for it is "soul's gravity, the essence of who somebody is, and which as such is inscrutable to human eyes" that "becomes manifest in love." This love manifests in that same gratefulness, that basic gratitude, that gives rise to praise and which in turn gives rise to love: Paul's consternation in the face of the law and his apocalyptic embrace of sin ("the worse it gets, the better it will be") is thus overcome.

This, Arendt (LOTM2: 97) might work well enough for Augustine, but it will not do in "the modern age—which Nietzsche, rightly, I think called 'the era of suspicion.' When men could no longer *praise*, they turned their greatest conceptual efforts to *justifying* God and His Creation in theodicies." Here we see that lineage mentioned above, though no names are named beyond Nietzsche's as the one who offers the diagnosis of the gap between the beginning of this chronological thread and its end. For Augustine, as for Pindar in the fragment Arendt quotes in the letter to Scholem mentioned above, it is both necessary and sufficient to praise; for Leibniz, this is no longer possible: the horrors of the seventeenth century demanded some sort of justification. All the same, Arendt (LOTM2: 97) argues that "Augustine, too, needed some means of redemption for the Will," since divine "grace would not help once he had discovered that the brokenness of the Will was the same for the evil and for the good will." As we saw in the discussion of "New Augustinianism" in the Introduction, contemporary followers of Augustine see in Arendt's version of this argument in

[1] For more on this letter and its importance for Arendt's claim that *Eichmann* is, for her, a sort of modern theodicy, see Robaszkiewicz and Weinman (2022: 98, 103–5, 116–18).

her *Liebesbegriff* a straightforward error in presenting his views. Our concern, however, is not so much about the extent to which Arendt was right or not regarding Augustine; rather, we are trying to see how—for Arendt—engaging Augustine offers a pathway beyond what she sees as a dead end in Pauline theology insofar as the love-of-neighbor offers a view of how a this-worldly ethic can be reconciled with Christian eschatology.

Once more, in a version of the distinctive lineage that she draws from Plato through Augustine, Duns Scotus and Leibniz to Bergson, Arendt (LOTM2: 101) stresses what she sees as the "first intimation of certain consequences that Duns Scotus much later will draw from Augustinian voluntarism" that she reads out of books 11 and 12 of *Confessions*; namely: first, that "the Will's redemption cannot be mental and does not come by divine intervention either"; second, that "redemption comes from the act which—often like a "*coup d'état*" in Bergson's felicitous phrase—interrupts the conflict between *velle* and *nolle*; and, finally, that "the price of the redemption is, as we shall see, *freedom*." Arendt's reading—and there is some sleight of hand here, for sure, which we will not examine closely here—thus yokes the life-philosophy of Bergson with which she begins *Willing* as discussed above with Duns Scotus' embrace of contingency, discussed in Chapter 3, and then yokes both to Augustine's embrace of love and praise as the answer to the irresolvable conflict Paul introduced in his depiction of grace, original sin, and the (un)freedom of the will.

As Arendt (LOTM2: 102) succinctly concludes this line of argument: "In Augustine, as well as later in Duns Scotus, the solution of the Will's inner conflict comes about through a transformation of the Will itself, its transformation into *Love*." If we call to mind in this regard an observation regarding the particular phrase that Arendt borrows from Bergson—namely, that he describes the interruption of the usual "conflict between *velle* and *nolle*" as a "*coup d'état*"—then what might have become a bit blurry regarding the relevance of all this sifting through the weeds of Augustine's theology comes sharply into focus. Arendt here is offering a reading directed toward the political–theological in that distinctly late-Weimar sense we associate with Walter Benjamin and, perhaps above all, Carl Schmitt. How so? This *coup d'état* ("change-of-state") is, of course, a revolution in the root sense for which Arendt goes (in a phrase she consciously borrows from Benjamin) "pearl-diving" in *On Revolution*. In that work, she sees a divide that cannot be bridged between ourselves as those who lived in the age of revolutions: the revolutionary treasure is "lost" in that picture.

Here in *Willing*, written a decade or so later, however, it appears that Arendt (LOTM2: 7) is at least entertaining the possibility that "our tradition" might be able to teach us something, today, concerning how the will, understood with Augustine as "this faculty of being able to bring about something new and hence to 'change the world,'" and, perhaps more importantly still, how natality "can function in the world of appearances" that "relentlessly transforms all the spontaneity of its newcomers into the 'has been' of facts." In this telling, we hear an echo of the problem of the lost revolutionary treasure with which Arendt ends *On Revolution*: here, as there, it is a real question—and a *practical*, not a theoretical, one—if it is possible for the "pearls" on the ocean floor to be dredged up and polished off in order to be appreciated *not* for what they *were* but as objects of love and of individual and collective mobilization *now*. Arendt, throughout the 1960s—in works like *Eichmann*, *On Revolution*, and *On Violence* as well as in the essays collected in *Between Past and Future*—seems persuaded that the answer to this question is no. But here, in *Willing*, she seems to be holding out—dare one use the word—hope.

If there is such hope, and if hope is the right word, then in this particular case, the big puzzle that Arendt presents in the introduction to *Willing* is whether and how Augustine's philosophy of the will and the account of freedom based on a love that manifests in an unpredictable and revolutionary overturning of the usual concourse of affirmation and denial in the execution of the individual or collective will can be relevant when the world itself is no longer the Platonic fundamentally good world upon which Augustine insisted against Paul's apocalypticism. We have now reached the place in chapter 10 where Arendt points to what, precisely, in the transformation of the Will into Love might be the ground of such a rational hope, notwithstanding the fact that we live in a time when the world of appearances is the only world we have in common and Being, the ground of Augustine's confidence in the goodness of the world as everything that is, is—like Nietzsche's absent God—no longer available to us.

For Arendt (LOTM2: 102), Augustine (here Arendt quotes *On the Trinity*, Bk. XI, ch. ii, 5) stresses this transformation of will to love because of the "great advantage" loving has over willing, which "is not only Love's greater force in uniting what remains separate—when the Will uniting 'the form of the body that is seen and its image which arises in the sense' that 'is so violent that it can be called love, or desire, or passion,'" but also, and more importantly, "love, as distinguished from will and desire, is not extinguished when it reaches its goal but enables the mind to 'remain *steadfast* in order to *enjoy* it.'" The sempiternal character of love, the way in which in love the limited ensouled but also bodily being that is the human being can participate in the eternal and everlasting, is that in which the "great advantage" of the transformation of mere willing into the robust form of willing that is loving rests.

For this, reason, unsurprisingly, the chief end of loving is its very lastingness, as Arendt (LOTM2: 103) continues: "What love brings about is lastingness, a perdurance of which the mind otherwise seems incapable. Augustine [in *On the Trinity*, Bk. XII—MDW] has conceptualized Paul's words in the Letter to the Corinthians: 'Love never ends'; of the three that 'abide'—Faith,

Hope, Love—'the greatest [the most durable, as it were] is love (I Corinthians 13:8)." In Arendt's hands, this oft-quoted line from Paul, perhaps his most famous phrase among lay Christians and secular Americans alike, is no longer about the analogy between Christ's love for the Church and one's love for one's spouse—which is the "reading" of this and surrounding verses with which we are likely familiar from the ubiquitous quoting from this moment in scripture at weddings both confessionally devout and ecumenical and even secular. Rather, love—as Arendt reads Augustine—is a political–theological principle in which the human drive for justice is made manifest.

Fusing doctrine from Paul with Plato's argument concerning justice as its own reward and in particular the love of justice as the ground of acting justly in *Republic*, especially book 9, Arendt (LOTM2: 104) understands Augustine as transforming a materialist doctrine concerning the will and its weight into a perfected self-actualizing feature of the mind-as-will that manifests in love; for Augustine (*On the Trinity*, Bk. XI, ch. xi, 18), she writes, the will "is not understood as a separate faculty but in its function within the mind as a whole, where all single faculties, memory, intellect, and will—are 'mutually referred to each other,'" and for this reason and in this way, the will and the mind and the human being as such "finds its redemption in being transformed into Love." Paul's flirtation with what Luther would call an antinomian position in the arguments about law, sin, and grace that we saw Arendt discuss and cast as ultimately paradoxical in chapter 8 of *Willing* above is here, at last, overcome in her mind through the intervention of Augustine, who takes the Pauline teaching about grace and love and fuses it with a hybrid understanding of the materiality of the willing mind drawn from Stoic and Peripatetic arguments and the Platonic doctrine that one becomes just by loving justice.

How is this supposed to work? And why it is clear that the love in question, the perfected love in which the will itself is transformed, materially and spiritually, into love, is love of justice? Arendt (LOTM2: 104) explains by returning the analogy between the will and material bodies: "Augustine's Love exerts its influence through the 'weight'—'the will resembles a weight'—it adds to the soul, thus arresting its fluctuations. Men do not become just by knowing what is just but by loving justice." Arendt (LOTM2: 104) then yokes Augustine's position concerning love, expressed in *On the Trinity* (Bk. XI, ch. xi, 18), to his position about the soul being forged in the crucible of its choice of object of love (in *City of God*, Bk. XI, ch. xxviii): "Love is the soul's gravity, or the other way round: 'the specific gravity of bodies is, as it were, their love." In one of the most stirring and surprising interpretive moves made in her intertextual reading of *On the Free Choice of the Will*, *On the Trinity*, *Confessions* and *City of God* in this chapter, Arendt (LOTM2: 104) concludes that what remains operative in Augustine's last works after "the transformation of his earlier conception" of will from his early ones is "the Will's power of assertion and denial." In an echo of her reading of Augustine in *Liebesbegriff* to which she—very surprisingly and as is not always noticed—returns in the final chapter of part II of *Origins* (as we will discuss in a moment), Arendt (LOTM2: 104) concludes this line of argument with an appreciation of Augustine's understanding of love as an affirmative *act* of the will, arguing that "there is no greater assertion of something or somebody than to love it, that is to say: I will that you be—*Amo: Volo ut sis.*"

With this affirmation, I argue, Arendt unequivocally—if only indirectly and frustratingly inexplicitly—"throws in" with Augustine. There is, sadly, no passage to which I can point—no epilogue to the complete three-volume version of *The Life of the Mind*, say—where Arendt explicitly and definitively states that she is "with" Augustine on this point. Worse for my case, I know, are the clear statements regarding the unbridgeable chasm that has been formed by *Traditionsbruch*, the definitive break with tradition that is seen as announced by and in the work of Karl Marx. All the same, when Arendt (LOTM2: 109) concludes that—as she does in the very last line of the revised version of *Origins* that includes "Ideology and Terror" (OT: 479)—"Every man, being created in the singular, is a new beginning by virtue of his birth," she adds as a corrective or an extension of Augustine's claim that "if Augustine had drawn the consequence of the speculations, he would have defined men, not, like the Greeks, as mortals, but as 'natals.'" I understand this gesture to be one which makes clear how, in the overall project of *The Life of the Mind*, Arendt has come to a version of the Benjaminian pearl-diving among the coral at the ocean floor in which the lost treasures of the tradition that definitively ended (for her) with Marx might have some sort of afterlife, after all.

But what afterlife is there for Augustine and his/Arendt's principle of natality? The answer is hinted at when Arendt (LOTM2: 109) continues by arguing that if Augustine had "drawn the consequence" of his own argued about man as an initium, then "he would have defined the freedom of the will not as the *liberum arbitrium*, the free choice between willing and nilling," between affirming and denying, following Epictetus in revising Paul's doctrine of grace and predestination; rather, Arendt concludes, he would have defined the freedom of humans as natals, rather than mortals, which is to say, "as the freedom of which Kant speaks in the *Critique of Pure Reason.*" In this imagined reconstruction of the tradition, one which it appears *can* be a living view for us about the definitive break with tradition, we see Kant's freedom fused with Augustine's natality. But this does not mean, despite appearances, that Arendt is correcting Augustine with Kant, I would argue. Rather, she is saying that Kant's sense of the spontaneity of human reason—which manifests itself (in her reading) in the practice of synthetic judgment, as is crucial for the argument of the unwritten volume 3 of *The Life of The Mind*—is itself a handmaid to the ultimate principle for politics that can be gleaned from the tradition, as she sees: Augustine's (and her) principle of natality.

That we mistake the overall architecture of the argument of the obviously non-extant three-volume version of *The Life of the Mind* if we read volume 2 (and Augustine) in the service of volume 3 (and Kant) can be seen explicitly when comes to close her chapter on Augustine. Here, Arendt (LOTM2: 110) chooses—as we knew it had to be—her favorite moment in his *corpus* as the last work of part II of *Willing*, his celebration (in *City of God*, Bk. XI, ch. 32; Bk XII, chs. 20–22) of *each* human being as the beginning of beginning, as the origin of originality: "The distinction between an 'absolute' and a 'relative' beginning points to the same phenomenon we find in Augustine's distinction between the *principium* of the Heaven and the Earth and the *initium* of Man." This distinction between God as a ruling principle and source in contrast to human beings as a beginner of actions and teller of stories is, needless to say, a complex matter to which Arendt devoted a third of her *Liebesbegriff*, as we discussed in Chapter 1. The core point, however, is that Arendt sees in Augustine a unique and invaluable presentation of the difference between being a source or principle (as the Creator is of Creation) and being an actor or beginner, a novice, a newcomer who is a new-maker (as each human being is). This is familiar enough from *Liebesbegriff*.

What is distinctive here is that Arendt (LOTM2: 110) ends this section with a rephrasing of the point that addresses, and frankly criticizes, Kant directly: "And had Kant known of Augustine's philosophy of natality he might have agreed that the freedom of *relatively* absolute spontaneity is no more embarrassing to human reason than the fact that men are *born*—newcomers again and again in a world that preceded them in time." In other words, the antinomy of freedom and law might never have settled in human reason as an antinomy as it did in Kant's First Critique were it not for the fact that, ignorant of Augustine's embrace of the human being as a "*relatively* absolute spontaneous" actor—as *intitium*, but an *initium* that is never *principium*, Kant understood human reason as scandalized by the fact that action is both free and determined by law.

In this way, Arendt reframes the whole problem of judgment for Kant—and the undeniable power and centrality of the faculty of judgment for democratic life—not as that in which discussion of the will discharges and that to which questions of the will are to be submitted for arbitration. Rather, Kant and the faculty of judgment need to be submitted to the always-new practice of willing as action, as both the source and end of freedom. As Arendt (LOTM2: 110) concludes: "The freedom of spontaneity is part and parcel of the human condition. Its mental organ is the Will." It is true that we do, and we must, tell stories of past actions—ours and those of our fellow newcomers and those who were newcomers before—and that we judge the actions thus disclosed to us, *and* the actors who effected those actions. But none of that touches the true essential arena of freedom, and for that reason, the core of liberalism as a political theology. That core rests in the ever-new and unpredictable, unruled and ungovernable, practice of Augustine's will, which has been transformed into love; love of justice, embodied in the here and now, which is to say, the love of the world. What had been the intended title ("Love of the World") of what might be her most enduring work (whose actual title, "The Human Condition", in no accident, is mentioned in these closing lines of the chapter on Augustine in *Willing*) here manifests as the "pearl of pearls" in the sustained ocean dive that is *The Life of the Mind.*

At the outset of this line of argument, I suggested that if we insist that one cannot understand Arendt's sense of politics as power, as freedom, without accounting for her strange Augustinianism and carry this thought through irrespective of all the tensions inherent in it, then we will see both why and how exactly she offers an alternative to political theology in the sense of Benjamin and Schmitt. Having now seen the turn to Augustine in *Willing* as a corrective to, rather than a preparation for, the discussion of Kant in *Judging*, the question remains: how, precisely, is this a response to the political theology of Benjamin and his picture of divine violence as the rupture of the reproduction of law in "Critique of Violence" (1921) and the messianism found both there and in his "Theological–Political Fragment" (1920–1921) and "Theses on the Philosophy of History" (1940)?

This is neither the time nor the place to articulate a full account of how Arendt's Augustine presents a sympathetic rejoinder to Benjamin's weak messianism and its manifestation in the rupture of legal and administrative violence. Fortunately, Yotam Hotam (2023) has recently provided an account that addresses both Benjamin (chapter 2) and Arendt (chapter 4) as engaging in a critique of political theology. Of particular interest is how Hotam (2023: 148) argues that while "Benjamin's 'Critique of Violence' strongly separates divine potency from the political arena," arguing that "the only type of violence that can be considered justified, and thus rendered nonviolent, is one that eschews the political and relates to the divine," Arendt "like Benjamin argues against political violence" but does so "through the political category of authority (as the Romans understood it) that is inherently free of violence." In this way, Hotam (2023: 148) argues, Arendt articulates "a divine nonviolence that dwells in the political sphere—not separated from it." It is just this sort of reading of Arendt, as doing critical–political theology in response to Benjamin's mystical and messianic version of the same, that I have been trying to articulate in this work.

But how, precisely, does this divine non-violence dwell in the political, rather than separate from it? For Hotam (2023), as for me, the answer is to be found in the revolutionary tradition and in the *novus ordo saeclorum* analyzed in *On Revolution* and then again in *Willing*. As we saw in presenting Arendt's response to Schmitt's version of political theology in Chapter 4 above, there are certain aspects of Hotam's depiction of the role of tradition and authority as political for Arendt in which his account goes a bit astray in the details of how this "new order of the ages" figures in her critique of liberalism as a political theology. Here, though, Hotam seems to me to be precisely right to argue that what he figures as Arendt's critical theology is an internal differentiation from Benjamin's attempt at something like the same, in response to the positive, and directly political, theology of Carl Schmitt. Evidence for reading Arendt's interest in the *novus ordo saeclorum* as a response to Benjamin can also be found in her gesture to Bergson in the closing moments of section II of *Willing*, discussed just above.

To see why, we must return to the lineage she constructs from Plato through Augustine and Duns Scotus to Leibniz and then to Bergson as an attempt to work through Benjamin's episodic appeals to cathartic violence as a creative/destructive force, with which we also saw Arendt struggle in a much more critical discussion of Bergson and Nietzsche in our discussion of part III of *On Violence* in Chapter 5 above. Arendt herself, in the introduction to *Illuminations* (Benjamin 1968: 39–40), diagnoses Benjamin's appetite for collecting as "a certain destructive force" that is "active even in this passion for the past, so characteristic of heirs and late-comers," and which Benjamin himself recognized only "when he had already lost his faith in tradition and in the indestructability of the world." Where we might be inclined to understand the desire or need to collect the treasures of the past—to go "pearl-diving" in the evocative image that runs through Arendt's introduction—as one of preservation and protection, in Benjamin's case and perhaps perversely, this drive to collect actually manifests a destructive force that for Benjamin is a mystical and messianic presence haunting supposedly disenchanted modernity.

The basic appeal of this destructiveness is a highly sublimated version of the apocalyptic messianism celebrated in Benjamin's political–theological essays written in the immediate aftermath of the First World War. In these, as Peter Demetz puts it in his introduction to *Reflections*, the "anarchist mystic Benjamin sees the coming of the Messiah as abrupt, sudden, destructive, ending all human history and its barrenness by freeing pure, glorious, divine violence from contagion with myth or the regions below" (Benjamin 1968: xxvii). And it is, I am following Hotam in suggesting here, in response to this trajectory in Benjamin's work, from the divine violence of the 1920–1921 texts to the "*weak* Messianic power" of "Thesis II," written in spring 1940 as the walls were closing in, that Arendt offers in her return to the tradition in *Willing*. The ultimate aim, I believe, of her "pearl-diving" in *Willing* in particular is to motivate us as her readers to fulfill a promise that Arendt articulates in the first Preface for *Origins*, written in summer 1950. Here, Arendt (OT: ix) gestures in the prospect of a "new guarantee which can be found only in a new political principle, in a new law of the earth" that best answers to the totalitarian experiment on human nature. This, and this alone, Arendt (OT: ix) argues, can address "the reality in which we live" rather than "escape from the grimness of the present into nostalgia for a still intact past, or into the anticipated oblivion of a better future," and her choice of phrase "new law of the earth" makes patently clear that Arendt means for this book to be the answer, among other things, to those versions of political theology used for the justification, or the putative historical necessity, of totalitarian regimes.

What, of course, is *not* clear from this is what content this new law ought to have and precisely how, as Arendt (OT: ix) argues it must, its "validity this time must comprehend the whole of humanity while its power must remain strictly limited, rooted in and controlled by newly defined territorial entities." For many, this appears to be a call for the sort of human rights protections that make up the international human rights regime that began to develop with the formation of the United Nations precisely at the time she was writing, translating, and editing *Origins* for publication. But if we listen to the precise specifications Arendt lists—namely, (i) valid for "the whole of humanity," but also (ii) "strictly limited, rooted in and controlled by newly defined territorial entities"—then we can see at once that this cannot be right. Arendt is precisely *not* arguing for universal human rights overseen by global governance bodies drawn from the member nation states.

This becomes clearer still if we turn to what she says about human rights in the famous ninth chapter of *Origins*, titled "The Decline of the Nation-State and the End of the Rights of Man," and more particularly to what she says there about slavery. Arendt (OT: 297) argues: "Slavery's crime against humanity did not begin when one people defeated and enslaved its enemies . . . but when slavery became an institution in which some men were 'born' free and others slave, when it was forgotten that it was man who deprived his fellow-man of freedom, and when the sanction for the crime was attributed to nature." Note the role criminality—and this is figured as a crime against humanity, not against particular human beings—is here argued to play in relation of man to fellow-man; unstated but clearly operative here is precisely the ethical demand of neighbor-love. However much, in her later writings of the 1950s and 1960s, Arendt would come to minimize or reject love as a political principle, it is undeniably the root of the new law of the earth, universally valid but territorially limited, for which she is calling in *Origins* and to which she explicitly returns in *Willing*.

In this respect, as hideous and criminal as chattel slavery was, it points to the even-greater outrage wrought by the invention of "superfluous people" under totalitarianism. Arendt (OT: 297) continues:

> Not the loss of specific rights, then, but the loss of a community willing and able to guarantee any rights whatsoever, has been the calamity which has befallen ever-increasing numbers of people. Man, it turns out, can lose all so-called Rights of Man without losing his essential quality as man, his human dignity. Only the loss of a polity itself expels him from humanity.

This language of expulsion, as Arendt (OT: 297) is keenly aware, brings us to reflect on the divine warrant for the notion that there is a basic human dignity, whether that dignity is grounded in a human nature that is understood "in terms of the natural law or in terms of a being created in the image of God" and whether it concerns "'natural' rights or divine commands." Irrespective of the putatively secular or straightforwardly theological justification of the notion of a human right, Arendt (OT: 299) insists that "it is quite conceivable, and even within the realm of practical political possibilities, that one fine day a highly organized and mechanized humanity will conclude quite democratically that for humanity as a whole it would be better to liquidate certain parts thereof."

If there is to be an antidote to this, we are not to seek it in democratic procedures, which, as long as they privilege majoritarian decision-making above all might always allow for sure an annihilation of already dehumanized "others." It is this fundamental problem of politics, Arendt (OT: 299) argues, that "caused Plato to say: "Not man, but a god, must be the measure of all things." But can a god, or God, be of any help to "us," when we understand the relevant "we" as Arendt's post-Second World War contemporaries? In a passage just below this reflection and just before the end of part II of *Origins*, devoted to the analysis of imperialism, Arendt (OT: 301) offers a reflection on how the demand or command of the other (she uses the word "alien" in scare quotes) has or could have this divine underwriting: "The 'alien' is a frightening symbol of the fact of difference as such, of individuality as such, and indicates those realms in which man cannot change and cannot act and in which, therefore, he has a distinct tendency to destroy."

Immediately following this, Arendt (OT: 301–2) goes on to give the example of anti-Black racism in the United States: "If a Negro in a white community is considered a Negro and nothing else, he loses along with his right to equality that freedom of action which is specifically human; all his deeds are now explained as 'necessary' consequences of some 'Negro' qualities; he has become some specimen of an animal species, called man." We can quarrel with and about how Arendt exactly formulates the interplay of freedom and equality here, but what is clear from this characterization of the way that many white Americans perceive Black Americans is that they have projected what Arendt calls an "ethnic homogeneity" onto Americanness and then through that alienated (literally made-alien) Black Americans from that Americanness. As whites are the majority in the United States then as now, though not forever of course, Arendt's line of thinking is clear enough: there is no democratic solution—in the sense of majority-rule—to the propensity of human beings to recognize humanity only when it looks like them.

What does this have to do with God? Just above these comments on destroying that which is beyond our power to change or our capacity to act, and the specification of that phenomenon to race relations in the United States, Arendt

(OT: 301) offers one of her less-noticed references to Augustine: "This mere existence, that is, all that which is mysteriously given to us by birth and which includes the shape of our bodies and the talents of our minds, can be adequately dealt with only by . . . the great and incalculable grace of love, which says with Augustine, '*Volo ut sis* (I want you to be),' without being able to give any particular reason for such supreme and unsurpassable affirmation." These words seem to come out of nowhere in the context of chapter 9 of *Origins*, but for those who have been following Arendt in building up to Augustine's substitution of Love for the Will as a solution to the problems in Paul's account of grace and free will, this makes a great deal more sense. In the latter text, written a quarter-century after this chapter of *Origins*, which itself was written a quarter-century after Arendt's first sustained engagement in *Liebesbegriff*, Arendt makes explicit what is implicit here. Namely, the "new law of the earth" for which Arendt prophesizes—which means, in understanding the Hebrew Bible context with which she identifies in *Willing*, to make a moral argument for a better future state, not to share an eschatological vision—is one where each territorially defined new community recognizes itself the universal application of the command to love the neighbor.

This new law of the earth is given a clear specification in the comment on the politics of race in America shared in *Origins*. Here, Arendt is actually much more insightful than in some of her later writings on race in America, and relatedly it is here that we see the living relevance of Arendt's thinking about Augustine. Whether in *Origins* or *Willing*, in *The Human Condition* or *The Promise of Politics*, in *Liebesbegriff* or *Thinking*, in *Eichmann* or *On Violence*, in *On Revolution* or *Between Past and Future*, Arendt brings us time and again face-to-face with the central contradiction of we late moderns: how are we to live in this world as future-oriented beings with an inchoate and weary faith in a tomorrow that is meant to be better, more free and equal, more just than today and the time before, who nevertheless feel deeply and intimately the loss of a certainty and a home in the world that can come only from a tradition or heritage that comes, unlike ours, with a valid testament. Throughout this work, I have tried here to do justice to the fullness with which Arendt forces us to live with the tensions of the three antinomies (freedom/law; natality/tradition; secularism/theocracy) that constitute and are constituted by that living contradiction that liberalism is as a political theology.

In this Epilogue, I have tried to go a step further, a step beyond anywhere Arendt was willing to go in her published works, by showing how a return to the thread at which she was still pulling in her very last work (*Willing*) might yet lead us into the future in ways that are more promising. This particular thread—the one that goes back to Augustine by means of an embrace of Bergson whom she had earlier (in *On Violence*) rejected in strong terms—holds continuing promise, I believe, because it helps us makes sense of why time and again Arendt found herself pointing us toward Augustine's striking statement: *Volo ut sis* (I want/wish/will that you be). Crucially, this helps us to understand why we also find Augustine at the heart of the book (*Origins*) she wrote in the middle of her writing career, as well as the more obvious places where we would look. In one sense, it should come as no surprise to those of us who know Arendt as the thinker of plurality and natality; yet, there is a twist. For, taking Augustine's statement as her view—as I argue we must—means aligning her, in ways that seem uncomfortable or impossible, with the conviction that we should love our enemy. For, the command to will the being of the other must hold for all others, whether children of God or not, whether "friends" or not, whether fellow citizens or not. This, of course, is neighbor-love and it is at the very heart, or rather is the very heart, of the critical–political theology of Hannah Arendt. Even if she insisted on the opposite in more than one place, and even if she never claimed it as her view out loud and without qualification.

BIBLIOGRAPHY

Works by Arendt

Arendt, Hannah. 1953. "A Reply to Eric Voegelin: The Origins of Totalitarianism (A Review)." *Review of Politics* 15(1): 76–84.

Arendt, Hannah. 1958. *The Human Condition*. Chicago: University of Chicago Press.

Arendt, Hannah. 1959. "Reflections on Little Rock." *Dissent* 6: 45–56.

Arendt, Hannah. 1968. "Walter Benjamin: 1892–1940." In: Walter Benjamin. 1968. *Illuminations: Essays and Reflections*, pp. 1–48.

Arendt, Hannah. 1969. *On Violence*. New York: Harcourt Brace.

Arendt, Hannah. 1972. "Civil Disobedience." In: *Crises of the Republic*. New York: Harcourt Brace, pp. 49–102.

Arendt, Hannah. 1973 [1951]. *The Origins of Totalitarianism*. New York: Harcourt Brace.

Arendt, Hannah. 1978. *The Life of the Mind*. New York: Harvest.

Arendt, Hannah. 1990 [1963]. *On Revolution*. London: Penguin Classics.

Arendt, Hannah. 1993 [1968]. *Between Past and Future*. New York: Penguin.

Arendt, Hannah. 1994 [1965]. "Some Questions of Moral Philosophy." *Social Research* 61: 739–64.

Arendt, Hannah. 1996. *Love and Saint Augustine*, ed. Joanna Vecchiarelli Scott and Judith Chelius Stark. Chicago: University of Chicago Press.

Arendt, Hannah. 2005a. "What Remains? The Language Remains: A Conversation with Günter Gaus." In: *Essays in Understanding 1930–1954*. New York: Schocken, pp. 1–23.

Arendt, Hannah. 2005b. *The Promise of Politics*, ed. Jerome Kohn. New York: Schocken.

Arendt, Hannah. 2006 [1929]. *Der Liebesbegriff bei Augstin: Versuch einer philosophichen Interpretation*. Hildesheim: Georg Olms Verlag.

Arendt, Hannah. 2018. "Religion and Politics." In: *Hannah Arendt. The Modern Challenge to Tradition: Fragmente eines Buchs*, ed. Barbara Hahn and James McFarland. (vol. 6 of *The Complete Works: Critical Edition*, Barbara Hahn, Hermann Kappelhoff, Patchen Markell, Ingeborg Nordmann, and Thomas Wild, eds.). Göttingen: Wallstein Verlag.

Works by Others

Abbott, Andrew. 2016. *Processual Sociology*. Chicago: University of Chicago Press.

Adams, Julia. 2005. "The Rule of the Father: Patriarchy and Patrimonialism in Early Modern Europe." In: Charles Camic, David M. Trubek, and Philip Gorski (eds.). *Max Weber's Economy and Society: A Critical Companion*. Stanford: Stanford University Press, pp. 237–66.

Adams, Julia. 2010. "The Unknown James Coleman: Culture and History in Foundations of Social Theory." *Contemporary Sociology* 39: 253–58, doi:10.1177/0094306110367907.

Adams, Julia. 2011. "1-800-How-Am-I-Driving?: Agency in Social Science History." *Social Science History* 35: 1–17, doi:10.1017/S0145553200014164.

Adorno, Theodor W. 1977 [1931]. "The Actuality of Philosophy." *Telos*, 120–33.

Agamben, Giorgio. 1998. *Homo Sacer: Sovereign Power and Bare Life*. Stanford: Stanford University Press.

Allen, Amy. 2017. *The End of Progress: Decolonizing the Normative Foundations of Critical Theory*. New York: Columbia University Press.

Allen, Danielle. 2004. *Talking to Strangers*. Chicago: University of Chicago Press.

Arato, Andrew. 2017. *The Adventures of the Constituent Power: Beyond Revolutions*. Cambridge: Cambridge University Press.

Arvidsson, Matilda, Leila Brännström, and Panu Minkkinen (eds.). 2020. *Constituent Power: Law, Popular Rule and Politics*. Edinburgh: Edinburgh University Press.

Asad, Talal. 1993. *Genealogies of Religion: Discipline and Reasons of Power in Christianity and Islam*. Baltimore, MD: Johns Hopkins University Press.

Beiner, Ronald, ed. 1982. *Hannah Arendt's Lectures on Kant's Political Philosophy*. Chicago: University of Chicago Press.

Beiner, Ronald. 1996. "Love and Worldliness: Hannah Arendt's Reading of Saint Augustine." In: Larry May and Jerome Kohn (eds.). *Hannah Arendt: Twenty Years Later*. Cambridge, MA: Polity Press, pp. 269–84.

Benhabib, Seyla. 1996. *The Reluctant Modernism of Hannah Arendt*. Lanham, MD: Rowman & Littlefield.

Benhabib, Seyla. 2018. *Exile, Statelessness, and Migration: Playing Chess with History from Hannah Arendt to Isaiah Berlin*. Princeton: Princeton University Press.

Benjamin, Walter. 1968. *Illuminations: Essays and Reflections*, ed. Hannah Arendt. New York: Schocken.

Benjamin, Walter. 1978. *Reflections: Essays, Aphorisms, Autobiographical Writings*, ed. Peter Demetz. New York: Schocken.

Benton, Lauren. 2009. *A Search for Sovereignty: Law and Geography in European Empires, 1400–1900*. Cambridge: Cambridge University Press.

Bernal, Angélica Maria. 2017. *Beyond Origins: Rethinking Founding in a Time of Constitutional Democracy*. Oxford: Oxford University Press.

Bernasconi, Robert. 1996. "The Double Face of the Political and the Social: Hannah Arendt and America's Racial Division." *Research in Phenomenology* 26: 3–24, doi.org/10.1163/156916496X00012.

Bernstein, Richard J. 1983. *Beyond Objectivism and Relativism*. Philadelphia: University of Pennsylvania Press.

Bernstein, Richard J. 1996. *Hannah Arendt and the Jewish Question*. Cambridge, MA: MIT Press.

Bilsky, Leora. 2010. "The Eichmann Trial and the Legacy of Jurisdiction." In: Seyla Benhabib (ed.), *Politics in Dark Times: Encounters with Hannah Arendt*. Cambridge: Cambridge University Press, pp. 198–218.

Bloch, Ruth. 1985. *Visionary Republic: Millennial themes in American thought, 1756–1800*. Cambridge: Cambridge University Press.

Bloch, Ruth. 2007. "Religion and Ideological Change in the American Revolution." In: Mark Noll and Luke Harlow (eds.), *Religion and American Politics: From the Colonial Period to the Present*, 2nd edn. New York: Oxford University Press, pp. 47–63.

Blumenberg, Hans. 1985. *Legitimacy of the Modern Age*. Cambridge, MA: MIT Press.

Brown, Wendy. 2010. *Walled States, Waning Sovereignty*. New York: Zone Books.

Brown, Wendy. 2016. *Undoing the Demos: Neoliberalism's Stealth Revolution*. New York: Zone Books.

Butorac, Sean Kim. 2018. "Hannah Arendt, James Baldwin, and the Politics of Love." *Politics Research Quarterly* 71(3): 710–21, doi.org/10.1177/1065912918760730.

Butler, Judith. 1990. *Gender Trouble: Feminism and the Subversion of Gender*. London: Routledge.

Butler, Judith. 2012. *Parting Ways: Jewishness and the Critique of Zionism*. New York: Columbia University Press.

Butler, Judith. 2015 [2004]. *Undoing Gender*. London: Routledge.

Camus, Albert. 1991 [1954]. *The Rebel*, trans. A. Bower. New York: Modern Library.

Cane, Lucy. 2015. "Hannah Arendt on the Principles of Political Action." *European Journal of Political Theory* 14(1): 55–75.

Canetti, Elias. 1984 [1960]. *Crowds and Power*, trans. C. Steward. New York: Farrar, Straus & Giroux.

Canovan. Margaret. 1992. *Hannah Arendt: A Reinterpretation of her Political Thought*. Cambridge: Cambridge University Press.

Cavarero, Adrianna. 2013. "Rectitude: Reflections on Postural Ontology." *Journal of Speculative Philosophy* 27: 220–35, doi:10.5325/jspecphil.27.3.0220.

Cavarero, Adrianna. 2016. *Inclinations*, trans. A. Minervine and A. Sitze. Stanford: Stanford University Press.

Chacon, Rodrigo. 2012. "Hannah Arendt in Weimar: Beyond the Theological-Political Predicament?" In: Leonard V. Kaplan and Rudy Koshar (eds.), *The Weimar Moment: Liberalism, Political Theology, and Law*. Lanham, MD: Lexington Books, 73–107.

Coleman, James S. 1998 [1990]. *Foundations of Social Theory*. Cambridge, MA: Harvard University Press.

Crease, Robert P. 2022. "Missed Connection: James Baldwin's Hangup on Hannah Arendt." *Arendt Studies* 6: 29–42, doi.org/10.5840/arendtstudies202265.

Deckman, Melissa, E. J. Dionne et al. 2023. *A Christian Nation? Understanding the Threat of Christian Nationalism to American Democracy and Culture*, available at: https://www.prri.org/research/a-christian-nation-understanding-the-threat-of-christian-nationalism-to-american-democracy-and-culture, last accessed October 23, 2023.

Eisenstadt, Shmuel N. 1999. *Fundamentalism, Sectarianism, and Revolution: The Jacobin Dimension of Modernity*. Cambridge: Cambridge University Press.

Elkins, Stanley. 1976 [1959]. *Slavery: A Problem in American Institutional and Intellectual Life*. Chicago: University of Chicago Press.

Elshtain, Jean Bethke. 1995. *Augustine and the Limits of Philosophy*. Notre Dame, IN: University of Notre Dame Press.

Field, Douglas. 2015. "James Baldwin's Religion Sex, Love, and the Blues."

Flathman, Richard E. 2003. *Freedom and Its Conditions: Discipline, Autonomy, and Resistance*. New York: Routledge.

Forst, Reiner. 2014. *Justification and Critique: A Critical Theory of Politics*. Cambridge: Polity.

Foucault, Michel. 1990. *History of Sexuality*, vol. 1. New York: Vintage.

Foucault, Michel. 1991 [1975]. *Discipline and Punish: The Birth of the Prison*. New York: Vintage.

Foucault, Michel. 2003. *Society Must Be Defended: Lectures at the College de France, 1975–1976*. New York: Picador.

Frank, Jason. 2010. *Constituent Moments: Enacting the People in Postrevolutionary America*. Durham, NC: Duke University Press.
Fraser, Nancy and Honneth, Axel. 2003. *Redistribution or Recognition? A Political-Philosophical Exchange*. New York: Verso.
Furet, François. 1981. *Interpreting the French Revolution*. Cambridge: Cambridge University Press.
Gaff, Alan D. 2004. *Bayonets in the Wilderness: Anthony Wayne's Legion in the Old Northwest*. Norman: University of Oklahoma Press.
Gines, Kathryn T. 2014. *Arendt and the Negro Question*. Bloomington: Indiana University Press.
Gordon, Peter. 2020. *Migrants into the Profane: Critical Theory and the Question of Secularization*. New Haven, CT: Yale University Press.
Gregory, Eric. 2001. "Augustine and Arendt on Love: New Dimensions in the Religion and Liberalism Debates." *Annual of the Society of Christian Ethics* 21: 155–72.
Groscurth, Helmuth. 1970. *Tagebücher eines Abwehroffiziers 1938–1940. Mit weiteren Dokumenten zur Militäropposition gegen Hitler*, ed. H. Krausnick and H. C. Deutsch. Stuttgart: Deutsche Verlags-Anstalt.
Habermas, Jürgen. 1996. *Between Facts and Norms*, trans. W. Rehg. Cambridge, MA: MIT Press.
Habermas, Jürgen. 2015 [1976]. *Legitimation Crisis*. Cambridge: Polity.
Harth, Erica. 1992. *Cartesian Women: Versions and Subversions of Rational Discourse in the Old Regime*. Ithaca, NY: Cornell University Press.
Herrero, Montserrat. 2023. "Carl Schmitt's Political Theology of Revolution." *Open Theology*, doi:10.1515/opth-2022-0223.
Hobbes, Thomas. 2016 [1651]. *Leviathan*, Longman Library of Primary Sources in Philosophy. London: Routledge.
Honig, Bonnie. 1993. "The Politics of Agonism: A Critical Response to "*Beyond Good and Evil: Arendt, Nietzsche, and the Aestheticization of Political Action* by Dana R. Villa." *Political Theory* 21(3): 528–33.
Honig, Bonnie. 1995. "The Arendt Question in Feminism." Editor's Introduction to: *Feminist Interpretations of Hannah Arendt*. University Park: Pennsylvania State University Press, pp. 1–16.
Honneth, Axel. 1995 [1992]. *The Struggle for Recognition: The Moral Grammar of Social Conflicts*, trans. J. Anderson. London: Polity.
Honneth, Axel. 2011. *The I in the We? Studies in the Theory of Recognition*. London: Polity.
Honneth, Axel. 2018. *Anerkennung: Eine europaeische Ideensgeschichte*. Frankfurt: Suhrkamp.
Horkheimer, Max. 1976 [1937]. "Traditional and Critical Theory." *Critical Theory: Selected Essays*, 288–43.

Hotam, Yotam. 2023. *Critiques of Theology: German-Jewish Intellectuals and the Religious Sources of Secular Thought.* Albany, NY: SUNY Press.

Hunt, Lynn A. (ed.). 1991. *Eroticism and the Body Politic.* Baltimore, MD: Johns Hopkins University Press.

Hunt, Lynn. 1992. *Family Romance of the French Revolution.* New York: Routledge.

Ingram, David. 1996. "Novus Ordo Saeclorum: The Trial of (Post)Modernity or the Tale of Two Revolutions." In: Larry May and Jerome Kohn (eds.). *Hannah Arendt: Twenty Years Later.* Cambridge, MA: Polity Press, 221–50.

Jourdan, Annie. 2004. *La Révolution, une exception française?* Paris: Flammarion.

Kalyvas, Andreas. 2008. *Democracy and the Politics of the Extraordinary: Max Weber, Carl Schmitt, and Hannah Arendt.* New York: Cambridge University Press.

Kampowski, Stephan. 2008. *Arendt, Augustine, and the New Beginning: The Action Theory and Moral Thought of Hannah Arendt in the Light of Her Dissertation on St. Augustine.* Grand Rapids, MI: Eerdmans.

Kantorowicz, Ernst. 1955. "Mysteries of State: An Absolutist Concept and Its Late Mediaeval Origins." *Harvard Theological Review* 48: 65–91.

Kantorowicz, Ernst. 2016 [1957]. *The King's Two Bodies: A Study in Medieval Political Theology.* Princeton: Princeton University Press.

Kiess, John. 2016. *Hannah Arendt and Theology.* London: Bloomsbury.

King, Richard H. 2012. "On Race and Culture: Arendt and her Contemporaries." *Politics in Dark Times: Encounters with Hannah Arendt*, ed. Seyla Benhabib. New York: Cambridge University Press, 113–34.

King, Richard H. 2015. *Arendt and America.* Chicago: University of Chicago Press.

Knopf, Richard. C. (ed.). (1960). *Anthony Wayne: A Name in Arms.* Pittsburg, PA: University of Pittsburgh Press.

Kotsko, Adam. 2018. *Neoliberalism's Demons: On the Political Theology of Late Capital.* Stanford: Stanford University Press.

Kottman, Paul. 2012. "Novus Ordo Saeclorum: Hannah Arendt on Revolutionary Spirit." In: Graham Hammill and Julia Reinhard Lupton (eds.), *Political Theology and Early Modernity.* Chicago: University of Chicago Press, pp. 143–58.

Lara, Pía (ed.). 2001. *Rethinking Evil: Contemporary Perspectives.* Los Angeles: University of California Press.

Leanza, Matthias. 2022. "The Imperial Origins of Nation-States: Revisiting Hannah Arendt's Genealogy of Totalitarianism." *Sociological Forum* 38: 144–68, doi: 10.1111/socf.12871.

LeSure, Ainsley. 2021. "The White Mob, (In)Equality Before the Law, and Racial Common Sense: A Critical Race Reading of the Negro Question in 'Reflections on Little Rock.'" *Political Theory* 49(1): 3–27.

Long, Michael G. (ed.). 2024. *Bayard Rustin: A Legacy of Protest and Politics*. New York: New York University Press.

Mathewes, Charles. 2001. *Evil and the Augustinian Tradition*. Cambridge: Cambridge University Press.

Mathewes, Charles. 2007. *A Theology of Public Life*. Cambridge: Cambridge University Press.

Mathewes, Charles. 2010. *Republic of Grace: Augustinian Thoughts for Dark Times*. Grand Rapids, MI: Eerdmans.

McCormick, John P. 1999. *Carl Schmitt's Critique of Liberalism: Against Politics as Technology*. Cambridge: Cambridge University Press.

Landes, Joan. B. (1988). *Women and the Public Sphere in the Age of the French Revolution*. Ithaca, NY: Cornell University Press.

Landes, Joan B. (2001). *Visualizing the Nation: Gender, Representation, and Revolution in Eighteenth-century France*. Ithaca, NY: Cornell University Press.

Lukes, Steven. 2005 [1974]. *Power: A Radical View*. London: Macmillan.

Mouffe, Chantal. 2005 [1993]. *Return of the Political*. London: Verso.

Mouffe, Chantal. 2018. *For a Left Populism*. London: Verso.

Moten, Fred. 2018. *The Universal Machine*. Durham, NC: Duke University Press.

Moyn, Samuel. 2008. "Hannah Arendt and the Secular." *New German Critique* 105: 71–96.

Moyn, Samuel. 2023a. "Hannah Arendt among the Cold War Liberals." *Journal of the History of Ideas* 84(3): 533–58.

Moyn, Samuel. 2023b. *Liberalism against Itself: Cold War Intellectuals and the Making of Our Times*. New Haven, CT: Yale University Press.

Murrin, John. M. 2000. "The Jeffersonian Triumph and American Exceptionalism." *Journal of the Early Republic*, 20: 1–25.

Neiman, Susan. 2001. "Theodicy in Jerusalem." In: Steven E. Aschheim (ed.), *Arendt in Jerusalem*. Berkeley: University of California Press, 65–90.

Neiman, Susan. 2002. *Evil in Modern Thought*. Princeton: Princeton University Press.

Nelson, Eric. 2019. *The Theology of Liberalism: Political Philosophy and the Justice of God*. Cambridge, MA: Harvard University Press.

Pateman, Carol. 1988. *The Sexual Contract*. Stanford: Stanford University Press.

Plaetzer, Niklas. 2023. "Refounding Denied: Hannah Arendt on Limited Principles and the Lost Promise of Reconstruction." *Political Theory* 51(6): 955–80.

Rae, Gavin. 2019. *Evil in the Western Philosophical Tradition*. Edinburgh: Edinburgh University Press.

Rana, Aziz. 2010. *Two Faces of American Freedom*. Cambridge, MA: Harvard University Press.

Reed, Isaac Ariail. 2017. "Chains of Power and their Representation." *Sociological Theory* 35: 87–117, doi:10.1177/0735275117709296.

Reed, Isaac Ariail. 2020. *Power in Modernity: Agency Relations and the Creative Destruction of the King's Two Bodies*. Chicago: University of Chicago Press.

Reed, Isaac Ariail and Michael Weinman. 2018. "Agency, Power, Modernity: A Manifesto for Social Theory." *European Journal of Cultural and Political Sociology*, doi: 10.1080/23254823.2018.1499434.

Robaszkiewicz, Maria and Weinman, Michael D. 2022. *Hannah Arendt and Politics: A Critical Introduction*. Edinburgh: Edinburgh University Press.

Robinson, Cedric. J. 2000 [1983]. *Black Marxism: The Making of the Black Radical Tradition*. Chapel Hill: University of North Carolina Press.

Roochnik, David. 2016. "Aristotle's Topological Politics." In: G. C. Kellow and N. Leddy (eds.). *On Civic Republicanism: Ancient Lessons for Global Politics*. Toronto: University Toronto Press, pp. 41–58.

Rodowick, David. 2021. *An Education in Judgment: Hannah Arendt and the Humanities*. Chicago: University of Chicago Press.

Rubinelli, Lucia. 2020. *Constituent Power: A History*. Cambridge: Cambridge University Press.

Rustin, Bayard. 2003. *Time on Two Crosses: The Collected Writings of Bayard Rustin*, ed. Devon W. Carbado and Donals Weise. New York: Cleis Press.

Sala-Molins, Louis. 2006. *Dark Side of the Light: Slavery and the French Enlightenment*, trans. J. Conteh-Morgan. Minneapolis: University of Minnesota Press.

Santner, Eric. 2011. *The Royal Remains: The People's Two Bodies and the Endgames of Sovereignty*. Chicago: University of Chicago Press.

Scheuerman, William E. 1999. *Carl Schmitt: The End of Law*. Lanham, MD: Rowman & Littlefield.

Schmitt, Carl. 2005 [1922]. *Political Theology*, trans. George Schwab. Chicago: University of Chicago Press.

Simpson, Peter L. P. 2018. *Political Illiberalism: A Defense of Freedom*. London: Routledge.

Smith, Philip. 2003. "Narrating the Guillotine: Punishment Technology as Myth and Symbol." *Theory, Culture & Society* 20: 27–51.

Spieler, Miranda F. 2009. "The Legal Structure of Colonial Rule during the French Revolution." *William and Mary Quarterly* 66(2): 365–408, at: http://www.jstor.org/stable/40212057.

Staudigl, Michael. 2017. "Alfred Schutz and Phenomenology of Religion: Explorations into Ambiguous Territory." *Human Studies* 40(4): 491–99, at: http://www.jstor.org/stable/44979951.

Styfhals, Willem. 2019. *No Spiritual Investment in the World: Gnosticism and Postwar German Philosophy*. Ithaca, NY: Cornell University Press.

Styfhals, Willem and Symons, Stéphane. 2019. *Genealogies of the Secular: The Making of Modern German Thought*. Albany, NY: State University of New York Press.

Suuronen, Ville. 2022a. "Nazism as Inhumanity: Carl Schmitt and Hannah Arendt on Race and Language." *New German Critique* 49(2(146)): 15–48, doi:10.1215/0094033X-9734791.

Suuronen, Ville. 2022b. "Carl Schmitt's Confrontation with the Work of Hannah Arendt: A Debate on Totalitarianism, Power, and Banality of Evil." *Global Intellectual History*, doi:10.1080/23801883.2022.2074866.

Taubes, Jacob. 2009. *Occidental Eschatology*. Stanford: Stanford University Press.

Thurman, Howard. 1996. *Jesus and the Disinherited*. Boston, MA: Beacon Press.

Vatter, Migel. 2021. *Living Law: Jewish Political Theology from Hermann Cohen to Hannah Arendt*. New York: Oxford University Press.

Vega, Facundo. 2017. "On the Tragedy of the Modern Condition: The 'Theologico-Political Problem' in Carl Schmitt, Leo Strauss, and Hannah Arendt." *European Legacy* 22(6): 697–728, doi:10.1080/10848770.2017.1334987.

Voegelin, Eric and Henningsen, M. 2000. *Modernity without Restraint*. Columbia, MO: University of Missouri Press.

Volk, Christian. 2015. *Arendtian Constitutionalism: Law, Politics and the Order of Freedom*. London: Bloomsbury.

Wagner-Pacifici, Robin. 1986. *The Moro Morality Play: Terrorism as Social Drama*. Chicago: University of Chicago Press.

Wagner-Pacifici, Robin. 2000. *Theorizing the Standoff: Contingency in Action*. New York: Cambridge University Press.

Wagner-Pacifici, Robin. 2005. *The Art of Surrender: Decomposing Sovereignty at Conflict's End*. Chicago: University of Chicago Press.

Wagner-Pacifici, Robin. 2010. "Theorizing the Restlessness of Events." *American Journal of Sociology* 115(5): 1351—86.

Wagner-Pacifici, Robin. 2017. *What is an Event?* Chicago: University of Chicago Press.

Walzer, Michael. 1993 [1973]. *Regicide and Revolution: Speeches at the Trial of Louis XVI*. New York: Columbia University Press.

Weinman, Michael. 2016. "Living Well and the Promise of Cosmopolitan Identity: Aristotle's *Ergon* and Contemporary Civic Republicanism." In: G. C. Kellow and N. Leddy (eds.), *On Civic Republicanism: Ancient Lessons for Global Politics*. Toronto: University Toronto Press, 59–71.

Weinman, Michael. 2022. "Thinking With and Against Arendt about Race, Racism, and Anti-Racism: Beyond Origins and "Reflections." *Arendt Studies* 6: 75–87, doi: 10.5840/arendtstudies202267.

Weinman, Michael and Vormann, Boris. 2020. "The Good City and its True Costs: Planetary Urbanisation through an Aristotelian Lens." In: Bryan Turner, Hannah Wolf et al. (eds.), *Urban Change and Citizenship in Times of Crisis*; London: Routledge, 11–28.

Young-Bruehl, Elisabeth. 1982. *For Love of the World*. New Haven, CT: Yale University Press.

Zerilli, Linda. 2005. *Feminism and the Abyss of Freedom*. Chicago: University of Chicago Press.

Zerilli, Linda. 2016. *A Democratic Theory of Judgment*. Chicago: University of Chicago Press.

INDEX

EU Authorised Representative:
Easy Access System Europe Mustamäe tee 50, 10621 Tallinn, Estonia
gpsr.requests@easproject.com

Printed and bound by CPI Group (UK) Ltd, Croydon, CR0 4YY
01/10/2026
02226084-0001